Research on Gender and Sexualities in Africa

This book is a product of the CODESRIA Gender Institute.

Research on Gender and Sexualities in Africa

Edited by

Jane Bennett
Sylvia Tamale

CODESRIA

Council for the Development of Social Science Research in Africa
DAKAR

Council for the Development of Social Science Research in Africa
Avenue Cheikh Anta Diop, Angle Canal IV
BP 3304 Dakar, 18524, Senegal
Website : www.codesria.org
ISBN: 978-2-86978-712-4

Typesetting: Alpha Ousmane Dia
Cover Design: Ibrahima Fofana

Distributed in Africa by CODESRIA
Distributed elsewhere by African Books Collective, Oxford, UK
Website: www.africanbookscollective.com

The Council for the Development of Social Science Research in Africa (CODESRIA) is
an independent organisation whose principal objectives are to facilitate research, promote
research-based publishing and create multiple forums geared towards the exchange of
views and information among African researchers. All these are aimed at reducing the
fragmentation of research in the continent through the creation of thematic research
networks that cut across linguistic and regional boundaries.

CODESRIA publishes *Africa Development*, the longest standing Africa based social
science journal; *Afrika Zamani*, a journal of history; the *African Sociological Review*; the
African Journal of International Affairs; *Africa Review of Books* and the *Journal of Higher
Education in Africa*. The Council also co-publishes the *Africa Media Review*; *Identity,
Culture and Politics: An Afro-Asian Dialogue*; *The African Anthropologist, Journal of African
Tranformation, Method(e)s: African Review of Social Sciences Methodology*, and the *Afro-
Arab Selections for Social Sciences*. The results of its research and other activities are also
disseminated through its Working Paper Series, Green Book Series, Monograph Series,
Book Series, Policy Briefs and the CODESRIA Bulletin. Select CODESRIA publications
are also accessible online at www.codesria.org.

CODESRIA would like to express its gratitude to the Swedish International Development
Cooperation Agency (SIDA), the International Development Research Centre (IDRC),
the Ford Foundation, the Carnegie Corporation of New York (CCNY), the Norwegian
Agency for Development Cooperation (NORAD), the Danish Agency for International
Development (DANIDA), the Rockefeller Foundation, the Open Society Foundations
(OSFs), TrustAfrica, UNESCO, the African Capacity Building Foundation (ACBF)
and the Government of Senegal for supporting its research, training and publication
programmes.

Contents

Preface

Jane Bennett & Sylvia Tamale

As part of its central commitment to the initiation and support of sophisticated knowledges generated within the African context and capable of complex and strategic engagement with the economic, political, and social challenges we face, the Council for the Development of Social Science Research in Africa (CODESRIA) has long acknowledged the importance of the politics of gender and sexuality to new research. In 1991, an extraordinary conference on the ways in which gender analysis transforms the disciplines of economics, history, agriculture, psychology and education, resulted in *Engendering Social Sciences in Africa*, edited by Ayesha Imam, Amina Mama, and Fatou Sow. The collection, published in 1997, remains one of the most valuable theoretical contributions to feminist research on the continent, and CODESRIA has continued to engage with African feminist and gender-focused scholarship ever since.

One of CODESRIA's strategies in this regard has been the commissioning and hosting of annual residential programmes – Gender Institutes – aimed at strengthening the scholarship and analytical skills of young researchers. The Institutes are thematised, and for the two consecutive ones in 2012 and 2013, CODESRIA chose to create a programme which would address not only the power of gender analysis within fields ranging from media studies to health and violence. Both institutes further examined the meaning of sexualities as they complicate, deepen, and enrich the options for innovative and analytically rigorous research.

'African Sexualities' was the chosen theme for both the 2012 and 2013 Gender Institutes. It was the first time since the inauguration of the Gender Institute in 1994 that the exciting theme of sexuality was receiving serious attention at the Council, and this had a number of implications. Firstly, the theoretical value of addressing sexualities as 'African' entailed careful consideration. As Desiree Lewis points out, there is a longstanding colonial scholarship on 'African sexualities,' where questions of ritual, socio-cultural practice and family dynamics have been interpolated into discourses on hygiene, 'otherness,' and health (Lewis 2011: 201-

202). Such discourses have in the twentieth century been integrated into many developmental approaches to the well-being of people in diverse continental contexts. Moreover, policy discussions on the prevention of HIV have been particularly complicit in imagining African-based people as sexually 'different,' in some homogenised way, from those in other parts of the globe. 'Behavioural change' thus became the silver bullet intervention for HIV prevention. Notions of hypersexuality, men's indifference to the health of their women sexual partners, abusive sexual practices helpful to 'curing AIDS,' and a delight in 'risky sexual behaviour' have, among other things, dominated the socio-medical landscape concerning the sub-Saharan African understandings of the shape of the epidemic (Campbell 2009). To posit, therefore, that in 2012-2013, new continental scholarship needed to re-imagine the question of sexualities entailed a rigorous analysis of historical and contemporary discourses on African-based embodiment, political and social systems, and languages was something novel and interesting.

This was not the only theoretical challenge to the conceptualisation of the Institute on 'African Sexualities.' Jane Bennett's chapter in this collection takes up the way in which much work concerning gender on the continent has been dismissive of engagement with sexualities, locating an interest in sexualities as merely 'fashionable' or – worse? – 'Western'. Such challenges, usually ignorant of the theoretical frameworks of such giants as Franz Fanon or Nawal el Saadawi, demand that curricula on 'African sexualities' ensure grounding in aspects of debates within the broad trajectory of pre-21st century African scholarship.

And a third theoretical challenge to shaping the Institute's programme on 'African Sexualities' came from the sheer breadth of the field. It would have been possible to focus on questions of law, policy, history, psychology, media, culture, education, economics, religion, geography and environmental studies, development, medical humanities, ad *infinitum*. The decision to focus two Gender Institutes on the same theme was a response to this challenge. The 2012 programme chose to focus on questions of law and policy, media, and social movement building (political studies, if you like), while the 2013 programme prioritised questions of history, language and culture, and development. While this by no means covered the spectrum of what could be explored through the theme of 'African Sexualities,' the range at least allowed for a wide range of young researchers to participate.

The theoretical challenges of designing the Gender Institute's programme are complex, but perhaps less so than the challenges of ensuring that the opportunity to participate is offered as widely as possible to young continental researchers. Given that very few universities take gender and sexuality seriously within their range of degree programmes, finding brave young writers interested in the question of 'African Sexualities' was not easy. Beyond the need to ensure that both French and English researchers could access the programmes (the need to accommodate speakers of Portuguese, Arabic, and other languages remains on CODESRIA's agenda), lies the reality that it is usually only in development studies or health, that young researchers are likely to encounter theoretical debate on sexualities. Overall, while over 200 young researchers applied to the Gender Institutes of 2012 and 2013, only a handful – despite obvious enthusiasm and intellectual acumen – were at a point in their doctoral, or post-doctoral research, to participate in what the Institutes could offer in three weeks of each Institute.

As directors of the Gender Institutes, we had the privilege of engaging, in 2012, with 16 intelligent young participants from 10 African countries, and in 2013, with 15, from nine countries. In both years, participants came from higher institutions in Anglophone and Francophone countries, and were both men and women at different levels of their careers. In 2012, Professor Sylvia Tamale, the director, was assisted by three highly experienced resource persons, while in 2013, Professor Jane Bennett was privileged to work with three more assistants.[1]

The Institutes were dynamic, and sometimes difficult, spaces. The terrain of sexualities studies is renowned for the epistemological, trans-disciplinary, and often 'personal' demands made on researchers who must sometimes be prepared to abandon deeply entrenched assumptions about human 'being' and social organisation. It is impossible, for example, to explore the links between globalisation, tourism, and sexuality if one holds immutable prejudices about sex-work, and impossible to understand links between political power, social change, and sexualities if one has been persuaded that 'polygamy is wrong' or 'young women who desire sexual pleasure, openly, are immoral.' Finding the language to explore new theoretical concepts without discouraging participants or causing unproductive debate, is a balancing act of patience, exploration, discipline, and an overarching commitment to the long-term value of the task. The 31 young researchers engaged in the two Institutes went to work with aplomb, imagination, and dignity, and we rehearse here only one example of their collective courage.

In one of the Institutes, one young man from Côte d'Ivoire arrived, full of energy, with an interesting research agenda on questions of violence, gender, and sexuality in his own environment. In an early session where participants were introducing themselves, he spoke of his anxiety about a young son. He felt his four-year old showed strong signs of femininity, and he was deeply distressed about what such 'gender non-conformity' meant. He explained he had scolded and even once beaten the boy, but was now at his wits' end. He asked the other participants for guidance, and many gave advice: 'Wait. It may just be a phase;' 'Maybe he is just copying his older sister, whom he admires;' 'You musn't scold him; he will become afraid of you, and if this is a problem, he needs to be able to speak to you freely.' Three weeks later, as participants left to return to their home countries, the Director of the Institute received an sms from this participant. It read, 'Thanks to all the participants. I want to tell you that at the airport, I bought a doll for my son.'

The Director wept. It was clear that the materials on transgender justice in African contexts, on the intransigence of many gender norms, and on the need for our radical revisioning of the links between gender and sexualities had been of importance to the researcher/father. While, of course, questions of transgender concern issues of gender identity (which cannot be conflated with sexualities research), in pedagogic practice, learning in one area often revolutionises ideas in another. It may have been his co-participants' non-judgmentalism, or it may have been a discussion of the sexual and gendered fluidities visible in the history of Senegal[2] which shifted anxiety to something else, but there is no doubt that both parental strength and research competence had been deepened.

All the participants were engaged in their research projects, and one of the goals of the Institutes was to support participants in writing up some of their ongoing work as a chapter for this collection. Not every participant was ready to do this (some were still designing methodologies or completing literature reviews); however in this collection we are delighted to include new work from seven participants, young researchers working in Zimbabwean, Ghanaian, Tanzanian, Ugandan, and Kenyan contexts.[3] Also included in the volume is the work of, at least, one resource person.

Because participants were engaged in research at differing academic levels (Masters, PhD, post-doctoral, and as young faculty beginning new research careers after completing doctoral work), their approaches to research, and the scope of what it was they were ready to write about for this collection ranged widely. This is visible in the chapters that follow: some are fairly short, while others extend their discussion much further. It is unusual for an edited volume not to standardise the length of chapters; as co-editors, however, we took the decision to recognise that participants at the two Gender Institutes varied so much in where they were in their careers that a 'one-size-fits-all' editorial approach would not work. Hence, while a chapter such as that written by Molly Manyonganise on the experiences of HIV-positive 'virgins' in Zimbabwe runs to some 5,000 words, Claire Coultas' chapter on the narrative of intimacy among young Tanzanians is twice that length. Both, however, have much to offer to contemporary research on questions of youth, sexuality, and the meaning of sexual and gendered discourses still trapped within the languages of public health advocacy campaigns around HIV prevention.

The collection opens with four chapters which explore aspects of the contemporary theoretical debates that informed the design of the Gender Institute's programmes. Jane Bennett's piece reviews the links in recent African feminist research between questions of gender and those which arise when sexualities are taken seriously, and simultaneously challenges the notion that sexualities research is merely or monolithically 'Western'. Sylvia Tamale's chapter argues that far from reading legal, religious, and 'cultural' discourses as oppositional to one another, it is essential to find theoretical approaches that understand and respect both the tensions and the synergies that connect them. As far as she is concerned, rigorous research on sexualities within the African contexts cannot afford to neglect these intersections. Signe Arnfred's chapter focuses on the destabilising notions of 'African-based women' as passive victims of heterosexual patriarchy, people without sexual desire, power, pleasure or influence. As the chapter explains, such notions have fallen out of development and public health discourses on gender and sexuality, and contemporary research needs to critique simultaneously and revolutionise them. A focus on questions of sexual pleasure is one route, here. Babere Chacha's piece reminds us that, while moving beyond colonial and development-inspired stereotypes of gender and sexuality is key to twenty-first century scholarship, the historical gaze cannot be abandoned and the deconstruction of ideas about 'secrecy' or 'silence' – both well-circulated within research on sexual norms and practices – demands both historical knowledge and local analysis.

The seven chapters which follow respond to different notes sounded by the opening discussion. Valerie Opiyo's chapter on performances of sexuality in urban Nairobi explores the public display of feminine sensuality through young women's responses to wearing 'G-strings'. Are these to be read as engagement with neoliberal versions of hypersexualised femininity or as indices of resistance to constricting norms around respectability and sexual passivity for women? Daniel Fiaveh's piece explores heterosexual women's power in negotiation with men for their own sexual pleasure, weaving into his research, based in Ghana, an interest both in 'silence' and in women's influence over when and how sexual interactions take place to their own satisfaction. Adebayo Mosobalaje pushes the envelope of inquiry into representation of desire and pleasure through an exploration of both traditional and contemporary Yoruba music, concluding that 'the erotic *juju* is a veritable site of contestation of meaning, negotiation of identities and, thus, a political struggle'.

The interest in language and sexuality is picked up in Pauline Mateveke's chapter on the use of Shona in sexual activity between men and women in Harare, Zimbabwe. She argues, on the basis of her research with both women and men, that during flirtation and sex itself, the 'respectability' of English is preferred by women while men partners relish the 'dirtiness' of Shona. Mateveke draws on this distinction to interrogate what she sees as a form of internal colonisation among her research interviewees: why, she asks, should Shona be regarded as 'vulgar' (and hence sexually exciting to her men interlocutors)? Prince Guma's piece on the influence of African feminist thought on Ugandan political discourses of gender suggests that without feminist epistemological work, moving beyond notions of women as sexually 'chaste', 'modest,' or 'respectable' is difficult. He grounds his argument in a brief survey of some feminist campaigns within Uganda. While his chapter concentrates more on struggles for gender equality within the political sphere than on questions of sexuality, he reminds us that without these struggles, it would be impossible now to recognise the centrality of sexuality to understanding the limitations of demands for women's political power within state structures and the need to move away from the 'add-a-woman-to-a-parliamentary-bench.'

This collection of chapters seeks to complement the work of recent scholars, such as in Charmaine Pereira's *Changing Narratives of Sexuality* (2014), Sokari Ekine and Hakima Abbas (eds), *Queer African Reader* (2013), and *Women, Gender and Sexualities in Africa,* edited by Toyin Falola and Nana Amponsah (this emerges from a 2010 conference at the University of Austin, Texas, at which many African-based researchers and writers were present). It seeks simultaneously to challenge approaches to understanding the politics of gender and sexualities which do not recognise the diverse legacies of African feminist work as foundational to questions of valuable research on 'African sexualities'. As Aminata Diaw, one of CODESRIA's Executive Secretariat members and a powerful interlocutor within both the 2012 and 2013 Gender Institutes argues, 'Today, the pursuit of power and rights for women is embedded in the calling into question of this boundary between the public and the private spheres by demonstrating that the private is in itself political'. It is theoretical work on questions of sexuality which not only affirm Diaw's conviction but extend her recognition of the salience of the 'private' towards a deeper political theorisation of 'men' as well as of 'women'. The chapters in this collection are all motivated by the hope of researching gender and sexualities, within African contexts, with those who are heterosexual and those who are not, with those whose gender-identities conform to normative models, and with those who refuse – in the name of a less violent, more economically and politically just world – constraints on the possibilities of being sexual, being gendered, being human.

Notes

1. The three included Prof. Jane Bennett (University of Cape Town, South Africa), Prof. Aretha Asakitikpi (Covenant University, Nigeria) and Prof. Signe Arnfred (Roskilde University, Denmark). In 2013, these were Prof Cheikh Niang (University of Cheikh Anta Diop, Senegal), Prof Babare Chacha (Laikipia University, Kenya), and Dr. Awino Okech (Kenya).

2. Prof Niang's work on questions of gender fluidity in Senegalese villages formed a part of the curriculum in 2013, where he also taught a week's worth of the programme.

3. This collection profile work completed by English-writing researchers. It is our hope that a separate volume will showcase work from the French-writing participants and professors in the two institutes.

Contributors

Jane Bennett is the director of African Gender Institute at the University of Cape Town. Her research interests include questions of sexualities, gender, and violence within African contexts, and also questions of African feminist theorising and strategic activism. She has co-edited, and co-written several books, including *Jacketed Women* (with Charmaine Pereira), and *The Country We Want To Live In* (with Nonhlanhla Mkhize, Vasu Reddy and Relebohile Moletsane). She also writes fiction (*Porcupine* is her most recently published collection of short stories), and works with a number of NGOs in Southern Africa.

Sylvia Tamale is a leading African feminist who teaches law at Makerere University in Uganda. Her research interests include 'Gender, Law & Sexuality,' 'Feminist Jurisprudence' and 'Women in Politics.' Prof. Tamale has published extensively in these and other areas, and has served as Visiting Professor in several academic institutions globally and on several international human rights boards. She was the first female dean of the School of Law at Makerere. She is the editor of African Sexualities: A Reader (2011).

Signe Arnfred is a sociologist and a gender scholar. She works at Roskilde University, Denmark. Between 2000 and 2006, she was located at the Nordic Africa Institute in Uppsala, Sweden, coordinating a research programme on Sexuality, Gender and Society in Africa. Her fields of interest are sexualities in Africa and postcolonial feminist thinking. Her most important books are *Re-thinking Sexualities in Africa* (2004) and *Sexualities and Gender Politics in Mozambique* (2011).

Babere Kerata Chacha is the director, External Linkages and a senior lecturer in the Department of Public Affairs and Environmental Studies at Laikipia University. He has a PhD in History from Egerton University. He has been a fellow of School of Oriental and African Studies, University of London, St. Antony's College, Oxford, and Wolfson College Cambridge. He has taught as an Adjunct Lecturer at the University of Eastern Africa, Baraton, and Kenya Military Academy. His research interests include women studies, social history, environmental history and sexuality. Currently, Chacha is extensively engaged in human rights research and sexuality.

Valerie Agutu Opiyo is a part-time Lecturer in Communication and Media studies in Nakuru, Kenya. She has a Master of Arts Degree in Project Management from University of Nairobi and a Bachelor's Degree in Media Studies from Egerton University. She was formerly an Adjunct Lecturer at Presbyterian University of East Africa. Her research interests include community service delivery, sexuality, youth, women gender studies and media.

Daniel Yaw Fiaveh is a sex sociologist/anthropologist with interest in the construction of masculinities, representation of men and boys, sexual cultures, and social cultural construction of sexual practices. His current research focuses on penile discourses and conceptualizations in Africa. He founded the Centre for Men's Health and Sex Studies; a not-for-profit established to promote research on men's health and sex studies. Daniel is an alumnus of the University of Ghana, Legon and the Graduate Institute of International and Development Studies, Geneva [Department of Anthropology and Sociology of Development]. He has authored papers in high impact journals and received several fellowships.

Adebayo Mosobalaje holds a PhD in English and teaches Literature in English at Obafemi Awolowo University, Ile-Ife, Nigeria. His areas of interest include Dramatic Literature, Literary Theory, Oral Literature, Popular Culture, Cultural Studies, Masculinity and Gender Studies. He has published in reputable journals both within and outside Nigeria.

Pauline Mateveke is a lecturer in the Department of English and Media studies at the University of Zimbabwe. Pauline's research interests are in Literature and gender related issues, sexualities and women's studies. Her PhD research focuses on the literary and musical representation of Zimbabwean female identity formation during Zimbabwe's post-2000 era.

Prince Karakire Guma is a researcher, scholar-activist, urban imaginer and social critic. He has independently engaged in ethnographic surveys and has written peer-reviewed articles with reputable journals. His research interests cover key social, economic and political processes shaping the African continent. Prince was 2013-2014 research fellow of the Harry Frank Guggenheim (HFG) Foundation's 'Young African Scholars' programme; the 2013-2014 Research Fellow of the International Association for the Study of Sexuality, Culture and Society's IASSCS, on the Ford Foundation's Emerging Scholars International Research Fellowship Program.

Molly Manyonganise holds a Master of Arts Degree in Religious Studies from the University of Zimbabwe. Currently, she is a senior lecturer in the Department of Religious Studies and Philosophy at the Zimbabwe Open University. Her research interests comprise religion and politics, gender and religion.

Claire Coultas is a social science and health researcher knowledgeable and trained in a wide variety of quantitative research techniques, the development and evaluation of M&E systems, and the design of communication materials and toolkits. She is particularly interested in the social, cultural, and health system issues surrounding community health, especially sexual, and is a proponent of the use of participatory and qualitative methods in the study of these. Ms Coultas has extensive experience working with youths in Tanzania and in rural village communities. She also has experience working with small and start-up NGOs and is knowledgeable about their problems and the challenges of working effectively with them. Ms Coultas holds a BSc in Human Sciences and MSc in International Primary Health Care both from the UK.

1

'Fashionable Strategies':
Travels in Gender and Sexuality Studies

Jane Bennett

Fatou Sow, one of the most renowned and prolific feminist researchers and writers in Africa, recounts an occasion that took place almost exactly twenty years ago at the celebration of CODESRIA's 20th Anniversary. She observed that in ' reflecting on the role of the intelligentsia and ideology in the development crisis, Professor Samir Amin haphazardly denounced the struggle for women's liberation, cultural challenges, environmental concerns, and so on as 'fashionable strategies' (Sow 1997:31). At the time, Amin's approach to taking the study of gender seriously would probably have been shared by many of his colleagues, and his scorn was, as we know, robustly rejected by a very wide range of African-based feminist theoreticians and activists. *Engendering Social Sciences in Africa* (1997), a collection of essays edited by Ayesha Imam, Amina Mama and Fatou Sow, published papers drawn from a diverse set of disciplines (economics, education, history, and others) through CODESRIA in 1997. The collection encapsulated part of the contemporary intellectual response to Amin's wariness about the project of revolutionising gender norms and remains, to my mind, one of the most important books on twentieth-century theory on the potential of social sciences research.

It is quite possible that intellectual resistance to the notion of taking gender seriously as part and parcel of the design and creation of excellent research remains in some quarters of continental academic institutions. Whether such resistance would, however, now be expressed as a resistance to what is *fashionable* is doubtful. Different forms of marginalisation have arisen (such as the frequent tokenisation of the value of research which explores the dynamics of gender), and within feminist circles themselves, powerful debates on the ways in which 'gender talk' has become co-opted as a facet of neo-liberal government policy-making make for interesting reading. Fierce negotiations for credibility, influence, and value characterise all theoretical work worth its salt. Within the twenty-first century, there is a very rich array of African-based intellectual engagements with the dynamics of gender in diverse contexts and a vibrant, even occasionally ferocious, network of debates. I had not, however, heard the term *fashionable* used of this work for a long time.

Then, in May 2012, I did hear it. The Gender Institute of CODESRIA has been the home for high-level teaching on the relationship between gender and many fields of interest (the media, climate change, development, and so on) for over a decade. In 2012, under the directorship of Sylvia Tamale, the Gender Institute sought to tackle the question of researching African sexualities. Applications to participate in the Institute came from a very diverse set of disciplinary and contextual backgrounds, and those selected included men and women working in sociology, religious studies, development, history, geographical sciences, critical literary studies, and public health. The men and women all came from universities across the continent where they have worked as committed intellectuals and teachers. The focus of the Institute generated immediate debate as early as the first day of the programme. Several participants suggested that the question of 'African Sexualities' as a route into excellent research and theory-building was 'very dubious', 'pandering to what is seen as fashionable,' and 'only of interest in the West; we have more serious things to talk about.'

Given that the Gender Institute, like other CODESRIA teaching programmes, welcomes controversial and direct input from participants and teachers alike, these perspectives proved simply a useful way of initiating discussion. By the end of the programme, evaluations suggested that none of the participants any longer doubted the value of taking the politics of sexuality seriously within social and humanities sciences. However, the similarity between the 1990s rejection of the idea that the politics of gender should be taken seriously by African intellectual work and the participants' vocabulary of resistance to discussion of sexualities ('fashionable,' 'Western,' 'not serious') was interesting.

This chapter seeks to offer a contribution to discussions about intellectual work on sexualities in African contexts as 'Western' and largely unimportant to the paradigms we need to strengthen social and humanities sciences in African higher education and research institutions. The chapter is organised into two sections, through which I develop an argument about the need to be wary of the simplistic deployment of an 'African'/'Western' binary, while simultaneously asking for a rich and intellectually resilient continentally-driven set of discourses concerning sexualities research. The first section asks questions about the temptation to homogenise 'the West', and the second offers a very brief review of influential work on gender and sexualities within contemporary African research contexts.

Sexualities Research 'in the West'?

Over the past thirty years, global research focusing on questions to which an understanding of sexualities is core has grown enormously. The research has been carried out in several disciplines, including demography, health, sociology, and cultural studies. Leading international journals grounded in very different approaches have made this subject a key preoccupation. They range from the renowned *British Journal of Medicine* (a google search of the journal's contents over the past 20 years using the term 'sexuality' comes up with 1,034 hits) to *GLQ: A Journal of Lesbian and Gay Studies*, which regularly publishes research on the politics, cultures, and dynamics of sexualities. *Culture, Health and Society, and Sexualities*, in particular, are well known for their editorial support of research which recognises the importance of medically-grounded work (such as the need to prevent the transmission of HIV between men having sex with other men) but which insist on sexualities research as always engaged with the micropolitics of local, stubborn, and complex contexts in which the possibilities of ready categorisation or straightforward generalisation are rare. The position of these journals has shown, too, that while the urgencies of the HIV pandemic continue to deserve the attention of researchers, sexualities research cannot be imagined solely within the scope of viral transmission, 'vulnerability', and 'risk'. Political questions of epistemology inform the range of topics catalysed by an interest in sexualities and their constellation into fields of allied enquiry. Within medical research, of course, research around sexualities may readily deploy concepts of dysfunction, a-typicality, and illness; within postmodern cultural studies, communities of researchers accept ideas about race, intersectionality, margin, or economy as critical points of entry into a new question or concern.

The roots of contemporary research and theory on sexualities within Europe and the United States of America are multiple and tangled. While a predictable chasm exists between contemporary research on sexual health generated from within the medical sciences and research on the meaning of sexualities within political economies and cultural dynamics, the work of leading researchers (such as Roz Petchesky, Sonia Correa, Carole Vance, Gary Dowsett, Peter Aggleton, and Diana di Mauro) is informed by public health, economics, political studies, and history. It would probably be safe to say that the influence of Foucault on understanding the interactions between sexualities, language, and power undergirds most canonical theory here. It is also safe to suggest that there are multiple tensions between feminist work (largely rooted in the recognition of reproduction, and the vulnerability to privatised violence, as critical political zones), queer theory (largely driven by the challenge to heteronormative approaches to identity, health, and epistemology), and the work of post-colonial writers (such as Jacqui Alexander, Anne McClintock, and Paul Gilroy) who read the project of colonialisms – and neo-colonialisms – as inherently both sexualised and gendered.

One body of 'Western' writing on the politics of sexualities, often overlooked in the homogenisation of 'the West', is the extraordinary work done since the 1970s, by poets, novelists, and theorists who worked from what came to be termed an 'intersectional' paradigm (the term was coined by Kimberlè Crenshaw 1989). All these writers identified themselves as African-American, Latina, and/or 'women of colour', and their epistemological approach to the creation of knowledge was deeply grounded in the recognition of how the state was organised through the deployment of race, class, and gender. Their analysis was extraordinarily influential, as they suggested that the DNA of what it meant to experience humanity in the West rehearsed, remembered, recreated (and sometimes resisted) the terms of injustice on which the state had been founded and through which it continued to sustain itself. Theorists in this school include Audre Lorde, Gloria Anzaldua, Cherrie Moraga, Barbara Smith, Beth Ritchie, Barbara Christian and June Jordan. No curriculum on political questions of sexuality in 'the West' can be considered valuable without factoring in their voices.

A different strand but equally important body of literature on sexualities, is rooted in the (initially) historical work that came to underlie the queer theory on the ways in which cultures of heteronormative language about desire and the body have erased the possibility of significantly changing the past. From Jeffrey Weeks' analysis of the construction of the 'invert' in nineteenth-century Britain to the work of Gilbert Herdt (1996) on what it may be possible to learn from colonial American records of indigenous people's gender and sexuality categorisations and socio-political organisation, the field of what has come to be instantiated as 'queer studies' is full of debate. Some of the underlying theoretical insights of this work, such as the notion of sexuality as fluid, inhospitable to categorisation, and a zone targeted for institutional and state-level control, have travelled very widely.

A final area of 'Western' research in the first decade of the twenty-first century warrants mention here. The report of a global meeting on 'Repoliticising Sexual and Reproductive Health and Rights', held in 2010 in Langkawi, Malaysia, suggests that the broad agenda of the 1994 International Conference on Population and Development (ICPD) is still something for which international, national and local actors in the sexual and reproductive health and rights movement have to fight. The programme emphasises the centrality of sexual and reproductive health to sustainable and equitable development processes, and defines 'health' in a breadth that allows researchers, policy advocates, and activists to link notions of rights to questions of sexual and reproductive health. The report is particularly interested in how macroeconomic frameworks have failed, by and large, to take on board the critical recognition that people's economic potential is embedded in conditions productive of 'the body'. Such conditions may entail security and conflict and/or access to housing or clean water. They simultaneously entail the operation of sexual and reproductive dynamics. While the report concludes with a range of innovative ideas concerning possible re-engagements with the basic ICPD agenda, it is undeniable that a thread of concern about the contemporary shape of access to sexual and reproductive rights, especially those of young women, runs through its pages.[1]

The past two decades have seen (often in connection with the attempt to prevent HIV transmission) new discourses on the importance of understanding sexualities, and new medical opportunities (such as the HPV vaccine). However, the combination of global economic instability, war and conflict, the rise of fundamentalist notions of the human personality, and rapidly changing knowledge economies have impacted heavily on the possibility of securing global sexual and reproductive health and rights, especially for women and girls. Ideas about sexual and reproductive rights flow from Western development discourses in rather complex ways. Nearly 20 years ago, at the 1994 ICPD conference which initiated the idea of sexuality as a right, Senegal, then occupying a vantage position in the leadership of the Organization of African Unity (OAU), provided support for the connection between taking sexuality seriously and designing policies on health in the continent. The position of OAU regarding the crucial importance of reproductive and sexual health placed it in alliance with Southern NGOs, such as Development Alternatives with Women for a New Era (DAWN) which argued for the linkage of the right of women to have control over their sexual/reproductive bodies to the possibility of economic development. There were also several African countries that refused to link 'rights' and 'choices' to sexuality, fearing that such ideas threatened religious guidelines on gender, sex, and marriage, and fearing, too, that 'Western' constructions of individualised rights aimed at epistemological and material recolonisation (Klugman 2002). One year after the ICPD conference, the language of the Beijing Declaration and Platform for Action eventually read,

> The human rights of women include their right to have control over and decide freely and responsibly on matters related to their sexuality, including sexual and reproductive health, free of coercion, discrimination and violence. Equal relationships between women and men in matters of sexual relations and reproduction, including full respect for the integrity of the person, require mutual respect, consent and shared responsibility for sexual behaviour and its consequences.

The vector through which most development research on questions of sexuality in Africa has been driven since then is, of course, the twenty-year-long battle against the transmission of HIV. Although many African delegations at the UN Beijing Conference on Women in 1995 articulated, through ferocious debate, the possibility of understanding sexualities as part and parcel of women's rights to equality, the epidemic overwhelmed all questions linking health, sexuality and policy for a decade afterwards. In the West, due to the near total erasure of realities of heterosexual transmission of the virus, the connection between the language of rights and questions of sexualities circulated primarily around lesbian and gay rights or (increasingly) around the right to the termination of pregnancy for heterosexual women. In sub-Saharan African contexts, however, development discourses constructed an unending flow of 'people sexually at risk' of contracting HIV. These include sex workers, truck drivers, migrant workers, young and undereducated women, men who have sex with men (MSM).

From this perspective, heterosexuality became a zone under intensive medical surveillance: pregnant women in dozens of countries served as the data-base for statistics on prevalence, and heterosexual activity was categorised fiercely through the vocabulary of 'safety' and 'risk.' In South Africa, for example, a delayed response to the need to address the transmission of HIV and the treatment of HIV-positive people meant that intensive NGO/civil society work had to turn towards a very particular conflict with the state. In most countries in the Southern African Development Community (SADC), public health discourses around 'populations at risk' of the transmission of the HIV came to include dangerously stereotypic notions about masculinity and femininity, such as the idea that 'men' are 'naturally irresponsible sexual partners' or that marriage was a 'safe' zone from HIV transmission because young mobile men, sex workers, and young women were usually the ones involved in transactional sex and, thus, the most vulnerable to infection. Much NGO and civil society work sought to tackle naïve readings of gender, poverty, and sexuality, but in doing so, it has been argued that the politics of sexual and reproductive health and rights took a back seat to the debates around HIV transmission and treatment.

At the same time, vigorous attempts have been made to propagate the ideals of sexual and reproductive rights across diverse spheres. For example, new NGOs have been formed to spearhead educational and policy projects, legal reform continues around questions of the prevention of violence against women, and networks of activists and researchers have continued to insist on connection and strategic coordination across the sub-Saharan region (such as the work done by Just Associates – JASS). Interest in several 'constituencies' fuel this work: sex workers, lesbians, men who are HIV-positive, women affected by gender-based violence, women with HIV and those who care for them (usually also women), and women fighting for reproductive choice and security. It is undeniable that the state is hardly the one funding this kind of work; a wide range of Western foundations do so. Such funding support ranges from the gigantic resources of the PEPFAR initiative[2], on which hundreds of NGOS working against the transmission of HIV depend, to minuscule grants made under stringent conditions to marginalised communities (such as those given to Genderdynamix in Cape Town to support refugees from a dozen countries living under threat becase of their gender identity choice).

Amid the different contexts that present themselves under this discourse, the meaning and role of 'the West' have become both painful and tangled. It could be argued that the politics of sexuality has become live threads within the civil society, as research and advocacy work is carried out within the contexts of the resources provided by the West. It has been suggested that where funding is threatened, NGOs tremble, academic research opportunities disappear, and 'the fashionable' relinquishes its allure? Is this really so? I think not

Contemporary Writing on Gender and Sexualities Within African Contexts

Many writers attest to the vibrancy, complexity and visibility of sexuality as a zone of pleasure and social negotiation within the poetry and oral cultures with which they are familiar. In an article about masculinity within his own 'Shona' family, in the 1960s, Chenjerai Shire writes that wives' evocative poetry to husbands on their desirability stressed the pleasure husbands were expected to give them sexually (Shire 1994). Despite this, mid-twentieth century African intellectual work that takes sexuality seriously engages with it as a political force through which the most vicious of systemic brutalities can become part and parcel of social organisation. Also, Fanon's *Black Skin, White Masks*, published in 1952, uses a psychoanalytic approach to heterosexual desire generated from within the crucible of French colonial epistemology, and argues that 'the black man's desire for 'white' includes sexual fantasy, idealisation, sexual longing and a self-hatred that splits him from himself. His demand for a black self-consciousness (a consciousness) ripped away from Manichean notions of race and hierarchy includes faith that 'love' itself may be possible: 'Today I believe in the possibility of love; that is why I endeavour to trace its perfections, its perversions' (Fanon 1952:75). Nawal el Saadawi's *Memoirs of a Woman Doctor* (1960), a fictional account of what a 'woman doctor' encountered among rural Egyptian villages stresses that heterosexuality for poor women constitutes a terrain of assault, choicelessness, and physical/psychological damage. In this case, heterosexual norms are shaped by specific patriarchal values about the value of women's bodies, and no sense of sexuality as a zone of intimacy, relational excitement, or joy can be found in the book.

The truth is that it has sometimes been difficult to manage the politics of gender and sexualities together, especially where development-oriented discourses about 'women's empowerment' have dominated research. Within African feminist writing over the past two decades, there has however been a strong thread of research and writing which seeks to combine epistemological commitment to 'undoing' patriarchal and colonial versions of gender with the recognition that sexualities comprise a critical terrain for theory and activism. Leading contemporary research voices here are Charmaine Pereira, Kopano Ratele, Sylvia Tamale, Desiree Lewis, Elizabeth Khaxas, Patricia Mcfadden, Zanele Muholi, Zethu Matebeni, Hakima

Abbas and Akosua Ampofo, although many others contribute (in both disciplinary and transdisciplinary work) to the discussions. The researchers named here do not share foci or approaches (Muholi, for example, researches as a visual artist, a photographer, and works mainly with black lesbians in South Africa; Ampofo, now the director of the Institute of African Studies at the University of Legon, Ghana, originally came from the background of development studies. Her research has taken on questions of reproductive choice, and of masculinities). But a survey of their work has shown a passionate engagement with the activism of research, with the urgency of writing which tackles the politics of gender and sexualities within African contexts and with an eye attuned to researching the politics that has often been done in the name of 'culture', the exotic and the sub-human. As Lewis begins her piece on 'Representing African Sexualities',

Although the American cartoon [she reproduces a cartoon of a 'black man' gazing lustfully at a 'white woman'] ...was produced in the nineteenth century, it features images that still haunt our conceptual landscape, whether within or beyond Africa. The cartoon portrays recurring stereotypes of black bodies and sexuality: the image of the lewd black man; the pure white female body; the portrayal of the black/African body as grotesque, uncivilized and crudely sexual, even when formally dressed (Lewis 2011:199).

It is not only the image of the poor HIV-positive black woman, abused and abandoned, whose hegemony over the meaning of gendered-sexuality-in-Africa deserves deconstruction; it is also that case that a very long legacy of anthropological, epidemiological, and development-oriented research exists, rehearsing notions of gender as static, 'traditionally' brutal, irrational and superstitious in matters of sexualities, and identically deployed across African contexts.

In the past few years, a small number of volumes edited by feminist writers, presenting research on the politics of gender and sexualities in African contexts have been published. These include two books edited by Steyn and van Zyl, from South Africa; *Re-thinking Sexualities in Africa* (edited by Signe Arnfred of the Nordic Africa Institute 2005), *African Feminist Politics of Knowledge* (published in 2010, and edited by Akosua Ampofo and Signe Arnfred). Similarly, Sylvia Tamale's *African Sexualities: A Reader* (2011) has been published by Pambazuka Press, and *Queer African Reader*, edited by Sokari Ekine and Hakima Abbas, was published in 2012. Also, Jane Bennett and Charmaine Pereira's edited work entitled, *Jacketed Women,* a collection of essays on research methodologies in qualitative study of gender and sexualities, was published in 2013, while Charmaine Pereira's edited collection, *Changing Narratives of Sexuality* was published by Zed Press in early 2014.

The collections all profile the possibilities of research which is unafraid to tackle questions of gender and sexualities outside the framework of HIV transmission and 'traditional' rites: questions of who is having sex, with whom; questions of pleasure; questions on the impact of post-flag democratic change – or militarism – on sexualities; questions about masculinities; questions about sexual commodification; and about queer theory and experience. As research, the collections offer an enormous amount to those of us also working as writers, and especially to those of us who work as teachers and supervisors of young writers and researchers, whether as independent thinkers, in universities or in research-inclusive NGOs. *African Sexualities: A Reader* opens with two chapters, both of which address what it means to research the politics of sexualities and gender in African contexts, both with a sense of the colonial (and indeed occasionally current) gazes which configured African embodiment as simultaneously exotic and bestial and with a commitment to exploring the ethics and methodologies of contemporary work. Tamale writes, 'a good sexuality research project does not view methodology as a mere appendage .... or a "way of carrying out an enquiry"' (Tamale 2011:29). She argues further that in the consideration of research methodology 'researching and theorising sexualities beyond the tired polemics of violence, disease and reproduction and exploring their layered complexities beyond heterosexual normativity and moral boundaries will lead to fresh conceptual insights and paradigm shifts' (Tamale 2011:30).

What this brief survey suggests is that *fashion* is not what is driving an interest in the politics of gender and sexualities in African contexts of research and writing. In the same years that these collections were written (between 2004 and 2012), many debates have sprung up within different countries concerning the independence of women, and the meaning of their sexual and reproductive rights. Within the constitutional reform process of Kenya, for example, debates on access to the termination of pregnancy were vocal and integral to voting politics; within the uprisings of Egypt and Tunisia, questions of women's rights surfaced continually as indices for the meaning of the revolutions underway, and in many countries policy-making and religious discourses have drawn on homophobia to generate support for sitting presidents or aspiring political actors. At the same time, escalating economic challenges have placed heavy burdens on civil society organising, making it even more difficult to sustain even basic service delivery in programmes targeting survivors of sexual violence or domestic abuse. Far from there being 'extra' funding available from international or regional donors for work on gender and sexualities, the 2008 fiscal crisis impacted funding in this arena very heavily – many programmes have seen cutbacks, withdrawals, and enormous battles around the sustainability of projects providing support to sex workers, to MSM projects, to educational programmes, and to organisations supporting research on gender and sexualities. Despite this, research in the area is strengthening, and the reason for this must be acknowledged as the relevance of the issues to questions of economic resilience, democratic governance, and to the ability of those in the social sciences to work with integrity and applied common sense.

Bringing it Home

Presenting theoretical arguments through a review of dominant research voices is one way of opening up a discussion on the importance of clarifying what we mean when we work with the politics of gender and sexualities in social sciences in Africa. A different approach could look at a particular research initiative in order to suggest that these politics are not only 'researchable' but fundamental to the lives of upcoming young researchers and writers – students in higher education systems. This section presents one such project, hosted through the African Gender Institute (AGI) between 2010 and 2011, in which faculty and students from five universities participated (the University of Namibia, the University of Botswana, the University of Zimbabwe, the University of the Witwatersrand, and the University of Cape Town). The project was initially managed by Susan Holland-Muter in the African Gender Institute and created, with colleagues in all the other universities, five research teams that took on board the challenge of addressing the covert curriculum around the production of 'conventionally gendered and sexual' students.

In brief, to differing extents, SADC-based universities face a number of challenges: challenged economies, rising number of young people with a strong desire for class mobility through higher education, campus structures which are too small (in many ways) to accommodate these numbers, and the question of the 'brain drain' which pulls researchers, teaching faculty and prospective students away from national university spaces towards international ones. At the same time, the gender parity of students admitted to universities has become more equitable, women are increasingly present in non-traditional areas of study (medical science, business, and the sciences more broadly), and women are more visible within higher echelons of university leadership.

We argued in designing the project that the young women who are accepted into universities in the region are thus faced with complex double messages. On the one hand, their academic institutional cultures increasingly recognise their equality with men and their intellectual potential; on the other hand, their contexts include high levels of vulnerability to sexual violence, stereotypes of hypersexual femininity, and strong – usually conservative – expectations around their identities as future 'girlfriends', 'wives, and 'mothers'. The territory they negotiate as gendered and sexual people is one fraught with opportunity, challenge, anxiety, and excitement, and it is one which constitutes much of the 'informal curriculum' of any higher education institutional culture. And yet, as Bennett and Reddy point out, this is a territory very poorly represented within formal university curricula. Even with education in medical sciences (degrees in medicine, surgery, and nursing), there is very little opportunity to explore the politics of the body beyond questions of disease and intervention.

Between 2010 and 2011, the AGI ran a project on strengthening the sexual and reproductive health and rights (SRHR) leadership of young women based at five different SADC universities: the University of Zimbabwe, the University of Botswana, the University of the Witwatersrand, the University of Namibia, and the University of Cape Town. The project was based on previous work aimed at supporting African feminist writers, researchers and NGO activists in their understanding of the politics of sexuality and gender and in their deployment of different concepts, including that of SRHR, in their own work. We recognised the need to move into work directly engaging the young women who were so frequently the topics of discussion about gender-based violence, the impact of economic stress on options for sexuality, and the meaning of reproductive rights in politically troubled contexts. University teams of faculty and student researchers were built and each one developed a research action project which undertook to raise consciousness about what young women were experiencing around questions or sexuality on their campuses and to find an 'action' through which to address issues of insecurity, lack of control, fear, or discrimination.

A number of socio-economic realities needed consideration when taking the lives and experience of young Southern African women seriously. At the risk of homogenisation (clearly, given vast political diversity across Southern Africa, it is not altogether wise to conflate 'Southern African' in this way), current constructions of gender – the meanings of 'manhood' and 'womanhood' – are currently in intensive contestation. The negotiation of 'masculinities' and 'womanhood' intersects with the dynamics of escalating poverty and unemployment, juxtaposed against the concerted efforts by state efforts to facilitate people's access to new opportunities for education, professional opportunities, and interaction with global cultural notions of desirable gender identities.

As is well known, a second issue that colours all contemporary exploration of sexualities and reproduction in Southern Africa remains the prevalence of HIV and the number of people dying of AIDS. The challenges of HIV and AIDS can be readily enumerated: the struggle to contain and prevent new transmissions, the politicised and fraught terrain of treatment, the economic implications of home-based care for the ill and dying, the challenge of loving and nurturing children (and others) left in the wake of death, the imminent collapse of certain hospital systems and the strain on all medical resources, the disappearance of teachers, nurses, labourers, fathers, politicians, singers, from their posts. It is also true that significant victories have been achieved: some excellent legislation on non-discrimination towards HIV positive people, vibrant (if occasionally infuriating) debate at governmental and NGO levels, and ongoing work at every level of society to illuminate the severity of the epidemic as a threat to the very foundations of democracy. Those engaged as feminist activists and researchers have, for the past decade, been vigorously embedded into the work of addressing the challenges of living in a country in which issues of sexualities and gender are dominated by the realities of the HIV and AIDS epidemic.

There has been some success here, and it is now recognised in many circles that most Southern African women, especially young women and married women (categories which may overlap) do not have enough power over the negotiation of heterosexual sex to create conditions of 'safety' for themselves and their partners. This is also especially true for poor women. There is also increasing recognition of the ways in which escalating poverty is transforming sexuality (heterosexualities and other performances of sexuality) into the terrain of transaction, where all players are vulnerable to commodification – who buys, and who sells, what are contextually defined, vulnerable to 'market volatility'.

Such transactions are not coded as sex work but as legitimate, expected, exchange within sexual (especially heterosexual) relationships. These dynamics present particular challenges to young men and women, placing them at the forefront of SRHR challenges.

These challenges encompass, of course, the vulnerability of young women to gender-based violence. It is recognised that confronting gender-based violence entails not only a solid set of legal instruments and an excellent system for their implementation, but simultaneously knowledge of women's and girls' rights not to be targeted as sexual prey. The corollary of this would be to say that SRHR work in Southern Africa demands a focus on women's and girls' confidence, authority, and capacity to negotiate relationships in terms of their own survival and safety.

Questions of reproductive health and rights are intertwined with all discourses on young women's sexuality. Even in contexts such as South Africa, where access to information and contraception is fairly easily available, it remains an expectation that reproduction is a 'woman's business', and negotiating the dynamic between health, pleasure, reproductive choice, and security is part of all sexually-active young women's lives. As a political space, this has been undercut by questions around 'safe sex' which pertain to the prevention of the transmission of HIV (except in debates about the termination of pregnancy), but just as new fundamentalist discourses have stressed the immorality of having sex outside marriage, so have they also deepened opposition to young women's unquestioned access to contraception.

The results of the project (some of which were published in issue 17 of Feminist Africa) not only confirmed how important it was to focus on young women within universities but also how severely their experiences of SRHR were marked by challenges around reproductive health and rights. Although their country contexts differed, the young women involved worked with questions of gender-based violence and policy, the politics of space and sexuality, the meaning of HIV-prevention campaigns, and the politics of gender and sexual pleasure. Working in teams, they developed very interesting action research projects in these areas.

The projects all demanded a refocusing on the 'reproductive health and rights' areas of our gender and sexuality discourses. While these areas are, of course, deeply embedded in questions of sexuality (choice, identity, orientation, behaviours, norms, knowledges), the 'older' researchers (the faculty) in the project were sometimes taken aback by the levels of distress spoken of by the younger women in relation to reproductive health concerns. The politics of condom usage, the fear of 'becoming sterile' if one masturbates, the stigmatisation suffered by becoming pregnant at teenage, and the need to negotiate for one's own reproductive 'safety' without making this a topic of conversation with a male partner, were among the 'late-night discussions' within the project. What was dramatically clear was the disjunction between the academic confidence of young women participants and their sense of impotence around the possibility of controlling their own bodies sexually. An equally clear disjunction was visible, despite the participants' diversity, between their relative willingness to explore ideas of sexual pleasure and to discuss together so-called 'taboo' areas of sexual experience and desire, and their reluctance (initially) to take active leadership within campus cultures around the promotion of ordinary (by now; the Beijing Conference was held in 1995) ideas about women's rights to control their own fertility, sexual pleasure, and sexual experience. The project itself dispelled this reluctance and students initiated extraordinary action-projects (for example, the University of Namibia team tackled the campus environment vigorously around ongoing gender-based violence; the University of Cape Town team hosted highly successful evenings of dialogue on sexual pleasure, for young women and young men). The project is planned to continue into a new phase; what is important to note here is that the research done around questions of gender and sexualities in the five institutions addressed fundamental questions about what it actually takes to support and strengthen young researchers. We often speak with anxiety about 'brain drains' and the Northern pull of our best graduate and undergraduate researchers; what this research project reveals is how the cultures of some of our own spaces, in their intellectual disinterest around questions of gender and sexualities, may fuel that pull (not that Northern environments are likely to be more hospitable; far from it; but the notion that they might be, if one was 20 years old, is compelling).

Conclusion

This chapter was stimulated by the opportunity to work with the CODESRIA Gender Institute in 2012, and it owes much to the laureates who participated and shared their work and thoughts, and to Professor Tamale who directed the Institute. Its argument is simply, in the end, that it is important to have at one's fingertips a general sense of what has actually been created 'in the West' around questions of sexuality and how this both does, and does not, influence research in our own contexts. Much of what has been written in the past few years, especially by African feminist scholars on questions of gender and sexualities, is well aware of 'Western' scholarship but rooted in the dominant political, economic, legal and cultural debates of African contexts and seeking cross-continental synergy.

The importance of this synergy cannot be overstated; the concluding section argues that without it, we risk the attrition of our most vivacious, innovative, and self-assured young scholars.

Notes

1. Report available online at http://www.rhmjournal.org.uk/publications/langkawi-report.pdf . Accessed on 2 January 2013.
2. The U.S. President's Emergency Plan for AIDS Relief (PEPFAR) is an initiative of the United States government introduced in 2003 to combat the HIV & AIDS epidemic around the world.

References

Ampofo, Akosua Adomako and Signe Arnfred, eds, 2010, *African Feminist Politics of Knowledge: Tensions, Challenges, Possibilities,* Uppsala: The Nordic Africa Institute.

Arnfred, Signe, ed., 2005, *Rethinking Sexualities in Africa,* Uppsala: The Nordic Africa Institute.

Herdt, Gilbert, ed., 1996, *Third Sex, Third Gender: Beyond Sexual Dimorphism in Culture and History,* New York: Zone Books

Imam, Ayesha, Amina Mama and Fatou Sow, eds, 1997, *Engendering African Social Sciences,* Dakar: CODESRIA

Crenshaw, Kimberlé, 1989, 'Demarginalizing the Intersection of Race and Sex: A Black Feminist Critique of Antidiscrimination Doctrine, Feminist Theory and Antiracist Politics', *University of Chicago Legal Forum,* pp. 139-67.

Lewis, Desiree, 2011, 'Representing African Sexualities,' in Sylvia Tamale, d., *African Sexualities: A Reader,* Oxford: Pambazuka Press

Tamale, Sylvia, 2011, *African Sexualities: A Reader,* Oxford: Pambazuka Press.

2

Exploring the Contours of African Sexualities: Religion, Law and Power

Sylvia Tamale

Introduction: Linking Religion, Culture, Law and Sexuality

Plurality is simultaneously the boon and the bane of Africa. The cultural diversity and richness found between and within the continent's religious and cultural communities lend to its versatility and beauty. Our historical and colonial legacy of pluralistic legal systems and multi-religious traditions hold both advantages and disadvantages. The plurality is further multiplied and problematised by the many permutations of religious beliefs/jurisprudence and the evolution of culture. It becomes even more complicated when one considers that organised religions on the continent operate at a global scale, albeit with a distinctly African flavour when transplanted to the continent.

African religious and cultural plurality spawns many contradictions and some absurdities. So one can only imagine the complexity involved in exploring varied African sexualities within such shifting paradigms and crosscurrents of discourses.[1] In order to make sense of such exploration, we approach the topic from a common ground where the plurality of laws, culture, religions and religiosity finds convergence in their engagement with sexualities in Africa. Such common ground can be found in the twin forces of patriarchy and capitalism – forces that support and reinforce each other, while also introducing new tensions and contradictions to the situation.

I use the term 'African sexualities' in this chapter not because I am unaware of African people's heterogeneity and the significance such differences hold. I know that because of the rich and diverse socio-cultural, as well as some political differences across African societies, the statuses of African peoples differ based on gender, class, race, ethnicity, religion, age, sexual orientation and so forth. However, my reference to Africans as a collective in relation to sexuality stems from two important factors. First, is to highlight those aspects of cultural ideology – the ethos of community, solidarity and *ubuntu* – that are widely shared among the vast majority of people within the geographical entity baptised 'Africa' by the colonial map-makers. More importantly, the term is used politically to call attention to some of the commonalities and shared historical legacies inscribed in cultures and sexualities within the region by forces such as colonialism, capitalism, imperialism, globalisation and fundamentalism.[2] The African philosophy of Ubuntu or humaneness refers to understanding diversity and the belief in a universal bond and sharing.[3] Justice Yvonne Mokgoro of the South African Constitutional Court elaborated this difficult-to-translate concept as follows:

> In its most fundamental sense it translates as personhood and 'morality.' Metaphorically... [it describes] the significance of group solidarity on survival issues so central to the survival of communities. While it envelopes the key values of groups solidarity, compassion, respect, human dignity, conformity to basic norms and collective unity, in its fundamental sense it denotes humanity and morality.[4]

And we speak of sexualities in the plural in recognition of the complex structures within which sexuality is constructed and in recognition of its pluralist articulations on the continent.[5]

A careful mapping of religions on the continent reveals that 86 per cent of its population subscribe to the imported monotheistic Abrahamic religions of Islam and Christianity.[6] All Abrahamic faiths believe that God is male, described in their different holy scriptures. They are also messianic in that they anticipate the coming of a God-sent messiah. Islam had penetrated the continent by the twelfth century while serious attempts to introduce Christianity only happened in the eighteenth century.[7] Historically, the process of proselytisation subverted, overthrew and demonised African traditional religions (ATR) which formed an integral part of African sexual culture.[8] Nevertheless, and despite the concerted effort to undermine its relevance to the African psyche, it is important to note that ATR currently exercises considerable influence on the populations and the tendency is for a significant number of people to practise them concurrently, even if discreetly, with the messianic religions.[9] Makau Mutua refers to this debilitating phenomenon as being 'suspended between a dim African past and a distorted, Westernised existence'.[10] This constitutes one of the inherent contradictions (and hypocritical deceptions) of plurality referred to earlier.

Although most African traditional religions are also monotheistic,[11] their Supreme Being is beyond gender – being neither male nor female and they are non-messianic.[12] Moreover, ATR is not located in sacred text and cannot be isolated from people's holistic and everyday existence. In that sense, ATR can be viewed as 'religion-plus', a modus vivendi. It is, as John Mbiti tells us, 'lived (not read), it is experienced (not meditated), it is integrated into the life of the people: wherever they are, their religiosity, their religion, is with them.'[13] In other words, African traditional religions cannot be delinked from culture. For that reason, it is important to emphasise the distinction made in this chapter between 'religion' and 'religiosity.' Religion refers to 'a system of beliefs, practices, institutions, and relationships that provide the primary source of moral guidance for believers' (e.g., Christianity, Islam, Hinduism & Judaism).[14] On the other hand, religiosity is one's pious conformity to a religion through practice and conduct (e.g., how often one goes to church/mosque).[15] Both are of significance in understanding the diverse ways in which African peoples translate their sexualities within the contemporary world.

While noting the above distinction, it is also important to recall that several philosophers of ATR argue that there is continuity between the Abrahamic religions and ATR, and indeed there are elements of convergence and mutual appropriation in the two forms of religion.[16] The positive convergence between ATR and notions of Christianity includes the belief in a Supreme Being that is responsible for the creation of humans and other living things and communication between the Supreme Being and the spirits on behalf of humans. But the perceived negative spiritual entities of ATR have also been actively incorporated into the image of the Christian Devil.[17] The commonalities between Islam and ATR are seen in the practices of polygyny, male circumcision and bride wealth and their admission to evil forces.[18] However, a significant rupture between the Abrahamic religions and ATR is that while the former often views the female body as the seat of sin, moral corruption and a source of distraction from godly thoughts,[19] ATR celebrates and valorises the female body as a reproductive/sexual icon.

The influence of messianic religions on African sexualities (practices, feelings, ideas, fantasies, excitements and aesthetics) has been enormous. Traditional sexual practices that were informed by ATR and indigenous culture have been seriously threatened. This chapter will demonstrate that the positive conceptualisations of African sexualities (including the African female body) have largely been negated and overtaken by the state-supported advocacy of the messianic religions. Mutua explains how African traditions were delegitimised by a new socio-political and religious order:

> Africa – from top to bottom – was remade in the image of Europe complete with Eurocentric modern states. Christianity played a crucial role in this process: weaning Africans from their roots and pacifying them for the new order. Utilizing superior resources, it occupied most political space and practically killed local religious traditions and then closed off society from other persuasions... Islam, which had invaded Africa at an earlier date, was equally insidious and destructive of local religions. Its forceful conversions and wars of conquest together with its

prohibition of its repudiation, were violative of the rights of Africans as well…
Progress, culture, and humanity were identified entirely in Islamic or Christian
terms never with reference to indigenous traditions.[20]

Far from suggesting that African cultural norms or ATR were universally egalitarian,
I argue that many sexual practices that were acceptable in pre-colonial, pre-Islamic
and pre-Christian Africa were encoded with the distinctive tags of 'deviant,'
'illegitimate' and 'criminal' through proselytisation and acculturation. African
sexualities were reduced to a universalised, essentialised culture and integrated into
the wider 'enlightened' culture.

Throughout this chapter, any reference to 'law' should be understood broadly
to include codified or statutory law, as well as religious laws and uncodified
customary laws rooted in culture.[21] All countries on the continent have pluralistic
legal systems where codified law – formally or informally – operates side by side
with customary law and/or Sharia (Islamic law). Even where it is not explicitly
stated that religion has the force of law, many religious principles find expression
in the legal codes of most jurisdictions and are often used to justify and legitimise
culture and law. Hence, in most African states, Christian and Islamic laws have
been effectively domesticated. Indeed, the lines that separate law, culture and
religion in Africa can sometimes be extremely blurred. Given how critical law and
sexuality are to the lives of Africans, it is surprising how little scholarly attention
has been paid to the intersection between these areas of our existence and how the
complex relationships are played out. How do/can organised religion, personal
spiritual convictions, culture and the law shape, challenge and potentially
transform the sexualities of African peoples? How are religious norms and values
institutionalised within African sexualities? How do people come to accept the
rules that govern their sexuality and what explains the actions of those that resist/
subvert such rules?

In addition to this introduction, the chapter is divided into four parts. The
second section provides a discursive framework within which to articulate the
conceptual link between power and knowledge in the construction of African
sexualities. The third section illustrates how law, culture and religion are used to
strip certain people of sexual citizenship. The fourth discusses the growth of the
sexual rights movement on the continent, tracing its activism from the margins
and demonstrating the small but significant gains that it has so far tucked under
its belt, and the final section constitutes the concluding remarks.

Law, Culture and Religion Viewed through the Lens of Power

As the old adage goes, 'knowledge is power.' The saying can be interpreted in
multiple ways: that knowledge equips one with potential power or that knowledge
itself is power. In other words, behind the mask of knowledge lies real power
dynamics. Knowledge reflects the 'truths' of the powerful, of those that pen and

record history. The Italian theorist, Antonio Gramsci,[22] introduced the concept of 'hegemony' to illustrate how systems of power are constructed through knowledge. Hegemonic power convinces people to subscribe to the social values and norms of an inherently exploitative system.[23]

Contrary to popular belief, sexuality is not exclusively driven by biology; a very significant part of it is socially constructed through legal, cultural and religious forces driven by a politico-economic agenda.[24] Sexuality is very much a socio-cultural invention that is closely linked to power and to the processes of subjugation; as Africans, how we 'do' and experience sexuality is heavily influenced by society and culture. How and with whom we have sex, what we desire, what we take pleasure in, how we express that pleasure, why, under what circumstances and with what outcomes, are all forms of learned behaviour communicated *inter alia* through the institutions of culture, religion and law.[25] It is through these social institutions and social relationships that sexuality is reified or given meaning.

So, who 'sets the agenda' and imparts these 'sexual truths' as the universal norm? These are mainly people who, at a particular historical point in time, exercise power and control discourse – politicians, media houses,[26] cultural leaders, religious leaders, mainstream educationists, multilateral institutions – using tools such as the law, culture, religion, media and educational textbooks to disseminate and legitimise these 'truths', thereby enforcing compliance. 'Truth' frameworks about good, respectable, normal sexuality as well as those for bad, immoral and unnatural sexuality are constructed by hegemonic discourses.[27]

Apart from the social and historical contexts that inform African sexualities and its relationship to law, culture and religion, there are also some developments at the international level that have cast their shadow over this phenomenon. During the past fifty years or so in North America and Europe, there has emerged a newfangled school of natural lawyers who seek to integrate a distinctive approach of Catholicism into law and legal systems.[28] Proponents of New Natural Law, such as John Finnis,[29] have breathed fresh life into anachronistic arguments against contraception, abortion, sexual activity outside of the heterosexual marriage (e.g., fornication, masturbation, homoeroticism, adultery and prostitution[30]) and sexual acts between spouses that lack reproductive potential. Jurists such as Nicholas Bamforth and David Richards have challenged this school of thought for its fundamentalism which is rooted in patriarchal religious authority.[31] During the same period, fundamentalist doctrines also took root in Islam with moral teachings and sacred interpretations of gender and sexuality similar to those of the new natural law. And despite the doctrinal differences between the two religions, they often come together and lock arms when defending 'conservative' perspectives on sexuality. Such reinvigorated religious fundamentalism has infiltrated Africa via a highly organised born-again evangelical movement and Christian groups as well as conservative branches of various Islamic sects.[32]

The adjective 'conservative' is advisedly placed in quotes, because when used in relation to religions, it masks the political interests behind the so-called traditional interpretations of the sacred writings of these religions. The preference in this chapter is for the term 'political religions' instead of 'conservative religions' in order to highlight the current role of such religions in dictating African sexual politics.[33] As Charmaine Pereira reminds us:

> While some dimensions of sexuality may always remain private, it is clear that sexuality is not, in its entirety, a private affair. Sexual politics are played out as much in the exercise of political authority as they are in intimate relations. Indeed, the intertwining of sex, violence and masculinity in the exercise of power by public office-holders is evident even (perhaps especially) among those who feel free to use religion for political ends.[34]

Several historical-anthropological scholars have long erased the mythical line that tries to separate religion from the secular in Africa. They have demonstrated that religion, politics and the market have occupied the same sphere since the colonial period.[35] Religion greatly influences the development of social justice and ethical norms in our societies. Indeed, there is hardly any African state that strictly applies secularism; the tendency is to adopt an institutionalised and organic union between religion and the state.

When we speak about African sexualities, we are relying on discourses of law, culture and religion and the way that these structure their realities. Disciplinary power, in the Foucauldian sense,[36] fashions African people to conform to the mainstream notions of sexuality, thus 'voluntarily' colluding with patriarchal-capitalist sexual moral standards. One of the most radical examples of such self-surveillance can be seen in the acts of young women voluntarily submitting themselves for virginity test in search of public approval. In South Africa and Zimbabwe, for example, many young women 'voluntarily' submit themselves for such tests in a bid to gain public approval, respond to demands for communal belonging and on account of the dignity and pride associated with it.[37] It is all part of the contradictions between bodily integrity, self-surveillance and religiosity.

It is thereby invaluable in facilitating our critical rethinking of how African people become subjects when we assume the gendered/sexualised identities that are constructed for us within the three power structures under scrutiny. Like elsewhere in the world, the 'truth regimes' about sexuality in Africa are largely penned by the nib of legislation, custom and religion. The 'master frames' (or scripts) of sexuality that law, culture and religion construct for African people push many who do not conform to the very margins of society – sex workers, rape survivors, the youth, homosexuals, widows, single-mothers, people living with HIV & AIDS, etc. Their bodies become sites for political inscription even as they are constituted as the sexual 'other.'

In this era of the HIV & AIDS pandemic, political Christianity and Islam, especially, have constructed a discourse that suggests that sexuality is the key moral issue on the continent today, diverting attention from the real critical moral issues for the majority of Africans such as financial security or the plunder, misuse, disuse and misappropriation of public funds. The wanton and fraudulent diversion of public funds by the powerful that prevent the masses from accessing basic human needs such as healthcare, clean water, education, nutrition, shelter, jobs, clothing, information and security is the number one moral issue preoccupying the minds of the average African. Employing religion, culture and the law to flag sexuality as *the* biggest moral issue of our times and dislocating the *real* issue is a political act and must be recognised as such.

The ideological premises from which African religions and sexualities operate dictate a separation of the public and private realms. They emphasise domesticated female bodies designed primarily for reproduction and social production on the one hand, and public male bodies on the other. At the same time, because religion in most African states is practically in the public square, it forms part of the mechanism that regulates women's domesticated bodies and sexuality. During the last four decades three major developments have operated to (re)shape sexualities in Africa: (a) the growth of the human rights and feminist movement; (b) the HIV & AIDS epidemic; and (c) the cultural/religious fundamentalisms which grew out of a backlash against the rights of women and sexual minorities. The various forces and interests involved lead to gendered contradictions and double standards regarding acceptable sexual behaviour. The past four decades have also seen the growth of 'new social movements' based on gender and sexuality that have raised serious critiques and trenchant resistance to dominant sexuality ideologies.[38] We now move to a discussion of how these developments have played out in law and society.

The Sexual Citizen: Between Desire and the Law

It is against this backdrop that we can now analyse how African people experience and express themselves as sexual beings. Note that gender relations and sexuality (for the two are inseparable) play a crucial role in creating and sustaining patriarchy and capitalism.[39] Male dominance and female subordination from the level of the family unit, to the community and state levels, has to be maintained for the survival and supremacy of the two systems. How does an African subject – particularly one who does not conform to the dominant model of sexuality – articulate their sexuality in the public sphere? How can they strike a balance between claims for rights and freedoms in the public realm and demands for the protection of separate 'private' sexual spaces? How do the law, culture and religion 'unsettle' sexual citizenship?

The need to control and regulate women's sexualities and reproductive capacity is crucial in patriarchal-capitalist societies at two levels. First, as one of the central tenets of the institutionalisation of women's exploitation, such control consolidates male domination through their control of resources and their relative greater economic power over women. The patriarchal family engenders these economic relations whereby the man, as head of the household, exercises control over the lives of women and children who are virtually treated as his property.[40]

In this way, heteronormativity forms one of the essential power bases for men in the domestic arena. Capitalism required a new form of patriarchy than that which existed in pre-colonial Africa – one that embraced a particular (monogamous, nuclearised, heterosexual) family form.[41] It is essential that the man's acquired property and wealth is passed on to his male offspring in order to sustain the system of patriarchy. Hence, it becomes important to control women's sexuality in order to guarantee the paternity and legitimacy of children when bequeathing property. To this end, the monogamy of women is required, without necessarily disturbing men's polygynous sexuality. Such double standards are clearly reflected in legislation across Africa: e.g., the crime of adultery applying to wives and not husbands. In fact, the double standards seen here reflect the culture in the Bible where the sin of adultery applied to married men only when they had sex with another man's wife.[42] (This is wrong. Pls check the references again) The inconsistency in sexual morality is also seen in the offence of prostitution around the continent that penalises only the sellers (the majority being women) and not the buyers (read men) of sex.

At another level, capitalist patriarchal societies are characterised by a separation of the 'public' sphere from the 'private' realm. The two spheres are highly gendered with the former representing men and the locus of socially valued activities such as politics and waged labour, while the latter is representative of the mainly unremunerated and undervalued domestic activities performed by women. This necessitated the domestication of women's bodies and their relegation to the 'private' sphere, where they provide the necessities of productive and reproductive social life *gratuitously* (thus subsidising capital)[43] and are economically dependent on their male partners.[44] In Africa, the process of separating the public-private spheres preceded colonisation but was precipitated, consolidated and reinforced by colonial policies and practices. Where there had been a blurred distinction between public and private life, colonial structures (e.g., law, religion) and policies (e.g., educational) focused on delineating a clear distinction guided by an ideology that perceived men as public actors and women as private performers. Where domestic work had co-existed with commercial work in pre-colonial satellite households, a new form of domesticity, existing outside production, took over. Where land had been communally owned in pre-colonial societies, a tenure system that allowed for absolute and individual ownership in land took over. At the same time, politics and power were formalised and institutionalised with male public actors in control. The Western capitalist, political ideology (i.e., liberal democratic theory) that was imposed on the African people focused on the individual, submerging the African tradition that valued the collective.

Statutory and religious jurisprudence in Africa, as well as its reinterpreted customary laws, are largely built on a heteronormative-reproductive ideal[45] with a presumed masculine juridical subject. I refer to 'reinterpreted' customs because during the process of colonisation, many of the entrenched African cultural norms were distorted by the colonialists and their patriarchal African collaborators to suit the new form of patriarchy required for the capitalist mode of production.[46] All three current legal regimes construct and reconstruct the African sexual terrain with particular emphasis on 'public morality'.[47] They dictate rules that govern marriage, divorce, adultery, transactional sex, incestuous sex, dress codes, and so forth.

There are several scriptural examples from the messianic religions to illustrate this point. Most of them find practical expression based on the patriarchal-capitalist interpretations of the Bible and the Qur'an. Messianic religions are well known for their restraining influence on sexuality. Compared to ATR, Christian and Islamic doctrines and sermons (as opportunistically and patriarchally interpreted) encourage sexual purity and virtue (especially for women). Whereas ATR generally tolerated practices such as masturbation, fornication, infidelity, adultery, non-penetrative sex, prostitution and homoerotics, the messianic religions condemned them as sinful.[48] Religious leaders from all denominations are extremely vocal and influential within the sexual surveillance system around the continent. Additionally, the religious and political leadership regulate and police African sexualities by highlighting their negative aspects. By keeping sexual pleasure in the background and foregrounding the risks and dangers associated with sexuality, practices of self-surveillance, particularly for women, are intensified. The concepts of sin (religious), taboo (cultural) and criminalisation (legislation) play a crucial role in constructing sexualities and the manner in which African people experience it, ultimately exercising a regulatory and controlling role.

A good example of how religion conjoins with politics and law in constructing African women's sexuality is seen in the 2008 Nigerian bill 'for an Act to prohibit and punish public nudity, sexual intimidation and other related offences in Nigeria.' The bill was presented by the chairperson of the senate committee on women and youth affairs, Senator Eme Ufot Ekaette in a bid to regulate women's dress code. It was introduced in the wake of several arrests of women wearing trousers and skimpy clothes in Lagos. Pastor Enoch Adeboye, the general overseer of the Redeemed Christian Church of God, the largest Pentecostal church in the country, had also addressed the issue of moral laxity and social corruption among his congregation, condemning women's clothing and banning his female congregation from wearing trousers and revealing clothes.[49] But it was clause 16 of the bill that was most revealing:

The roles of religious bodies in moral rejuvenation of our country is by this Act hereby guaranteed:

a. The Ministries of Information, Cultures and National Orientation shall develop policies and programmes for the integration of religious bodies in the reformation of the society for moral uprightness;

b. religious bodies shall be encouraged in teaching moral uprightness to its adherents.

Analysing the bill, Bibi Bakare-Yusuf writes:

> [T]he senator collapses various distinct issues into a confused and spuriously unified account. First, she assumes that there is a causal relationship between nudity and sexuality. Second, women's sartorial agency is assumed to always be directed at men and is held to be an invitation to an erotic encounter that might often lead to unwanted consequences. Women must therefore be disciplined and protected from any potential masculine sexual terror that acts under provocation. Finally, the senator assumes that the judicial system must be based on a religiously grounded morality, which can be universalised regardless of differences... The unclothed body, which in many Nigerian cultures was previously read in a non-sexual way, is now overburdened with sexual meaning and anxiety that acts as a prelude to sexual intercourse.[50]

The Nigerian bill illustrates the elaborate system that legal regimes deploy to reward those who conform to the rules and punishes those who transgress them. The text and implementation of the laws largely exercise double standards and discriminate against women.[51] At the same time, it is notable that they also invoke the notions of religious piety and sexual morality in order to justify what is clearly an effort at the reinforcement of patriarchal dominance.

Recalling that the messianic religions stress the impurity and inherent sin associated with women's bodies, Ruether informs us, 'Most human religions, from tribal to world religions, have treated woman's body, in its gender-specific sexual functions, as impure or polluted and thus to be distanced from sacred spaces and rites dominated by men'.[52] It is not by coincidence that penal codes around the continent reduce religious sexual transgressions into punishable criminal offences thereby laying down the laws of sexuality, ensuring that all citizens (believers and nonbelievers alike) adopt the hegemonic sexual discourse. Through the intersection of religion, the law and reinterpreted customs, the complexity of African sexualities (particularly women's) is instrumentalised, controlled and regulated by the patriarchal state.

Generally classified under the label 'Offences against Morality', sex laws are enumerated in African penal codes prohibiting and/or regulating various sexual relations. Not only do these laws universalise sexuality but they squarely place issues of 'sexual morality' between consenting adults within the realm of the state and the public. Such offences are often prejudicial to women and seek to maintain their subordinate status in society. Most of these laws found their way into African penal codes as direct imports from the legal regimes of former colonial powers. Ironically, while most victimless sex offences have been decriminalised in former colonial metropoles such as Britain, France, Portugal, and Belgium, African jurisdictions maintain the moral surveillance regimes with enthusiasm. For example, while the offences of criminal adultery, pornography, prostitution, abortion, sodomy and elopement were all struck out of the penal codes of these western countries, they remain intact in most of Africa. The legal protection of rape in marriage was also lifted in all these countries.

Equally antiquated are sexist defences available to sex offenders such as 'mistaken belief'[53] and 'general immoral character'[54] as mitigating factors in rape cases. Alternatively, the cautionary rule in cases of sexual assaults that require corroboration of the evidence provided by the complainant.[55] Under the Sharia, the rules of evidence dictate that the testimony of a female is only worth half of the value of a man's testimony. The injustice built into the evidentiary requirement of 'corroborating evidence' in rape trials (based on the assumption that women and girls fabricate rape) and admissibility of the complainant's sexual history were highlighted in the highly publicised Jacob Zuma rape trial in South Africa in 2006.[56] Such rules turn the constitutional presumption of innocence until proven guilty in criminal cases on its head. Adultery as a crime or even as a ground for divorce has long been repealed in the countries that exported this law to Africa. However, most of these outmoded sex laws continue to enjoy currency in many African jurisdictions. In its most violent manifestation, stoning-to-death for adultery, for example, is still a legal form of punishment in northern Nigeria's (mis)interpretation of Sharia. This issue was thrown into sharp relief by the infamous case of Amina Lawal.[57]

The offence of prostitution criminalises sex work in all but one African nation. Senegal, which legalised prostitution in 1969, keeps a tight regulatory leash on those engaged in the trade. Historically, the reasons for such a status in this former French West African colony was not a result of a liberal government but rather, attempts to protect French colonial administrators from contracting sexually transmitted diseases (STDs) from native women.[58] The continued total prohibition of sex work in African states is justified on two main grounds: (a) that prostitution promotes social immorality; and (b) that prostitution poses a public health hazard to society, particularly STDs such as HIV. The morality argument buckles in the face of the apparent double sexual moral standards that most African penal codes set for men and women; the law targets and penalises only the sellers of sex (mostly women), letting the clients (mostly men) off the legal hook.

Professional public health literature indicates that the continued enforcement of prostitution laws only exacerbates the problem of public health. Indeed, this is borne out by the statistics of HIV adult prevalence rates; 0.7 per cent in Senegal compared to Uganda (6.5 per cent), South Africa (17.8 per cent), Botswana (24.8 per cent), Lesotho (23.6 per cent) and Swaziland (25.9 per cent).[59] The contradiction in the socio-cultural legal regimes is clearly seen in that most African countries now include sex workers among the 'most at risk' populations in their multisectoral AIDS strategies, yet they maintain the prohibitive legal regime.[60] Studies on adult sex work on the poorest continent in the world show that those engaged in the trade do so primarily for economic reasons and to meet the appeal of financial autonomy.[61]

A good example to illustrate how the Messianic faiths supplanted African cultural values pertaining to sexuality is seen in the labelling of same-sex erotic relationships as deviant. Indeed, the strength and influence of the hegemonic sexual discourse are clearly demonstrated in the area of homoeroticism. In Africa, not only does the discourse construct same-sex relations boldly as 'unnatural' but also as distinctly 'un-African' – an import from decadent Western societies. Political religions and reinterpreted culture are the chief inscribers of same-sex sexuality as 'un-African' and deploy it within the discourse of 'sin'. Hence, Africans engaged in same-sex sexual practices are viewed as undeserving aping sinners. In collaboration with state political leaders, the deviant-defining rule is reinforced and firmly entrenched in the public sphere. President Mugabe of Zimbabwe described homosexuals as 'worse than dogs and pigs' and is one of several African politicians who link homosexuality to Western imperialism. Others include Presidents Arap Moi of Kenya, Sam Nujoma of Namibia, Bingu wa Mutharika of Malawi, Olusegun Obasanjo of Nigeria and Abdoulaye Wade of Senegal – all of whom are on record for espousing homophobic bigotry and policies. Legislation provides the final authoritative and normalising framework for punishing and silencing 'deviant' individuals.

A respectable body of scholarship exists that suggests that prior to the proselytising influence of the Messianic religions, there was a general tolerance, even acceptance of homosexuality in Africa.[62] The enigmatic history of same-sex relations not only indicates that they were invested with ritualised significance (e.g., for healing, spiritual and magical powers) but they were also accepted as age-structured and erotic sexual pleasure in many African cultures. By re-writing the history of African sexualities, the power elite seek to obliterate same-sex relations to bolster their control over the political and social context; to maintain the heteronormative hegemonic hold on women. Such revision facilitates the control of the nation's very identity. How is it even possible to talk about an African sexual morality in a continent as pluralistic and layered as Africa?

It is against such a background that it is important to appreciate that the current homophobic upsurge and the legal winds of re-criminalisation of same sex relations that are sweeping across the African continent from Dakar to Djibouti and from Cairo to Cape Town are not coincidental nor are they mere happenstance. Recent history has connected the religious and politically-inspired homophobia in African states to evangelical renewal movements (aligned with the neo-conservative right) in the United States. Zambian Rev. Kaoma argues that Africa has become a critical locale for these groups due to the demographic shift of the centre of global Christianity to the global south.[63] He claims that the U.S. Christian Right is using African churches, through the divisive issue of homosexuality, as proxies for U.S. culture war battles. They work hand-in-glove with African religious and political leaders to oppose progress in the rights of LGBT (lesbians, gays, bisexuals and transgendered) persons.

Far from being used by the American evangelical movements as suggested by Kaoma, there is a mutual benefit for both groups in spreading homophobic propaganda. The benefits are economic, populist and personality-driven, tinged with hypocritical self-righteousness. Homophobia has simply become a political tool used by conservatives to achieve their selfish agendas. The more important point to note is that anti-homosexuality rhetoric legitimises the standing of its proponents in mainstream thought and maintains their social relevance – whether in the West or in Africa. They have whipped up stigma, discrimination and violence against people engaged (or those perceived to be engaged) in same-sex relations. It is this hysteria that explains why the incidents of so-called 'corrective rapes' of lesbians to turn them into heterosexuals and other homophobic violence are on the rise around the continent.[64]

It is also worth noting that the homophobic gusts blow amidst rising inflation, high unemployment, corruption, repression and increased hopelessness among the African populace. Whether it is the draconian Anti-Homosexuality Act in Uganda (now defunct) or the Nigerian Same Gender Marriage (Prohibition) Act, all homophobic legislations around the continent enjoy populist support thanks to the hegemonic power structures. It was not accidental that the Ugandan bill was tabled in parliament against the backdrop of a conference to expose the 'dark and hidden' agenda of homosexuality organised by a fundamentalist religious NGO called the Family Life Network and funded by right wing American evangelicals.

All the new bills around the continent targeting homoerotic relations ride on the backs of existing legislative codes that criminalise 'unnatural' sexual relations in 38 of Africa's 54 states.[65] Even in South Africa – the only country on the continent that outlaws discrimination on grounds of sexual orientation – the legislative gains for sexual citizenship are constantly threatened by those who wish to reinstate the hegemonic discourse. In 2002, the then Deputy President Jacob Zuma launched the high-profile 'Moral Regeneration Movement' (MRM) which, as its name suggests, was meant to renew the spirituality and morality of the people of South Africa. The campaign, which was carried into Zuma's current presidential term, is implemented by the government in partnership with faith-based organisations. One of its programmes is to build stronger (heterosexual) family structures.[66] Indeed, President Zuma himself is on record for saying that same-sex marriages were '... a disgrace to the nation and to God', a taboo that could not be tolerated in 'any normal society.'[67]

Zuma's remarks go to the core of the negative links between state actors who are intent on constricting the space for civil action and the dominant religious movements, which likewise seek to propagate a particular version of piety and morality. Among African dictatorships, non-conforming sexualities have become a metaphor for immorality and form an effective instrument in the politics of distraction. Instead of blaming political mismanagement and corruption for high unemployment, the high cost of living and poor health facilities, the red herrings will crystallise, among other things, in the form of 'the vice of homosexuality' or 'the evil of prostitution'. And the red herrings are usually fished out of the sea of morality when political accountability is looming.

The irony seems lost on those who condemn same-sex relations as alien while simultaneously bolstering their arguments with 'foreign' religions such as Christianity and Islam. Is it not the mother of all ironies for a Bible-wielding African politician named 'David' and dressed in a three-piece suit, caressing an iPhone and speaking a colonial language to condemn anything for its un-Africanness? Another irony lies in the fact that, in African countries, ideological and political groupings, civic associations, cultural, linguistic and religious organisations that are staunchly opposed in their worldviews quickly rally together in their opposition to non-conforming sexualities. Hence 'progressive' social groups (e.g., children's rights activists) have become strange bedfellows with the most oppressive regimes in Africa in condemning and attacking such sexualities.

The capacity of African women to control their sexual and reproductive lives and to break free from the chains of domesticity is continually curtailed by law, culture and religion.[68] Despite the staggering abortion-related mortality rates[69] on the continent, unrestricted abortions are only legal in Tunisia (1973), Cape Verde (1983) and South Africa (1996).[70] In 2007, Nigeria's efforts to domesticate the UN Convention on the Elimination of All Forms of Discrimination against Women (CEDAW) were thwarted by the patriarch elite who dismissed the CEDAW bill as neo-imperialist. The words of Sonnie Ekwowusi echo those of many other African leaders:

> My humble submission is that Nigeria must not domesticate CEDAW... the *raison d'etre* of CEDAW, the main thrust of the 30-article CEDAW Convention, the whole live wire of CEDAW is centered in Articles 10(h), 12, 14(b) and 16, which are aimed at legalising abortion, sterilisation of women to control population, prostitution, under the soft language of family planning.... I trust that neither the Speaker nor the President of the Senate nor any member of the National Assembly would be deceived to yield to the mounting pressures to domesticate

CEDAW and legalise abortion in Nigeria, which run counter to the aspirations of the Nigerian people and the fundamental objectives and directive principles of state policy enshrined in our constitution. We are obliged to make it known to our countrymen and women that CEDAW is a lying snake which must be killed before it crawls into the house… Africa is for Africans. We must reject the use of African soil as a dumping ground for all sorts of evil by our neo-imperialists.[71]

Even when African states ratify the hard-won women-friendly Protocol to the African Charter on Human and People's Rights on the Rights of Women in Africa (Maputo Protocol), many of them do so with a specific reservation to article 14 relating to the 'right to health and control of reproduction.' Article 14 (2) (c) describes abortion as a human rights issue and calls for member states to authorise medical abortions 'in cases of sexual assault, rape, incest and where the continued pregnancy endangers the mental and physical health of the mother or the foetus.' A faith-based website is dedicated to 'fight against [Article 14 of] the Maputo Protocol.'[72] As I argue elsewhere, laws that restrict the abortion of unplanned pregnancies and force motherhood on women, mesh perfectly with the gender roles that the patriarchal-capitalist state has constructed for women, that is, childcare and homecare. It reinforces the basic notions of repronormativity and leaves little time and room for women to pursue goals outside the confines of domesticity. Thus, the status quo of 'private/domestic' women and the 'public/political' men is safely entrenched in African societies.[73]

Women are sometimes the unwitting reinforcers of the man-made negative discourse regarding our sexualities and the sexualities of 'failed' masculinities such as homosexuality. In analysing representations of African sexualities, Desiree Lewis suggests that the resilience of the reactionary constructions of our sexuality is because:

> [African] individuals often rely on conservative fictions of self to gain acceptance within communities, societies or nations. Both men and women may collude in perpetuating customary laws and practices. This happens not because women and men gain equal measures of power from these, but because many women are able to derive a seemingly enduring and meaningful sense of self and belonging through them. The survival of fictions of sexuality in the myths by which many live and structure their lives is probably the most obvious indicator of our need to interrogate representations of sexuality today.[74]

Given the taboos, silences and mysteries that surround sexuality, the hegemonic discourse remained the master narrative (or meta-narrative) of African sexualities for decades in post-independence Africa. Even mainstream women's rights activists generally shied away from the topic beyond the classics of sexual violence, disease and population control. The hegemony was broken in 2003 when the African Gender Institute at the University of Cape Town, in collaboration with the Institute of African Studies at the University of Ghana organised a pan-

African conference on mapping African sexualities.[75] In the next section of the chapter, I turn to some of the ways that African activists have interrogated and challenged (mis)representations of their sexuality in a bid to shift the normative sexual landscape that has been influenced by the dominant religious, cultural and legal discourses.

Out of the Margins: Challenging Structures of Sexual Oppression

Needless to say, not all Africans passively conform to the hegemonic or dominant sexual discourses constructed by the establishment. Indeed, the turn of the century witnessed the growth of social movements that put up a courageous challenge and provided different inflections to the various 'truths' regarding the sexualities of Africans. African communities that have been pushed to the margins of sexual citizenship, particularly women, have made real attempts to construct a counter-hegemonic sexual discourse through subversion, activism, advocacy and research.[76] Their navigation around hegemonic discourses always throws up critical issues of intersectionality whereby the interactive influences of culture, religion, gender, class, race, ethnicity, age, disability, and geographical location, on one's sexuality are taken into account. Inevitably, such complexities lead to counter-hegemonic intersectional discourses of sexuality that highlight, for example, the sexual rights of physically challenged young women or those of poor refugee homosexuals.

Sexual minorities seek to explode the sexual myths based in essentialist attitudes towards African sexuality (as represented in the singular) and demand for inclusion, justice and dignity. The pursuit of social change has coalesced at the national (e.g., INCRESE in Nigeria, Sister Namibia in Namibia and Sexual Minorities in Uganda), sub-regional (e.g., Justice Associates (JASS) in Southern Africa and The Mediterranean Women's Fund in the Maghreb sub-region) and regional (e.g., Feminist Africa, African Sex Workers Alliance-ASWA and Pan-African Positive Women's Coalition, Coalition of African Lesbians) levels and happens within the range of formal non-governmental organisations, community-based organisations and unregistered grassroots and volunteer groups. Within their diversity, the activist work of sexual minorities across Africa has made serious attempts to build horizontal alliances with mainstream human rights organisations and to link up vertically with international actors (e.g., the African Union, the European Union and the United Nations).

It must be remembered that African political struggles for sexual rights take place against the very powerful institutions of law, culture and religion and their terms of engagement remain contested. This means that activists have to devise creative ways of advancing their cause. For example, fitting their agenda within the frameworks of public health or development is found to be more strategic for some groups than espousing the language of 'sexual empowerment'.[77] The rights framework is similarly attractive to some sexual minorities on the continent for its holistic approach. This section demonstrates how activists have responded to counter essentialist 'truths' and hegemonic discourses about African sexualities. Today, sexuality is indeed on the cutting edge of human rights activism and research on the African continent.

In these struggles, the law is a double-edged sword. Even as states deploy it to construct the hegemonic discourse and to control and regulate the sexualities of African people, activists can also use it to challenge and overturn unjust practices and to effect fundamental change to the status quo.[78] Thanks to the activism of legal feminists, several African states have reformed their sex laws to sanction marital rape, the provision of which has been incorporated into the criminal justice systems of South Africa, Namibia, Zimbabwe, Seychelles and Lesotho. Not only do legal feminists and sexual activists around the continent lobby for law reform, they also engage in strategic action litigation to engender social change in the area of sexuality. For example, laws against special corroboration in rape trials have been abolished by courts in Kenya, Tanzania and Uganda and are facing serious challenge elsewhere.[79]

Strategic litigation has indeed proved to be a powerful, if rather slow, vehicle for challenging 'dangerous' sexuality regulatory laws. In Uganda, feminists successfully challenged a discriminatory law which criminalised extramarital sexual relations for wives but not for husbands (unless they had sexual relations with another man's wife). Hence, the regulatory agenda behind sex laws and the glaring double standards of sexual morality set out in the law have been clearly exposed. In South Africa, although sex work has not yet been decriminalised, the NGO, Sex Workers Education and Advocacy Task Force (SWEAT) won a significant victory when it got the high court in Western Cape to declare that the police was in violation of the rights and dignity of sex workers when they arrest them 'knowing with a high degree of probability that no prosecution will follow.'[80] Justice Burton Fourie elaborated:

> They [sex workers] are rounded up, arrested, detained and, virtually without fail, thereafter discharged without being prosecuted for any offence. I agree with the contention of applicant, that what the police are therefore targeting is not the illegality of sex work *per se*, but rather the public manifestations of it. The arrests of the sex workers therefore amount to a form of social control.[81]

In the oft-quoted case of *Sara Longwe v. Intercontinental Hotels*[82] a feminist in Zambia successfully challenged a hotel policy that prevented 'unaccompanied women' to access their hotel. This discriminatory policy was based on the assumption that women that patronised the hotel bar without male company were prostitutes; it was part of the oppressive patriarchal surveillance machinery.

The rights of homosexuals to human dignity and protection from inhuman treatment have been successfully tested in the Ugandan courts.[83] Through a constitutional law test case, the Ugandan penal code provision on adultery was also declared unconstitutional.[84] At the international level, the United Nations Working Group on Discrimination against Women recently urged governments around the world to repeal laws that criminalise adultery.[85] The emphatic statement said in part:

> Almost two decades ago, international human rights jurisprudence established that criminalization of sexual relations between consenting adults is a violation of their right to privacy and infringement of article 17 of the International Covenant on Civil and Political Rights… Given continued discrimination and inequalities faced by women, including inferior roles attributed to them by patriarchal and traditional attitudes, and power imbalances in their relations with men, the mere fact of maintaining adultery as a criminal offence, even when it applies to both women and men, means in practice that women mainly will continue to face extreme vulnerabilities, and violation of their human rights to dignity, privacy and equality.

The production of shadow reports critiquing the progress of African governments in implementing UN human rights treaties is another strategy that activists have adopted. For example, in 2008 a Nigerian NGO shadow report to the Committee on the Elimination of All Discrimination against Women (CEDAW) elaborated areas in which maternal health objectives could not be met due to failings in policy, legal and administrative areas.[86] Although such reports hardly cause a ripple in national law reform processes, they certainly draw the attention of the international community. They usually work to supplement other strategies mentioned above. At the regional level, landmark success was recorded in May 2014 through a resolution adopted by the African Commission on Human Rights prohibiting discrimination and violence against lesbians, gays, bisexuals and transgendered (LGBT) individuals.[87] Resolution 275 acknowledges the universal rights of LGBT individuals and condemns the increasing incidence of violence on the basis of sexual orientation and/or gender identity. It urges states parties to enact appropriate laws to end all acts of violence and punishment. Moreover, the resolution also calls on states parties to ensure that LGBT rights defenders work in an enabling environment.

During the past three decades reproductive justice has also been realised in some African countries (e.g., Algeria, Botswana, Burkina Faso, Ghana and Ethiopia) where abortion laws have been liberalised in some form.[88] The 1985 Abortion Amendment law in Ghana, for instance, expanded the conditions under which legal abortions could be procured, including pregnancies that result from rape, incest or defilement of a mentally challenged woman.[89] Similar conditions were incorporated into the highly restrictive Ethiopian criminal code in 2004.[90] In both cases, advocates that lobbied for law reform worked within the frameworks of public health and human rights.

Creative and unique methods of resistance and contestation of hegemonic sexual discourses have been adopted across the continent, including silence. There is a legitimate silence surrounding the sexualities of African people whose citizenship has been rendered fragile – a silence that is ambiguous and not able to be engaged. However, the construction of counter-hegemonic discourses of African sexualities is also evident in poetry, novels, artworks, theatre, cinema and photography.[91] For example, a documentary film entitled, *Not Yet Rain*, was produced in Ethiopia to highlight the evils of unsafe abortions. In that documentary, the mother who lost her daughter to a back alley abortion narrates how the abortionist used a catheter wrapped around an umbrella to perform the procedure on her daughter. In Lusophone Africa, feminists have also engaged directly in the political reconstruction of hegemonic discourses on sexuality through critical and historical analyses of works of fiction. In their article, 'Cape Verdean and Mozambican Women's Literature: Liberating the National and Seizing the Intimate,'[92] Isabel Fêo Rodrigues and Kathleen Sheldon analyse novels to demonstrate the link between the political and the intimate arena of sexuality and motherhood.

More radical methods of resistance enlisted by sexual rights activists include the embodied acts of stripping naked – the traditional and powerful 'weapon' that African women have employed for centuries to articulate their anger towards injustice. Historically, women have used their gendered and sexualised bodies to protest extremities, including sexual oppression and their reclamation of their 'undisciplined' bodies. The shocking primordial exposure of women's nudity (or near nudity) in public acts of irreverence and parody has proved quite effective. Desiree Lewis argues that subversion of power through spectacle (such as women enlisting their bodies in resistance) signal a form of 'politics' beyond formal politics that undermines the foundations of the hegemony of repressive regimes.[93] Recently, in Uganda, a group of women activists stripped to their bras in front of the central police station in the capital city to protest against the sexual assault of a female opposition leader by the police force.[94]

In 2008, hundreds of South African women marched to a commuter taxi stand dressed in miniskirts to protest against the harassment for wearing miniskirts.[95] The protest had been sparked off by the treatment of a 25-year woman wearing a miniskirt who had been stripped, paraded naked and sexually assaulted by some drivers in Johannesburg.[96] Similar acts have been reported in Malawi, Nigeria, Democratic Republic of Congo, Sierra Leone, Kenya and a host of other African countries. These 'disciplinary' actions by men are part of the patriarchal surveillance apparatus to preserve the status quo and the spectacle performance by activists is a direct rejection of the dominant gender sexual paradigms. The gay pride parades staged in South Africa (and more recently in Uganda) also demonstrate the subversive power against heterosexist-patriarchal oppression.[97] The power in all the embodied subversive examples given above derives from the reversal of positions where the social superior is subjected to the position of spectator of the 'erotic' spectacle put on by the social inferior. It cannot be denied that those spaces of protest have a counter-hegemonic effect on society.

Finally, one important way that African sexual activists have directly responded to dominant religious discourses is by adopting analytical methodologies that engage in re-interpreting the sacred scripts in the holy books, particularly the Bible. This epistemological approach addresses the important question: *how do we know?* Generally referred to as 'African feminist hermeneutics', these feminist biblical scholars use the African context to analyse the Bible from a critical and scientific point of view, in the bid to expose its sexism.[98] Feminist interpretations of the Bible seeks to uncover the structures of exploitation and oppression embedded therein, to bring to central focus the role of women in history, theology, and ethics, to critique the images of women as portrayed by the writers of the biblical text *and* as explored by its interpreters. African feminist hermeneutics seek alternative theories and methods by which the 'meaning' of the biblical text is generated, and therefrom discuss the relative merits not only of the Bible's interpretation and application, but of the Bible itself. This scholarship is critical in equipping the movement with the liberation language and in offering an alternative discourse from a theological perspective.

Conclusion: African Religion and Sexualities – Toward a Sociolegal Reconstruction

Since the turn of the century, African intellectuals have given serious attention to analysing issues of sexuality on the continent. However, the scholarship is still very much a 'work in progress' with a clear paucity of theoretical and empirical investigations that draw links between law, culture, religion and sexuality. It is important to comprehend the central role that the control and regulation of African sexualities play in maintaining patriarchal-capitalist inequalities in order to strategise for effective social change. The chapter has attempted to illuminate the essentialist roles that law, culture and religion play in organising the moral, social and economic aspects of African sexualities. The pluralist nature of African legal systems both complicates and refines our understanding of sexualities simultaneously as an oppressive and potentially liberating force.

This chapter has further drawn attention to the growing presence of fundamentalist or political religions led by clergy with complex, often opaque, connections to key players from outside Africa and within, as well as to national politicians and, critically, the general population. As one of the most important forces that influence the belief systems that African people have, shaping and defining the deepest values that they hold, religion heavily impacts on sexual morality. The sexual morality espoused by most religions and the law perpetuates gender hierarchies, thereby depriving certain groups of their full citizenship.

When religious fundamentalism worms its way into law, policies, regulations and institutions, it becomes political fundamentalism and targets powerless minorities. Predictably, most of the campaigning and policy efforts of these fundamentalist actors constitute a focused attack on African women's bodily autonomy, integrity and dignity and the criminalisation and persecution of sexual minorities. The authority vested in religions and their leaders is often used negatively by people to justify oppressing, excluding, stifling, manipulating and controlling others. And yet, paradoxically, religion has also provided a fulcrum on which arguments for equality, freedom and liberty have been founded. We need only think of the struggles against colonialism, slavery or apartheid, racial discrimination or civil rights to recognise the role that religion-based movements have played in liberation.

The statutory law provides an indispensable tool in the hands of the powerful to maintain the hierarchical status quo. However, activists around the continent have demonstrated that the same law can be used to engender social justice and transformation. But shifting the broader forms of law found in culture and religion requires strategies that are better able to support people's appreciation of their day-to-day lives. Transformation of existing oppressive sexual scripts propped by religion and culture would require a nuanced approach that seeks to integrate people's local understandings within the human rights discourse.

Some African scholars, such as Abdullahi Ahmed an-Na'im, have devoted considerable time to examining how religion and culture can be legitimately transformed to accommodate human rights and constitutionalism. Given how much African people are entrenched in their traditional and religious beliefs, an-Na'im is convinced that any attempts to pursue reform must be adapted to local conditions.[99] In other words, it is only through people's conviction and agency that social change can happen.[100] Through what he terms 'internal cultural transformation' married to progressive religious interpretations, an-Na'im argues that it is possible to integrate human rights and constitutionalism into culture and religion. We must respect the fact that religion is a place where most Africans anchor their beliefs and values. As such, we should aim at reconstructing religion in a manner that makes it relevant to the needs of African people (particularly women) and work to un-learn the dominant hegemonic religious culture and re-learn a new liberating one. Mobilising religion as a source of rights will resonate with many African people.[101] The challenge is for activists and scholars to develop effective praxis-oriented methods of engendering legal and social change in the quest for sexual citizenship in Africa.

Notes

1. Sexuality, as used in this paper, encompasses a wide array of complex elements, including sexual knowledge, beliefs, values, attitudes and behaviours, as well as procreation, sexual orientation, and personal/interpersonal sexual relations. It touches a wide range of other issues including pleasure, the human body, dress, self-esteem, gender identity, power and violence. It is an all-encompassing phenomenon that involves the human psyche, emotions, physical sensations, communication, creativity and ethics. The pluralistic use of the term is in recognition of the complex structures within which sexuality is constructed as well as its pluralistic articulations. Sylvia Tamale, ed., *African Sexualities: A Reader* (Oxford: Pambazuka Press, 2011), esp. Sylvia Tamale, "Researching and Theorising Sexualities in Africa," in *African Sexualities: A Reader,* ed. Sylvia Tamale (Oxford: Pambazuka Press, 2011), 11-36.
2. Tamale, *African Sexualities: A Reader.*
3. Mogobe Ramose, *African Philosophy through Ubuntu,* Harare: Mond Books, 1999.
4. Quoted in Albie Sachs, *The Strange Alchemy of Life and Law,* London: Oxford University Press, 2009), 106-107.
5. Tamale, *African Sexualities: A Reader.*
6. See Pew Forum on Religion & Public Life, *Tolerance and Tension: Islam and Christianity in Sub-Saharan Africa,* Washington DC: Pew Research Center, 2010); David Barrett, ed.,*World Christian Encyclopedia: A Comparative Study of Churches and Religions in the Modern World,* 2 Vols. (Oxford: Oxford University Press, 2001). Out of a total population of 820 million in Africa, approximately 234 million (28%) are Muslims, while 470 million (57%) are Christians (Pew Forum 2010: i), with the remainder professing ATR.
7. Judith Trimingham, *The Influence of Islam Upon Africa* (London: Longmans, 1968).
8. Makau Mutua, *Human Rights: A Political and Cultural Critique* (Philadelphia: University of Pennsylvania Press, 2002).
9. Chimaraoke Izugbara, "Sexuality and the Supernatural in Africa," in *African Sexualities: A Reader,* ed. Sylvia Tamale (Oxford: Pambazuka Press, 2011); Pew Forum, *Tolerance and Tension;* Lamin Sanneh, "The Domestication of Islam and Christianity in African Societies," *Journal of Religion in Africa* 11(1) (1980): 1-12.
10. Mutua, *Human Rights,* 110.
11. Edwards Evans-Pritchard, *Nuer (African People) Religion,* (Oxford: Clarendon Press, 1956).
12. John Mbiti, "General Manifestations of African Religiosity," Paper Presented at the First Meeting of the Standing Committee on the Contributions of Africa to the Religious Heritage of the World," available at http://www.afrikaworld.net/afrel/mbiti.htm accessed 12 October 2012.
13. Ibid.
14. Abdullahi Ahmed An-Na'im, 'The Politics of Religion and the Morality of Globalization," *Religion in Global Civil Society,* Mark Juergensmeyer, ed., (Oxford: Oxford University Press, 2005), 24.
15. Meredith McGuire, *Religion: The Social Context,* 4th ed. (Belmont, CA: Wadsworth Publishing Company, 1997).

16. Frans Wijsen, 'Popular Christianity in East Africa: Inculturation or Syncretism?' *Exchange* 29(1) (200): 37–60; Matthews Ojo, 'The Contextual Significance of the Charismatic Movements in Western Nigeria,' *Africa* 57(2) (1988): 175–92; Sanneh, 'The Domestication of Islam and Christianity in African Societies'; Byang Kato, *Theological pitfalls in Africa*, Kisumu, Kenya: Evangel Publishing Company, 1975); John Mbiti, 'Christianity and Traditional Religions in Africa' in *Crucial Issues in Missions Tomorrow*, ed. Donald Mcgavran (Chicago: Moody Press, 1972); John Mbiti, 'The Encounter of Christian Faith and African Religion,' *Christian Century* 97(27 Aug. 1980): 817–20.

17. Birgit Meyer, 'Christianity in Africa: From African Independent to Pentecostal-Charismatic Churches,' *Annual Review of Anthropology* 33 (2004): 447- 474; Yvan Droz, Yvan (1997), 'Si Dieu veut ... ou suppôts de Satan; incertitudes, millénarisme et sorcellerie parmi les migrants kikuyus,' *Cahiersd'Etudes Africaines* 145 (1997): 85–114.

18. William Arens, 'Islam and Christianity in Sub-Saharan Africa: Ethnographic Reality or Ideology,' *Cahiers d'études africaines* 15(3) (1975): 443-456.

19. Joan Entwistle, *The Fashioned Body: Fashion, Dress and Modern Social Theory* (Cambridge: Polity Press, 2000), 84; Bibi Bakare-Yusuf 'Nudity and Morality: Legislating Women's Bodies and Dress in Nigeria,' in *African Sexualities: A Reader,* ed. Sylvia Tamale (Oxford: Pambazuka Press, 2011), 122.

20. Mutua, *Human Rights,* 109, 110.

21. It must be noted, however, that in most African legal systems and jurisdictions customary law is overridden by received colonial laws Mutua, *Human Rights.*

22. Antonio Gramsci, *Selections from the Prison Notebooks of Antonio Gramsci,* trans Q. Hoare and G. N. Smith (New York:International Publishers, 1971); Antonio Gramsci, *Prison Notebooks: Volume I,* trans. J. A. Buttigieg (New York: Columbia University Press, 1992); Antonio Gramsci, *Prison Notebooks: Volume II,* trans. J. A. Buttigieg, New York: Columbia University Press, 1996).

23. Mark Stoddart, "Ideology, Hegemony, Discourse: A Critical Review of Theories of Knowledge and Power," *Social Thought and Research* 28 (2007): 191-225.

24. Arleen Dallery, "The Politics of Writing (the) Body," in Alison Jagger and Susan Bordo, *Gender, Body, Knowledge: Feminist Reconstructions of Being and Knowing,* New Brunswick, NJ: Rutgers University Press, 1989).

25. Ibid.

26. There are thousands of popular media houses that are privately owned by mainstream religions as well as Charismatic and Pentecostal denominations all over the continent. For example, in Uganda we have Top TV, Lighthouse TV, Channel 44 and over forty religious broadcasting radio stations.

27. Gayle Rubin, "Thinking Sex: Notes for a Radical Theory on the Politics of Sexuality," in *Pleasure and Danger: Exploring Female Sexuality,* ed. Carole Vance (London: Routledge, 1984).

28. Germain Grisez, Joseph Boyle and John Finnis, "Practical Principles, Moral Truth and Ultimate Ends," *American Journal of Jurisprudence*: 32 (1987): 99-151.

29. John Finnis, *Natural Law and Natural Rights* (Oxford: Clarendon Press, 1980).

30. We use the term 'prostitution' on account of the structured and stigmatised official/legal uses of the term. 'Sex work' is the preferred reference to adult transactional sex

in order to highlight its professional aspects and to move away from its derogatory associations.

31. Nicholas Bamforth and David Richards, *Patriarchal Religion, Sexuality and Gender: A Critique of New Natural Law* (New York: Cambridge University Press, 2007).

32. Kapya Kaoma, *Globalizing the Culture Wars: US Conservatives, African Churches and Homophobia* (Somerville, MA: Political Research Associates, 2009); Ayesha Imam, 'The Muslim Religious Right ("Fundamentalists") and Sexuality', in Pinar Ilkkaracan (Ed.), *Women and Sexuality in Muslim Societies,* (Istanbul: Women for Women's Human Rights (WWHR)/Kadmin Insan Haklari Projesi (KIHP), 2000); Paul Gifford, *The New Crusaders: Christianity and the New Right in Southern Africa,* London: Pluto, 1981).

33. Huma Ahmed-Ghosh, 'Introduction: Lesbians, Sexuality and Islam,' *Journal of Lesbian Studies* 16(4) (2012): 377-380.

34. Charmaine Pereira, '*Zina* and Transgressive Heterosexuality in Northern Nigeria,' *Feminist Africa* 5 (2005): 75.

35. Karen Fields, *Revival and Rebellion in Colonial Central Africa* (Princeton, NJ: Princeton University Press, 1985); John D. Y. Peel, 'The Pastor and the *Babalawo*: the Interaction of Religions in Nineteenth Century Yorubaland,' *Africa* 60(3) (1990): 338–69; John D.Y. Peel, *Religious Encounter and the Making of the Yoruba,* Bloomington: Indiana University Press, 2003); John and Jean Comaroff, *Of Revelation and Revolution: Christianity, Colonialism, and Consciousness in South Africa,* Vol. 1.(Chicago: University of Chicago Press, 1991); John and Jean Comaroff, *Revelation and Revolution: The Dialectics of Modernity on a South African Frontier*, Vol. 2. (Chicago: University of Chicago Press, 1997); Norman Etherington, 'Recent Trends in the Historiography of Christianity in Southern Africa,' *Journal of Southern African Studies.* 22(2) (1996): 201–19; Meyer, 'Christianity in Africa,' 2004.

36. Michel Foucault, 'Truth and Power,' in *Power/Knowledge: Selected Interviews and Other Writings, 1972-1977,* ed, Colin Gordon (Brighton: Harvester, 1980; Michel Foucault, *The History of Sexuality, Volume I: An Introduction,* Translated by R. Hurley, New York: Vintage Books, 1978); Michel Foucault, *Discipline and Punish: The Birth of the Prison,* trans. A. Sheridan (Harmondsworth: Peregrine, 1977).

37. Desiree Lewis, 'Gendered Spectacle: New Terrains of Struggle in South Africa,' in *Body Politics and Women Citizens: African Experiences,* ed, Ann Schlyter (Stockholm: SIDA, 2009).

38. Jane Bennett, 'Subversion and Resistance: Activist Initiatives,' in *African Sexualities: A Reader,* ed, Sylvia Tamale (Oxford: Pambazuka Press, 2011).

39. Tamale, *African Sexualities: A Reader.*

40. Friedrich Engels, *The Origin of the Family, Private Property and the State*, New York: Penguin Books, 1972); Barrett, *Women's Oppression Today.*

41. Eli Zaretsky, *Capitalism, the Family and Personal Life* (New York: Harper and Row, 1976).

42. See Deutronomy 22:22 and Leviticus 20:10.

43. Also by keeping women in a subordinate position, capitalism can justify and profit from paying women who work outside the home lower wages and employing them under worse conditions than men.

44. Zaretsky, *Capitalism, the Family and Personal Life;* Linda Nicholson, *Gender and History: The Limits of Social Theory in the Age of the Family* (New York: Columbia University Press, 1986).

45. Oyeronke Oyewumi, *The Invention of Women: Making an African Sense of Western Gender Discourse*, Minneapolis: University of Minnesota Press, 1997); Ifi Amadiume, *Reinventing Africa: Matriarchy, Religion and Culture*, London: Zed Books, 1997).

46. Capitalism, the Family and Personal Life;

47. Ayesha Imam, 'The Muslim Religious Right ("Fundamentalists") and Sexuality'.

48. See, for example, in the Bible: 1 Corinthians 6: 9-10; Matthew 19: 9; 1 Thessalonians 4: 3; Genesis 38: 9-10; Exodus 20: 14; Leviticus 19: 29; Leviticus 20: 13; and Deuteronomy 22: 22. And in the Qur'an: Sūrah 24: 2-3, 30-33; Sūrah 4: 15-16; and Sūrah 7: 81-84. In addition, there are several Islamic examples found in hadith books e.g., Sahih Buhari Vol. 3 Book 48 No. 817.

49. See 'Breaking News: No More Trousers for Redeemed Ladies, Adeboye Orders,' http://www.nairaland.com/71063/breaking-news-no-more-trousers   (accessed   5 January 2013).

50. Bakare-Yusuf, 'Nudity and Morality,' 117, 122.

51. Pereira, '*Zina* and Transgressive Heterosexuality in Northern Nigeria'.

52. Rosemary Radford Ruether, *Sexism and God-Talk: Towards a Feminist Theology* London: SCM Press, 1983), 7.

53. Mistaken belief is a defence available to individuals accused of sexual offences. If they can establish that they had an honest and reasonable mistaken belief of a fact (e.g., the age of the victim), they will be let off the hook.

54. Evidentiary rules allow a man accused of rape to put up the defence of 'general immoral character' on the part of the female victim in order to impeach her credibility.

55. This evidentiary rule requires the evidence of a complainant in cases of sexual assault to be independently corroborated. Hence, the court must always warn itself of the danger of convicting an accused rapist on the uncorroborated evidence of the complainant.

56. In the case of *The State v. Jacob Gedleyihlekisa Zuma*, the South African High Court allowed Zuma's lawyers to cross-examine the complainant about her sexual history, thereby violating her rights to dignity, privacy and equality. See Jake Moloi, 'The Case of S V. Zuma: Implications of Allowing Evidence of Sexual History in Rape Trials,' *South African Crime Quarterly* Issue 18: 25 (2006). Also see, Elizabeth Skeen, 'The Rape of a Trial: Jacob Zuma, AIDS, Conspiracy and Tribalism in Neo-Liberal Post-Apartheid South Africa,' BA Thesis, Princeton University (April 2007). Available at: http://www.friendsofjz.co.za/documents/The%20Rape%20of%20a%20Trial.pdf accessed Dec 26, 2012.

57. Pereira, '*Zina* and Transgressive Heterosexuality in Northern Nigeria'.

58. Kalala Ngalamulume, 'Le Péril Vénérien: L'État Colonial Français et la Sexualité à Saint-Louis-du-Sénégal, 1850-1920,'['The Venereal Peril: The French Colonial State and Sexuality in Saint-Louis, Senegal, 1850-1920'] in Conquêtes Médicales: Histoire de la Médecine Moderne et des Maladies en Afrique [Medical Conquests: the History of Modern Medicine and Diseases in Africa], ed. Jean-Paul Bado (Paris: Karthala, 2006).

59. UNAIDS Report on the Global AIDS Epidemic, available at: http://www.unaids.org/globalreport/Global_report.htm accessed Dec 18, 2012.

60. Sylvia Tamale, 'Paradoxes of Sex Work and Sexuality in Modern-Day Uganda,' *East African Journal of Peace and Human Rights* 15(1) (2009): 69-109.

61. African Sex Worker Alliance (2011), ' "I Expect to be Abused and I have Fear": Sex Workers' Experiences of Human Rights Violations and Barriers to Accessing Healthcare in Four African Countries,' Research Report available at: http://africansexworkeralliance. org/sites/default/files/ASWA%20Report%20HR%20Violations%20and%20 Healthcare%20Barriers%2014%20April%202011.pdf, accessed Dec 12, 2012; Tamale, "Paradoxes of Sex Work and Sexuality in Modern-Day Uganda".

62. Marc Epprecht, *Heterosexual Africa? The History of an Idea from the Age of Exploration to the Age of AIDS* (Athens: Ohio University Press, 2008); Marc Epprecht, *Unspoken Facts: A History of Homosexuality in Africa* (Harare: GALZ, 2008); Stephen Murray and Will Roscoe, eds., *Boy-Wives and Female Husbands: Studies of African Homosexualities* (New York: Palgrave, 1998); Gilbert Herdt, 'Representations of Homosexuality: An Essay in Cultural Ontology and Historical Comparison, Parts I and II,' *Journal of the History of Sexuality* 1(3) & (4) (1991): 481-505; 603-632; Boris de Rachewiltz, *Black Eros: Sexual Customs of Africa from Prehistory to the Present Day,* trans. Peter Whigham, New York: Stewart, 1964). Note that the concept, 'homosexuality' which originated and evolved from the West does not necessarily hold the same historical and contemporary meanings in the African context of same sex relations and typologies.

63. Kaoma, *Globalizing the Culture Wars.* Also see Kapya Kaoma, *American Culture Warriors in Africa: A Guide to the Exporters of Homophobia and Sexism* (Boston, MA: Political Research Associates, 2014).

64. Mary Hames, 'Violence against Black Lesbians: Minding our Language,' *Agenda* 25(4) (2011): 87-90.

65. Jessica Horn, 'Re-Righting the Sexual Body' *Feminist Africa* 6 (2006): 7-32

66. Louise Vincent, 'Moral Panic and the Politics of Populism,' *Representation* 45(2) (2009): 213-221.

67. Legogang Seale, 'Zuma's Anti-Gay Comments Lead to Backlash,' *The Star,* 27 September 2006.

68. Sa'diyya Shaikh, 'Morality, Justice and Gender: Reading Muslim Tradition on Reproductive Choices,' in *African Sexualities: A Reader,* ed. Sylvia Tamale (Oxford: Pambazuka Press, 2011); Sylvia Tamale, 'Gender Trauma in Africa: Enhancing Women's Links to Resources,' *Journal of African Law* 48(1) (2004): 50-61.

69. The World Health Organisation (WHO) reported that in 2008 the unsafe abortion mortality ratio in Africa was 80 per 100,000 live births, four times higher than the Asian region and eight times as high as in the Latin American and Caribbean regions (see 'Unsafe Abortion Incidence and Mortality: Global and Regional Levels and Trends during 1990-2008,' available at http://apps.who.int/iris/bitstream/10665/75173/1/ WHO_RHR_12.01_eng.pdf last accessed on Dec 15, 2012

70. In the three countries abortions are legally unrestricted during the first trimester of pregnancy and thereafter they can be procured under certain conditions.

71. 'Why Nigeria Must Not Domesticate CEDAW,' *The Guardian* (Nigeria), 18 July 2007.

72. See http://www.maputoprotocol.com/the-fight-against-the-maputo-protocol accessed 8 January 2013.

73. Sylvia Tamale, ëLaw, Sexuality and Politics in Uganda: Challenges for Womenís Human Rights NGOs,í in Makau Mutua, ed., *Human Rights NGOs in East Africa* (Philadelphia: University of Pennsylvania Press, 2009)

74. Desiree Lewis, 'Representing African Sexualities,' in Sylvia Tamale, ed., *African Sexualities: A Reader,* (Oxford: Pambazuka Press, 2011), 213.

75. Sylvia Tamale, 'Researching and Theorising Sexualities in Africa'; Amina Mama, 'Is It Ethical to Study Africa? Preliminary Thoughts on Scholarship and Freedom,' *African Studies Review* 50(1) (2007): 1-26.

76. Jane Bennett, 'Subversion and Resistance: Activist Initiatives'.

77. Bennett, 'Subversion and Resistance: Activist Initiatives'.

78. Sylvia Tamale and Jane Bennett, 'Legal Voice: Challenges and Prospects in the Documentation of African Legal Feminism,' *Feminist Africa* 15 (2011): 1-15.

79. Sarah Bott, Andrew Morrison, and Mary Ellsberg, ëPreventing and Responding to Gender-Based Violence in Middle and Low-Income Countries: A Global Review and Analysis,í *World Bank Policy Research Working Paper 3618* (Washington DC: World Bank, 2005); E.K.Quansah, ëCorroborating the Evidence of a Rape Victim in Botswana: Time for a Fresh Look,í *Botswana Notes & Records* 28 (1996): 231-238.

80. Justice Burton Fourie in *SWEAT v. The Minister of Safety & Security* (2009)6 SA 513 at 57.

81. Ibid.

82. 1992/HP/765. Also see, Sara Hlupekile Longwe, 'Case Study: Legal Action to Stop Hotels Discriminating against Women in Zambia,' *Feminist Africa* 15: 83-104 (2011).

83. See the cases of *Victor Mukasa & Yvonne Ayo v. AG* [Hct Misc. Cause No. 247 of 2006] and *Kasha Jacqueline, David Kato & Onziema Patience v. Rolling Stone Ltd. & Giles Muhame* [Hct Misc. Cause No. 163 of 2010]. The latest case of *Oloka-Onyango and 9 Others v. Attorney-General,* [Const. Pet. No. 8 of 2014] overturned the Anti-Homosexuality Act on a legal technicality.

84. See case of *Law and Advocacy for Women in Uganda v. Attorney General* [Unreported Const. Pet. No. 13 of 2005]. Also see Jamil Mujuzi, 'The Constitutional Court of Uganda and Women's Right to Equality: the "Adultery Judgment,"' *East African Journal of Peace & Human Rights* 16(2): 474-492 (2010).

85. Dated October 12, 2012. See full statement at: http://www.ohchr.org/EN/NewsEvents/Pages/DisplayNews.aspx?NewsID=12672&LangID=E last accessed 12 December 2012.

86. See http://www.fidh.org/IMG/pdf/BAOBABNigeria41.pdf accessed 26 Dec 2012. Also see Ann Godwin, 'Women Protest Against Delay in Passing Bill on Eliminating Discrimination,' *The Guardian* 16 November 2011.

87. See Resolution 275 on Protection against Violence and other Human Rights Violations against Persons on the basis of their real or imputed Sexual Orientation or Gender Identity available at: www.achpr.org/sessions/55th/resolutions/275/ [last accessed October 20, 2014].

88. Marge Berer, 'Making Abortions Safe: A Matter of Good Public Health Policy and Practice,' *Bulletin of the World Health Organization* 78(5) (2000): 580-592.

89. See Ghanaian Criminal Code (Amendment), 1985 (amending Criminal Code-29 of 1960), sections 58 & 59.

90. See Article 551 of the Federal Republic of Ethiopian Criminal Code as amended in 2004.

91. See e.g.,Tamale, *African Sexualities: A Reader.*

92. Isabel Fêo Rodrigues and Kathleen Sheldon (2010), 'Cape Verdean and Mozambican Women's Literature: Liberating the National and Seizing the Intimate,' *African Studies Review* 53(3) (2010): 77-99.

93. Desiree Lewis, 'Gendered Spectacle: New Terrains of Struggle in South Africa,' in *Body Politics and Women Citizens: African Experiences,* ed.Ann Schlyter (Stockholm: SIDA, 2009).

94. The police officers violently squeezed the breast of Ingrid Turinawe in the process of arresting her. See, John Njoroge, 'Police Arrest Women Activists,' *DailyMonitor,* April 23, 2012. Available at: http://www.monitor.co.ug/News/National/-/688334/1392006/-/avjh6iz/-/index.html accessed Dec 27, 2012

95. C. Lowe-Morna, C. 'Long and short of the miniskirt debate,'

96. See 'Hundreds of Women in Miniskirt Protest,' *Mail & Guardian,* 4 March 2008. Available at: http://mg.co.za/article/2008-03-04-hundreds-of-women-in-miniskirt-protest accessed 27 Dec 2012

97. Lewis, 'Gendered Spectacle.'

98. See, e.g., Sarojini Nadar, 'Power, Ideology and Interpretation/s: Womanist and Literary Perspectives on the Book of Esther as Resources for Gender-Social Transformation,' presentation at the School of Theology, University of Natal, Pietermaritzburg, 2003; Musa Dube, ed.*Other Ways of Reading: African Women and the Bible,* (Atlanta and Geneva: Society of Biblical Literature & WCC Publications, 2001; Musa Dube, *Postcolonial Feminist Interpretation of the Bible,* (St. Louis: Chalice Press, 2000); Dora Rudo Mbuwayesango, 'Childlessness and Women to Women Relationships in Genesis and in African Patriarchal Society: Sarah and Hagar from a Zimbabwean Woman's Perspective (Gen 16:116; 21:821),' *Semeia* 78 (1997): 2736; Teresa Okure, 'Feminist Interpretation in Africa,' in *Searching the Scriptures: A Feminist Introduction,* ed. Elizabeth Schüssler Fiorenza (New York: Crossroad, 1993).

99. Abdullahi Ahmed An-Na'im, *Human Rights in Cross-Cultural Perspectives: A Quest for Consensus* Philadelphia: University of Pennsylvania Press, 1992); Abdullahi An-Na'im, *Islam and the secular state: Negotiating the future of shari'a,* Cambridge: Harvard University Press, 2008).

100. This reasoning is in line with the perspectives of Western theorists Max Weber and Anthony Giddens.

101. Gerrie Ter Haar, *How God Became African: African Spirituality and Western Secular Thought* (Philadelphia: University of Pennsylvania Press, 2009).

3

The Power of Pleasure: Re-conceptualising Sexualities

Signe Arnfred

A new and needed focus on female sexuality as pleasure and desire is emerging, challenging previous approaches, which mainly saw female sexualities as areas of risk and danger. For a long time, research on sexualities in Africa was marked by colonial representations of 'African sexuality' as primitive, exotic and excessively sexual – i.e., profoundly Other, compared to European Christian norms of decency and morality – and/or by medicalised approaches centred on reproduction. Western feminist crusades in the 1970s and 1980s against Female Genital Mutilation focused on pain, suffering and sexual violence (perpetuating dynamics of Othering, in as far as previously over-sexed African women now were seen as pitifully de-sexualised) – and the HIV & AIDS pandemic, gaining ground in the 1980s and 1990s, engendered a re-medicalisation of African sexualities (Tamale 2011b:16-19). These approaches to sexuality are still dominant, but alternative voices are gaining ground. The point is not only to get a new focus, but to conceptualise issues of sexualities in different ways.

Two important contributions in this regard are Nkiru Nzegwu's chapter: "Osunality, or African Eroticism' in the volume on *African Sexualities*, edited by Sylvia Tamale (2011), and Bibi Bakare-Yusuf's chapter: 'Thinking with Pleasure' in the volume on *Women's Sexuality and the Political Power of Pleasure*, edited by Susie Jolly, Andrea Cornwall and Kate Hawkins (2013). An initial discussion of these two chapters will set the tone for the rest of the paper, which is based on a mixture of a (re-)analysis of data material from my own research in Mozambique and contributions by other researchers based on material from elsewhere in Africa. Taking off from the importance of re-conceptualisations – or even 'epistemic ruptures' (Adesina 2010:3) – the paper will strive to 'flip the dominant script'

(Bakare-Yusuf 2013:36) and come up with counter-narratives, i.e. different stories of female sexualities. The paper has a double focus: on conceptualisations, highlighting new ways to think about sexuality in Africa, and on data material focused on female sexual pleasure. Obviously, conceptualisations and narratives feed into one another: alternative concepts lead to new ways of seeing.[1]

Framing Alternative Approaches to Analysis of Female Sexualities

In her contribution to re-thinking sexualities in Africa, Nkiru Nzegwu (2011) frames a comparison between Africa and the West as a matter of two different logics, with reference to Cheikh Anta Diop's classical works, mapping out inherent differences between Indo-European cultures, on the one hand, and African cultures on the other: '[The] sexualised gender hierarchy of the West eroticises male dominance and female subjugation as sexual (...) making eroticism and sexuality a basis for women's moral anguish, conflict and downfall' (Nzegwu 2011:255). By contrast, in African cultures, 'sexual pleasure and fulfilment were equally expected for both women and men, and sensuality was neither pornographic nor the basis of women's subjugation and domination, as was the case in Europe' (Nzegwu 2011:254). Nzegwu points out 'the error in believing that terms such as erotic and sexual pleasure have the same meaning in the mother-centered African cultural universe as they do in the patriarchal European cultural universe,' maintaining that 'we do epistemological violence to Africa and the conceptual schemes of similarly situated cultures, when we fold their underlying matri-focal ideology and principles of complementarity into Europe's patriarchal structure' (Nzegwu 2011:256). 'African sexual ontology' Nzegwu asserts, 'is not Western sexual ontology in a black face; (...) it has its own defined history; (...) it is in fact quite progressive and a resilient stronghold of female power' (Nzegwu 2011:254).

In Yoruba contexts, this female power points back to Osun, the Yoruba divinity of 'fertility, wealth, joy, sensuality and childbirth' (Nzegwu 2011:258). Based on ancient sacred texts of Yoruba culture (Ifa divination) Nzegwu describes Osun as representing 'a pronatalist, female-centred, life-transforming energy (...) highly sensual and sexual' (Nzegwu 2011:258). Note here the interconnection of sexuality and fertility, which makes an interesting contrast to Western notions of sexuality as different from, even opposed to fertility and motherhood, epitomised in the Madonna/whore dichotomy: women as seen (by men) as either a-sexual mothers (morally elevated) or as sexual objects (morally debased).

From a similar position, also seeing sexuality as a stronghold of female power, Bibi Bakare-Yusuf draws a parallel between the Nigerian deity Osun and the biblical figure of Eve. Bakare-Yusuf makes a similar observation of different approaches to, and conceptualisations of, female sexuality. She, however, does not link them to geography (Africa/the West). Eve also represents female desire – with the well-known consequence of being expelled from the Garden of Eden. There is a tension at the heart of Christianity, Bakare-Yusuf says, in as far as 'desire manifests itself at the outset and is immediately cast out. At the moment of desire's coming to presence, it leads to expulsion. Fertility must be excised from any relation to an originary female desire or action' (Bakare-Yusuf 2013:34). In fact, as Bakare-Yusuf also points out, 'coitus is what leads to fertility and reproduction, and not the other way round' (Bakare-Yusuf 2013:34). Nevertheless, Christianity has managed to separate the two in the figure of Mary, and her miraculous conception, free of coitus: the Bible gives the terms of the Madonna/whore dichotomy. There is a point to keeping female desire subdued and invisible; the point is patriarchal power. 'For societies that have been subsumed under the panoptical gaze of Christian colonialism (...) occluding female originary desire (...) helps to reduce the opportunities for resistance. In other words, if female sexual pleasure and desire is highlighted, the supremacy of male desire, power and control are called into question' (Bakare-Yusuf 2013:35). In this optic, maintaining a focus on female sexual pleasure and desire has important political implications regarding resistance to patriarchal power. We may here recall Audre Lorde's assertion of the erotic as power. In Lorde's understanding, 'the erotic' is an inherently subversive force, a source of mobilization against oppression: 'In order to perpetuate itself,' she says, 'every oppression must corrupt and distort those various sources of power within the culture of the oppressed that can provide energy for change. For women, this has meant a suppression of the erotic as a considered source of power and information within our lives' (Lorde 1984:53). Lorde's insights have been brought into African sexuality studies by, among others, Patricia McFadden (2003), and Sylvia Tamale (2005).

This does not mean, of course, that female sexuality is not also an area of 'violence, sexual epidemics, population explosion, domination, mutilation, repression and lack of choice' (Bakare-Yusuf 2013:28). However, it is not only that. The dominant discourse in African studies and development contexts is this 'hegemonic discourse of sexual terrorism', as Bakare-Yusuf calls it (Bakare-Yusuf 2013:29). Furthermore, 'positioning women as weak or damaged subjects gives renewed legitimacy to patriarchally motivated discourses of control and protection' (Bakare-Yusuf 2013:30). The importance of counter-narratives becomes obvious. 'Telling stories about female sexual pleasure, agency and power allows us to uncover a tradition and community of powerful, feisty, indomitable women who will not be cowed by oppression or violation' (Bakare-Yusuf 2013:37).

Nzegwu actually tells such stories. The ways she does it, in a juxtaposition between African and Western logics, is, however, risky, open to misunderstandings and charges of essentialism. Nzegwu is aware of this danger, also inherent in Cheikh Anta Diop's scheme of two cradles of civilization (Diop 1959/1978) setting up patriarchal Indo-European cultures as against the mother-centred logic of African societies. Nzegwu defends her position in the following terms: 'Some might construe this reference to an African sexual universe and (...) African sexual ontology as a gross homogenisation of Africans, at best, and of essentialism at worst. I should state that I am well aware of the diversity of cultures and the heterogeneity of the peoples of Africa. However, recognition of differences does not automatically preclude identification of similarities,' she says, pointing to 'underlying structural commonalities in the patterns of beliefs, family systems, social ethos, ideology and practices that need to be articulated' (Nzegwu 2011:266). I both agree and disagree with Nzegwu here. Yes, there are lots of commonalities in patterns of belief, family systems, and so on, across Africa. However, the issue at stake has to do with sexual cultures, and yes, Western sexual cultures are heavily influenced by Christianity. But so are African sexual cultures, after colonialism, and particularly after being 'transformed and reconfigured by evangelical strains in the post-structural adjustment era of the 1980s' (Bakare-Yusuf 2013:33). After all, it is not a question of generalising about Africa (or about the West for that matter) but to replace misleading Western categorisations and assumptions of male dominance/female subordination with alternative, more inclusive conceptualisations, open to different realities.

The issue, thus, is how to *think* about male and female sexualities, deconstructing and *unlearning* dominant ideas and lines of thinking, in the field of sexuality as in gender relations in general. Seen in this light, re-conceptualisations of sexualities in Africa become a continuation of the general re-conceptualisation of gender and gender relations in Africa, initiated by African post-colonial feminist scholarship, and signposted in important conceptual contributions, e.g. by Ifi Amadiume (1987, 1997) and Oyèrónké Oyewùmí (1997, 2000, 2002) among others.

Epistemic Ruptures in Thinking about Gender

In his recognition of the importance of Amadiume's and Oyewùmí's scholarship, Nigerian sociologist, Jimi Adesina praises their work as 'producing epistemic ruptures in the global discourses around the sociological understandings of gender relations and how we understand 'gender" (Adesina 2010:3). What earns them this praise is first and foremost that they do not just 'deploy local data without challenging the received theories and conceptual frameworks, that is, they do not just continue the well-known international division of labour 'in which Africa and Africans supply the data and their Euro-American counterparts supply the theory' (Adesina 2010:3-4). On the contrary, what Amadiume and Oyewùmí have both done is that they 'allow their data to produce conceptual outcomes appropriate to its uniqueness. The result is an important epistemic shift in our understanding of a *global idea* of gender' (Adesina 2010:9). Appropriately, in my view, Adesina is pointing to *epistemic ruptures* in global ideas regarding gender, not just to the coining of concepts better suited to understanding particularly African realities. As arguments for his claim regarding 'epistemic ruptures', Adesina highlights the following aspects of Amadiume's and Oyewùmí's works.

There is, first, Amadiume's focus on matrifocality or matricentricity as an organising principle of society, not just as produced by instability or absent men, the context of the concept in previous anthropological writings (Adesina 2010:5). Actually, as Amadiume notes, for European anthropologists the idea of men *not* playing decisive social roles, was hard to grasp; 'the invisible, transitory or distant role of a man as father in African kinship was extremely difficult for the European mind to accept.' European writers, she says, 'kept looking for a man as father or a man as the axis around which all rotated' (Amadiume 1997:80). Contrary to this, the point for Amadiume in her focus on matrifocality is exactly the 'shift of focus from man at the centre and in control to the primacy of the role of the mother/sister in economic, social, political and religious institutions' (Amadiume 1997:80). In this change of focus, she too takes important inspiration from Cheikh Anta Diop's works, Diop being the first to talk and write about matriarchal understandings of African societies. For Amadiume, the use of concepts like 'matriarchy', matricentricity/matrifocality and 'the motherhood paradigm' helps her to avoid the trap of simply (like much conventional anthropology) taking patriarchy for granted: 'The recognition of the motherhood paradigm prevents the error of taking patriarchy as given, or as a paradigm' (Amadiume 1997:154). Adesina emphasises the aspects of female power: 'for Amadiume matriarchy refers to the exercise of power by women within their societies,' he says. 'In other words, matrifocality is not simply about mother-rights or a society or family being 'mother-centric', rather Amadiume shows how it reflects the domains of the legitimate exercise of power by women' (Adesina 2010:11).

Another point of epistemic rupture highlighted by Adesina is Oyewùmí's statement that 'gender was not an organising principle in Yoruba society prior to its colonisation by the West' (Oyewùmí 1997:31, Adesina 2010:8). Unlike gender, hierarchies of *seniority* would always be important, according to Oyewùmí. In Yoruba, Oyewùmí's native tongue, 'most names and pronouns are ungendered. (...) [Thus] it is possible to hold a long and detailed conversation about a person without indicating the gender of that person. (...) There is, however, considerable anxiety about establishing seniority in any social interaction (Oyewùmí 1997:40). Also, unlike 'gender', 'seniority is highly relational and situational in that no one is permanently in a senior or junior position; it all depends on who is present in any given situation. Thus, it is neither rigidly fixated on the body, nor dichotomised' (Oyewùmí 1997:42; Adesina 2010:8).

I agree with Adesina that Amadiume and Oyewùmí have greatly facilitated the opening of minds of feminists for alternative thinking; they have helped us *unlearn* what has previously been taken as basic terms of feminist scholarship (such as the centrality of gender, and presumed universal pattern of male dominance/female subordination). Moreover, even if neither Amadiume nor Oyewùmí is much concerned about sexualities, their innovative thinking has clear implications also for sexuality studies.

Female Initiation Rituals in Northern Mozambique

Now for the narratives. My involvement with the analysis of sexuality in Mozambique is a long story, starting in the early 1980s when I was working as an employee of the National Mozambican Women's Organization, the OMM (Organizacão da Mulher Moçambicana).[2] Mozambique, at that point, was a one-party state, and the OMM was closely linked to the governing party Frelimo. After a while, I realised that the OMM's story of women in Mozambique did not match the stories I heard from the women themselves, particularly those in the northern provinces of the country, to which OMM sent me on a research trip. The contradictions centred on different understandings of the female rituals of initiation – seen by Frelimo and the OMM as woman oppressive and degrading, reinforcing the subordinate status of women in relation to men, but experienced by the women themselves as very important, absolutely indispensable, central to their femininity, and (in my analysis) key in their power struggle with men. A power struggle, which had intensified after the coming to power of Frelimo with its socialist and astutely masculinist ideology (for more detailed analysis, see Arnfred 2011).

I tried to keep a focus on how things were seen and experienced by the women, taking this as a point of departure for my analysis. Part of this experience had to do with the ethnic groups in northern Mozambique being matrilineal – a fact that was (also) not known and not accounted for by Frelimo or by the OMM. The Frelimo/OMM understanding of women's lives seemed to have more to do with received ideas of women's emancipation (in this case, socialist theories from Friedrich Engels onwards) than with knowledge of gender relations on the ground. My attempts to explain, on my return to the OMM headquarters in Maputo, how I had come to see these issues, based on meetings with women of the north, had no impact whatsoever. The OMM leadership was more interested in listening to the bosses in Frelimo than to rural women in a distant province. It also complicated matters, of course, that in a certain sense the rituals *were* oppressive; only that this had nothing to do with relations between women and men, but more with relations between older and younger women. The older women were in power, the young initiates the underdogs. But once initiated, every woman could take part in future rituals of initiation, now in positions of increasing seniority (cf the point made by Oyewùmí above). Thus, the experience of the rituals was very different from the points of view of the initiates (being bossed around by older women) as compared to the points of view of all other participating women, who enjoyed themselves having a good time with juicy jokes, provocative dancing, sexual license and lots of laughter.

I came to see the female initiation rituals as very important for the women and for their unity and strength *vis a vis* men, particularly at the early 1980s historical juncture, shortly after the end of the war of liberation (from Portuguese colonial power) when male dominance (supported by Frelimo) was gaining ground even in the matrilineal north. Women felt squeezed and pressured to give up traditional rights rooted in matrilineal norms, such as easy access to divorce, and – in the case of divorce – of gaining custody of the matrimonial house and children. In such circumstances, women needed the unity of gender more than ever – unity that was created and enhanced by and through the rituals of initiation.

Preparations of the Erotic Body

I was intrigued by these rituals. It seemed to me that in the matrilineal setup of the northern provinces, particular emphasis was given to female sexuality. Young women were educated as sexual experts, instructed in how to seduce and have pleasurable sex with the male partners they needed to become pregnant. Of course, the entire range of sexual preparations of the young women's bodies – from the elongation of the *labia minora* (starting well before puberty, so that when getting to the rituals of initiation they have already reached the desired length), over the body tattoos/ scarifications (they are always referred to as tattoos in Mozambique) to the strings of glass beads (*missangas* in Portuguese) worn around the hips – in a patriarchal context might be interpreted as female subordination to male sexual pleasures. But nothing in my data indicated that this was the case. On the contrary, it was my clear impression that women, as masters and initiators of sexuality, were proud of their capacities, and that they themselves enjoyed the sexual encounters just as did the enchanted men. In this social setup, women emerged as sexual agents; men as the ones being seduced. Older women were the seasoned experts, particularly those whose business it was to act as experts of female initiation; these women would often also be diviners, with special gifts and capacities regarding making contacts and relations with the world beyond. Belonging to a lineage in these contexts are not just the living, but also the dead, the ancestors, and the yet unborn; women are seen to be central in reaching out to these segments of the lineage.

Below, I will elaborate on different aspects of preparations of the erotic body. The stories – in terms of fieldwork quotes – will focus on body tattoos/scarifications, on *missangas*, on elongated labia *(ethuna)* – all of this being body markings or adornments – and on perfumes, scents and erotic movements. For some of the stories, I'll go beyond my own fieldwork and beyond Mozambique, taking in material from other places in Africa, collected by other researchers. My data from Mozambique derive from two different sources. One part is obtained from my own interviews and investigations conducted from 1981 to 1984, when I was an employee of the OMM, and later (1998 to 2005) as an independent researcher. Another set of data derives from the OMM archives: a nationwide database on 'women's social situation' collected from 1983-1984 in preparation for the Extraordinary OMM Conference of 1984. Preparation for, and supervision of, this nationwide study was the very reason for my employment by the OMM.

Body Tattoos/Scarifications

It was my impression in the early 1980s that women's body tattoos were now less frequent, particularly in urban settings. However, I vividly remember when interviewing a group of women in a Maputo factory in 1981, how one participant after another laughingly pulled up their blouses, showing stomachs with all kinds of tattoo designs. These women, who were in their 30s and 40s had all been raised in the countryside in the southern provinces of Mozambique, only coming to the city as grown-ups with their husbands or as single/divorced mothers seeking jobs. When I subsequently attended several sessions of women's initiation rituals in the north of Mozambique where the initiates as well as some of the accompanying women undressed, I noticed that most accompanying women (in their 20s and 30s) had elaborate body tattoos, while as a general rule the young initiates (in their teens) did not. Of course some of the initiates might have acquired them later on. The body tattoos are folds of skin filled with charcoal powder. When healed they give an uneven body surface, which – cut in pretty designs – is/was considered having aesthetic value as well as important sexual functions. Previously, the design would show the bearer's identity and membership of a particular family or ethnic group, but nowadays there is a free choice of patterns (within certain limits) according to the preference of the girl. In some cases, the work is done by a tattoo-cutting expert, in other cases by the girls themselves. Here are some descriptions from the Province of Gaza (in the south) and Cabo Delgado (the north of Mozambique):[3]

> In every region, there would be women known as experts for cutting tattoos. Generally, they would use a piece of wire bent like a hook, together with a razor blade. They would cut the tattoos in accordance with the preference of the girl in question. The expert would oblige the girls or women for whom she worked to do her favours in return, by working in her field, fetching water or firewood for her, or pounding maize, etc. (Gaza Province 1983).

> When they grew up, the girls had to go into the bush, where there would be old women cutting them on the stomach, on the thighs and on the buttocks. The operation is very painful. The old women would have to grab the girl and hold her tight for her not to move. The women would make nice designs on the ground for the girls to choose from. Those girls who lacked the courage to endure the pain would flee; if the grandmother and the aunts did not get hold of her, when she reached the age of marriage it might happen that the husband would reject her. And even if he did like her, she wouldn't be considered a proper woman (Gaza Province 1983).

> Regarding the tattoos: they are found in all the districts of Gaza Province. The tattoos are made during the winter. There is a tendency now for the tattoos to disappear, but the custom continues in Massingir and Chiqualaquala [two remote and thinly populated districts of Gaza Province]. A woman, who was not tattooed was called the name of a black fish without scales; there was no respect for her (Gaza Province 1983).

> The women have tattoos on the stomach and on the thighs, which get men aroused very fast. There are no fixed times for making these tattoos: the first ones could be made when the girl is still in the initiation hut, and the next ones maybe after 2-3 months of marriage, and so on. A woman may have tattoos made throughout her life. (...) It is the women themselves who make the tattoos. They will arrange to meet at the river, and then they will make them on each other. They'll bring a knife and charcoal powder. It hurts a lot, their clothes will be full of blood. It is done on the back and the buttocks as well. When they have been cut like that they will have to wait for 2-3 days without having sexual relations with their husbands (Cabo Delgado Province 1982).

As for the functions of the body tattoos, there is a general agreement that they promote sexual pleasure for the man as well as for the woman. Like the other key sexual adornments, *missangas* and elongated labia, body tattoos promote eroticism and extended foreplay. This is what the women said:

> In the time of our ancestors the tattoos were important, and together with the *missangas* on the hips they attracted the man in such a way that he could not stay in bed very long before making love to the woman (Niassa Province 1983).

> The tattoos as well as the *missangas* (strings of glass beads around the hips) serve to motivate the man, as certain men do not know how to arouse the woman sexually; when they feel the need to have sex they take the woman by surprise, and under such circumstances she has little chance of reaching full orgasm, that is sexual pleasure. However, if the woman has tattoos on her body, if she wears missangas and if she has the elongated lips of the vagina, the man has to start by playing with these things. By his doing this the woman becomes prepared for the sexual act, resulting in satisfaction for both parties (Zambézia Province 1983).

Zambézia and Niassa provinces are parts of northern Mozambique, inhabited by matrilineal Makhuwa and Yao people. Body tattoos are, however, also popular in southern parts of the country, as seen from the many quotes from Gaza province above. Here the tattoos even have different names, depending on their positions on the body of the woman, indicating specific functions during the sexual encounter. Possibly, of course, tattoos also have names in other parts of the country; only they were not recorded. The following are the recorded names from Gaza Province (recorded in the OMM Extraordinary Conference preparation process):

XIVUIA NKATA	Meaning: come closer, my husband. These tattoos on the stomach are for the man to caress and touch before and after sexual intercourse.
MUVUSSA NKUZI	Positioned below the navel, these tattoos, characterised by small outstanding balls which will excite the man when he touches them, serve as preparation for the sexual act.

XIKOMA NKATA   Meaning: hold me tight, my husband. These tattoos
                      are in the hip-bone region of the back.

HUMULA NKATA   Meaning: rest well, my husband. These tattoos on the
                      thighs are for the penis to rest in a pleasant position
                      after sexual intercourse.

XIKOMBA NWINGUI   Tattoos on the frontal part of the legs, just above the
                      knees. They serve as a guarantee for the mother-in-
                      law that her son will not marry a slippery fish.

In Gaza Province it was also reported that 'the objective of the tattoos as a ritual practice is to create a good atmosphere in the general proceedings during the sexual act' (Gaza Province 1983). And in the northern Province of Tete: 'Besides pulling their labia the girls are making tattoos on the stomach, on the chest and on the thighs. All of this has, as its purpose, the creation of a situation that facilitates orgasm in the woman as well as in the man' (Tete Province 1983).

For a young girl, the choice of having body tattoos or not , like any other fashion, depends a lot on the attitude of her peers, and in general on the social surroundings. If all other girls have tattoos, and if you are called 'a fish' when you don't have them – well the trend is that the girls will want to be tattooed, however much it hurts. If, however, the tattooed body is ridiculed when compared to the body that is not – who then should bother? This is what they also said in Gaza Province:

> The young men of today don't like women with tattoos, and the girls themselves don't like them either. They feel embarrassed when practising sports and gymnastics and expose their body due to the type of clothing that goes with these activities; they are exposed to laughter (Gaza Province). And the province of Sofala (mid-Mozambique): The tattoos are already in a process of extinction. The girls that were born towards the end of the 1950s don't have them. Tomorrow they will be considered a disgrace (Sofala Province 1983).

As I saw them, body tattoos gave personality and expression to women's bodies. I had a strong experience of this during one of the sessions of female initiation rituals, in which I participated as an observer while conducting fieldwork in the district of Ribáuè, Nampula Province (in the north of Mozambique) from 1998-1999. I quote from fieldwork notes regarding a session of competitive dancing in which the initiates as well as a number of already initiated young women took part:

> The [competitive] dances and games reveal an atmosphere and feelings of play and sex, of fun and games with sexual overtones. Play and sex are interlinked, in a women-only setting displaying sexuality as a female way of expression and enjoyment. The women obviously have a good time; they are in their element, all in high spirits – apart from the *amwali* [the initiates] who have to keep their faces straight. The initial mutual embarrassment [*vis-a-vis* me as an observer] of the women's nakedness soon disappears, and before long I began to see their breasts

and tattoos as parts of their personalities, much more expressive, in fact, than the usual outfit of worn-out *capulanas*[4] and tattered T-shirts (Arnfred 2011:158).

Characteristic of the body tattoos is the focus on the sexual foreplay, as reported in the quotes above, emphasising sexual foreplay as a precondition for sexual satisfaction for the woman as well as for the man. Old ethnographic photos from other parts of Africa show women's bodies adorned by body tattoos – but I have not found much contemporary literature on the issue.[5] Like other kinds of body adornments, such as lip plugs, pointed teeth, face tattoos – all used in northern Mozambique some generations ago, body tattoos are on the road to extinction and thus not a topic of contemporary analysis.

As for *missangas* and labia elongation, the situation seems very different. Regarding these aspects of the eroticised female body I draw on material from other parts of Africa, in addition to my own research from Mozambique.

Hip Belts of Glass Beads – *Missangas*

In Senegal, *missangas* are called *bine bine,* and hip-belts of erotic glass (or clay) beads are found throughout Africa (Nzegwu 2011). The art of female eroticism – including *bine bine* – seems to be particularly well developed in Senegal. But let me first give a few quotes from the OMM conference preparation discussions in Mozambique from 1982-1983. One of the questions put to the participants sought their views on whether or not the existing customary norms and practices should be maintained. In the northern province of Niassa, women said this about the *missangas*: 'A custom that we feel ought to continue is the use of *missangas*, since the men, when they go to sleep, like to play with these, here around the hips of the wife' (Niassa Province 1983). From Nampula Province came this report: 'Regarding tattoos and *missangas*, the group stressed the importance of the continuation of these habits, as they attract the man and increase his force for making love to the woman' (Nampula Province 1983). In the province of Tete the women (and men) have similar opinions: 'The *missangas* have a special function in relation to the man, in as far as – besides adorning the woman's body – they will give him a very fast erection' (Tete Province, 1983). Even during the day when the beads are worn beneath women's clothing, their subtle presence is felt: 'Similarly the *missangas* worn around the waist; they are also not seen, but rather heard by the men walking by as ever so slight a tingle, causing irresistible sexual arousal' (Arnfred 2011:149). The importance of invisible assets, things which are not to be seen, brings to mind an observation made by Oyèrónke Oyewùmí regarding the way in which priority in the West is so often given to vision, to what is/can be seen. In Africa, Oyewùmí says, *hearing* plays a much more prominent role as against the Western 'concentration on vision as the primary mode of comprehending reality promot[ing] what can be seen over that which is not apparent to the eye,' (Oyewùmí 1997:15).

Eroticism is located in feeling and hearing, in hands and ears, and in scents: incense and perfumes are erotic devices in Mozambique as well as in Senegal. In Senegal, a particular ethnic group, the Lawbe, has specialised erotic paraphernalia and knowledge, among which scents and perfumes have a special standing. 'The eroticism of the Lawbe is most vividly expressed by the consummate art of their women to concoct a variety of scents ranging from the incense to the pearl belts soaked in a cocktail of diverse perfumes' (Ly 1999:47). Tshikala Biaya talks of 'a double girdle of shimmering, multicoloured pearls, *bine bine*, which evoke local forms of erotic play (...). This is the same type of pearls that is worn hidden under the *drianké's* loose-fitting *boubou*, from where it emanates intoxicating perfumes' (Biaya 2000:716). The Senegalese figure of the *drianké*, according to Biaya, is 'a titillating, plump and mature woman expert at *thiuraye*' (Biaya 2000:715). *Thiuraye* is a term for a series of erotic practices, including 'scented undergarments and girdles of fragrant pearls' (Biaya 2000:715). Francis Nyamnjoh describes *drianké́s* as 'reputedly good at business, well-to-do and generally in a position to flatter younger men with gifts and money. They are also experts at the art of seduction, with an impressive mastery of the traditional kit for seduction and eroticism in Senegal' (Nyamnjoh 2005:300). The *diskette*, on the other hand, is more 'Barbie-like' (Nyamnjoh 2005:301). Biaya describes the *diskette* as 'a young Senegalese woman with the slender body of a fashion model, who frequents the nightlife of urban discotheques and bars. Less expert than the mature, full-figured *drianké*, the *diskette* nonetheless carries a double erotic charge: a body type with global erotic purchase, stamped with the *thiuraye* seal of erotic sophistication and craft' (Biaya 2000:715).

Similar packages of erotic paraphernalia and skills are reported from Uganda by Sylvia Tamale, who has studied the roles of family and/or commercial *Ssengas*. *Ssenga* is originally the name for 'paternal aunt', having turned into an institution. 'The phenomenon of *Ssenga*,' Tamale says, 'represents one of the most powerful cultural inscribers on women's bodies among the *Baganda*' (Tamale 2005:12). *Ssenga's* are tasked with the sexual and cultural education of their nieces (and other young girls) and in Tamale's description of *Ssenga's* tutorials, we find again a whole array of erotic gadgets and capacities: 'Needless to say, sexuality featured prominently in *Ssenga's* tutorials, which would focus on erotic skills, sexual paraphernalia and aphrodisiacs in the form of herbal perfumes, sensual oils, sexual beads (*obutiti*) and so on' (Tamale 2005:17).

Elongated *Labia*

In the discussion of female initiation rituals during the OMM Extraordinary Conference preparation process and in my own 1980s study in northern Mozambique, a key topic of interest was the elongation of the *labia minora* – the small lips of the vagina. Men as well as women praised the practice of elongation in elaborate terms. In many places in Mozambique, the practice is known as *puxa-puxa (puxar* is 'pulling' in Portuguese). Young girls from the age of 8-10 are instructed by an older female relative, an aunt or a grandmother (never the mother herself) regarding how gently to pull the small lips of the vagina, applying a certain home-made pomade, with the purpose of making them longer; some five centimeters or the first two joints of an index finger, is the desired length. This work should be completed before the girl is submitted to the rituals of initiation. After the first instruction regarding how to proceed, the girl will be left to do the work on her own, or rather together with other girls, at some secluded place, where they will not be disturbed, and certainly not by men. In the countryside the girls go to a secret place in the bush; in the cities the bathroom of the apartment will serve the purpose.

This is how the practice of *puxa-puxa* was described in meetings and interviews during the OMM Extraordinary Conference preparation period:

> Groups of girls would go to the dense bush about 3 o'clock in the morning, each of them carrying a *capulana* to be used as cover once the work would start, because they would be sitting like somebody giving birth to a child. On the first day they would be given instructions by the *madrinhas* [older women in charge] about how to proceed, and after that each of the girls would continue on her own, using a certain pomade to facilitate the process. In the course of this work the *madrinhas* would monitor each one of the girls to see if they had been pulling satisfactorily, at the same time verifying that some of them had been doing too little work. It was strongly prohibited for a man to appear at the place where the girls went to pull their labia. If some man should happen to pass the place he would be driven back by handfuls of sand thrown at him, after which the place would be moved to somewhere else (Gaza Province 1983).

And a description from Sofala Province:

> The *madrinha* explains to the girl how to pull the small lips of the vagina; this is done in the morning and in the afternoon, that is twice a day. When the girl has learnt how to do it, she'll continue on her own in the bush with the other girls, bringing with her the oil of *npichi* mixed with the pounded roots of *nhacatamo-tama*. The work will only finish, when the *madrinha* sees that the *lábia* have reached the proper size (more or less five centimetres); she'll then order the girl to stop (Sofala Province 1983).

The pomade or oil used for the pulling is kept in a container, which is considered a very secret and female item, a kind of extension of the personality of this particular woman.

In the OMM Extraordinary Conference preparation process, labia elongation was eagerly discussed, and men and women generally praised the practice. Here are some quotes from what was said in some of the many public meetings held throughout the country. It is evident from several of the quotes that the elongated labia are supposed to enhance sexual pleasure for the woman as well as for the man. It is interesting to note that apparently kissing was not previously a part of erotic play:

> Regarding the elongation of the vaginal lips, it is the general feeling that this custom should be continued, as it has the advantage of working as a brake on the penis at the time of sexual intercourse, that is it secures the slow entrance of the penis, tightly fitting around it, so as to let the man as well as the woman feel aroused. The elongated labia are a great stimulation for the man; before starting sexual intercourse he will become excited by pulling the lips of the vagina. If the modern way of having sexual intercourse is kissing and embracing, it is the same thing we achieve with the lips of the vagina (Zambézia Province 1983).

> The elongated labia stimulate the man as well as the woman during the sexual act. Furthermore, the labia act as a substitute to kissing for those that are not used to kiss (Nampula Province 1983).

The elongated labia, along with the body tattoos and the *missanga* belts have their special functions during the erotic foreplay before penetration. The man is obliged to caress and play with the labia before 'entering' the woman, and obviously this kind of foreplay stimulates the woman as well as the man:

> This thing [elongation of the lips of the vagina] is practised simply in order to have sexual pleasure with your husband. (...) In addition to this, the elongated labia have another quality of making the penis rise faster. It is well known that some men have difficulties in getting an erection. For this type of men, it is important to begin by caressing the woman's vaginal lips to get stimulated and be able to feel himself more like a proper man (Nampula Province 1983).

> Without the elongated labia a man with poor erection will feel next to nothing in the woman. The labia serves as brakes, thus provoking pleasure for the man and contributing even more to the love between the man and woman (Tete Province 1983).

> The elongated labia have a crucial function. They make sure that the woman as well as the man get a good result from the sexual act. By dynamising the man's penis the elongated labia will create a good atmosphere through a process of mutual adjustment (Gaza Province, 1983).

Finally a quote from an elderly woman who evidently has not stopped enjoying sex:

> The initiation rites must continue, because people get pleasure from them. Through the initiation rituals, the man will know everything about how to treat his wife, he even will have learnt how to burn this fruit called *npichi*, which is used to smear the vagina in order to avoid sliding during the sexual act. I am an old woman, but when I apply this pomade, I become young, and whichever man grabs me would be satisfied sleeping with me. He would be so satisfied that the next morning he would pick up the hoe and go to the field, working to his heart's content (Zambézia Province 1983).

All of the quotes above derived from the OMM Extraordinary Conference preparation process, which covered the entire nation, in village squares, in cooperatives and in factory meeting halls. I was impressed by the way the men and the women were able to describe and discuss details of their sexual lives in these public fora. Here, at a village meeting in the public square, serious men would explain the advantages of the elongated labia and how they support and caress the penis during intercourse, and matron-like women would stress the importance of their own sexual satisfaction. The rituals of initiation were a taboo subject that could not be discussed in public, but regarding sex as such there seemed to be no prohibitions – and certainly much less than in similar Western contexts of my knowledge.

Also striking for me as an observer was that the practice of labia elongation made the girls acquainted with their potentials for sexual pleasure at a tender age, and furthermore that the experience of pulling would be undertaken in the company of other girls. This indicated to me a very different starting point for young girls regarding sexuality as compared to what was (and is) considered normal in most Western societies. Such differences support Nzegwu's point, when she says that women's sexuality is differently structured in Western countries (rooted in Christianity and patriarchy, and conceptualised by Sigmund Freud and others) as compared to (some) African contexts, where the practice of labia elongation and other aspects of erotic enhancements of female bodies provide young women with a very different take on their own sexualities – including different types of relations to other girls, relations where borderlines between friendship, mutual touching and sexual arousal seem more blurred and floating than in Western contexts. Insights in differences such as these make visible the limitations of Western approaches, pointing to the need for more inclusive (and less moralistic) conceptualisations.

Labia Elongation, Sexual Self-confidence and Categorisations

Prior to my encounter in Mozambique with labia elongation, I had never heard about it. There was an abundance of feminist (and other) literature on female genital mutilation (FGM) – but nothing on labia elongation. Could it be that to Western feminists, images of women in Africa in terms of risk and danger, violence and mutilation had greater purchase than images of sexual pleasure? Fortunately, today this situation is changing. Research on female sexual pleasure is emerging (e.g., Tamale 2005, 2011; Parikh 2005; Undie et al. 2007; Groes-Green 2011, 2013; Nzegwu 2011; Bagnol and Mariano 2011, 2012; Spronk 2012), including a documentary film, 'Sexy Uganda', made by a Dutch filmmaker, Sunny Bergman (Bergman 2011).

For a continued discussion of labia elongation, I take my point of departure in this film. A remarkable aspect of this documentary is first the way the young woman filmmaker approaches the issue of female sexual practices in Africa.

Being impressed by expressions of explicit female sexual initiative and enjoyment among African women in Holland, Sunny Bergman decides to go to Uganda to find out more about female sexualities and pleasures. She explores the topic with an open curiosity and a wish to learn from her Ugandan interlocutors – an attitude very different from the Othering gazes of the classical anthropologist describing unfamiliar sexual practices as exotic (at best) or repugnant (at worst), or the development practitioner who – even, or precisely when feminist – focuses on helping less fortunate and/or suffering sisters.

At one point in the film, Bergman disappears into the bathroom with a Ugandan woman friend for mutual inspection of elongated versus not-elongated labia. In another scene, she lets a Ugandan *Ssenga* pull her labia, showing her how she too can proceed with the pulling – just like instructions given to Baganda girls. In yet another scene, Bergman tells her Ugandan woman friend that in Dutch the labia minora are called 'shame lips' (same in Danish), and the Ugandan friend is surprised: 'Shame lips? Why? How can you be ashamed of your own body? You should be proud of what you have got, of the way you are as a woman!' If she knew how many young and older women in the West are ashamed of their own bodies... Bergman is impressed by the sexual self-confidence shared by young and older women in Uganda; older women talk proudly about their own sexual experience, whereas, as she says 'older women in Western countries aren't quick to dish out graphic sex stories. Here in Uganda they are proud, also of their labia.'

Interviewing in northern Mozambique in the early 2000s I had very similar experiences with older women, who saw themselves as owners of sexual knowledge and expertise. It is gratifying to see this experience confirmed and reinforced. Yet another aspect highlighted in the film is the mutual pulling of labia between female friends. This, too, is evidenced in Mozambique, in my own data as well as in the material Brigitte Bagnol and Esmeralda Mariano collected in 2005 in Tete Province: 'They pull each other so that it will not hurt, among friends, one in front of the other (...) They pull each other when they are young, only those who are not married' (Bagnol and Mariamo 2012:46). To a Western eye this mutual pulling comes very close to homoeroticism, but in local terms this has nothing to do with sexual orientation. 'Pulling each other is normal, like doing each other's hair,' the Ugandan women say in Bergman's film. It is body contact, not a big issue. And it is not sexuality.

The categorisation of what is sexual is thus culture specific. In Western contexts, a situation of two women manipulating each other's genitals certainly would be termed not just 'sexual', but 'homosexual'. But not in Uganda – and not in Lesotho, where Kendall came to the conclusion that, in Lesotho, two women could have intimate body contact without this being regarded as sexual, since there was no penis involved. 'It is impossible for two women to share the blankets [local euphemism for having sex],' she was told, 'you cannot have sex unless somebody has a *koai* (penis)' (Kendall 1999:162). Similarly, 'no *koai*, no sex means that women's ways of expressing love, lust, passion or joy in each other are neither immoral, nor suspect' (Kendall 1999:167). 'Sexuality' in Uganda (and Mozambique) might be defined in similar ways: as long as there is no penis involved, whatever takes place is body contact, not sexuality. Furthermore, also distinctions between homosexuality and heterosexuality seem to have Western roots, as also acknowledged by Marc Epprecht, who (writing on Zimbabwe) states that 'the homosexuality/heterosexuality dichotomy is a false one' (Epprecht 2004:11). Intimate body contact in Uganda, Mozambique, Lesotho, Zimbabwe – and presumably elsewhere in Africa – is categorised (locally) in different ways.

In Uganda, as evident from Bergman's film, and also from research conducted by Sylvia Tamale (2005) and Shanti Parikh (2005), labia elongation is treasured and widespread. A frequently used metaphor for elongated labia across countries is that they serve as 'doors' to the vagina: the man is not supposed to enter just like that, like 'entering a house without first knocking at the door,' or 'as if he was entering a bus' (quotes from Bergman's film). 'The labia are like doors' the young Malawi men and women interviewed by Chi-Chi Undie *et al.* (2007, Malawi) confirmed. Also in Mozambique the metaphor of the door is well known: 'References to elongated labia often use the metaphor of 'the door': Before having sex, partners must open 'the door'; 'the man cannot enter just like that'' (Bagnol and Mariano 2012:53). Thus the metaphor of 'the door' also indicates the importance of elongated labia in the sexual foreplay, central for sexual enjoyment maybe particularly for women, but also for men.

Not surprisingly, however, according to Parikh, Christian missionaries were not keen on elongation. 'For elder women,' she says, 'the decline of pulling is closely linked to the presence of British missionaries because, they recall, the missionaries believed that pulling was masturbation or body mutilation and, hence, uncivilised and immoral. Furthermore, female missionaries stationed at schools and health wards asserted that pulling promoted promiscuity by introducing girls at an early age to their genitalia and sexual sensation' (Parikh 2005:149). Certainly, as she says, 'foreign religions have interacted in complex and multiple ways with local ideas about sexual learning and morality through the colonial project aimed at 'civilising' African sexuality,' resulting in a situation where 'church and health centres became important interventions for reformulating African bodies, sexuality and moral codes' (Parikh 2005:150). This kind of re-categorisations of issues of bodies and sexuality in Africa have been going on for a long time, nowadays further enhanced by popular cultures such as discos, the media and internet. This is what Nzegwu calls 'epistemological violence'. 'What is the justification', she asks, 'for embracing a notion of eroticism that is steeped in an ideology of gender inequality, that promotes men's sexual hierarchy and the domination of women (...)?' (Nzegwu 2011:255).

Erotic Movements

In addition to body tattoos, scented *missangas* and elongated labia, instructions regarding erotic movements are also crucial in preparing young women for appropriate and fulfilling sexual lives. Particular sexual movements are encouraged; 'to remain motionless is no good' as stated in the quote below. All somewhat different from the Freudian idea of female passivity in sexual matters, and from the reassuring instruction, allegedly given to young ladies of Victorian times, facing their sexual debut: 'Just close your eyes and think of England.' In Mozambique, Uganda and elsewhere in Africa, women are expected to contribute actively to sexual intercourse, even to take the lead. Women's particular erotic movements and bedroom dances were celebrated in the OMM 1982-83 data material, as follows:

> During the initiation rituals, the girl is instructed regarding how the husband will behave in bed, and how the woman must follow his movements. To remain motionless is no good (Cabo Delgado Province 1983).

> While beating the drums, the old women instructed us on how to dance in order for us to learn the different ways of receiving the man for the sexual act (Niassa Province 1983).

> Among all of the instructions of the rituals of initiation, the *massaceto* is the most important, the dance where they instructed us how to move during the sexual act, in order to support the man in making the necessary movements (Tete Province 1983).

> The dance *maunho* is taught when the girl reaches her first menstruation. The *conselheira* [woman advisor] goes underneath and the girl goes on top of the lady, who then begins to move. The girl will follow her movements, learning how she is doing. The girl will also try the position underneath, learning thus the required movements (Sofala Province 1983).

> The girl will be lying on her back, the old woman on top of her, teaching her flexibility and all the gestures that go with the sexual act. Despite the efforts of the girls, sometimes they have difficulties in getting it all right. In such cases, the instructor will device punitive measures, such as fitting a needle into the mat underneath the girl to prick her during the movements and the gestures that she needs to make, thus forcing her to keep in the best position and make a good outcome of the exercise (Sofala Province 1983).

Also in Sunny Bergman's film from Uganda, women's sexual movements play a central role. Her female friends show her their bedroom dances, and her *Ssenga* instructs her regarding how to move her hips and pelvis in the proper way. A particular good position, according to the *Ssenga*, is to move the pelvis while elevated from the bed – as if a needle was sitting in the mattress.

The persons quoted in the OMM material are generally women, although a few male voices are also heard, as below:

> The girl is instructed to move in that way for the man to get an erection more quickly. Without this, when the girl has not been instructed, it is much more demanding on the man, having to do all the work by himself. In this way, he'll soon get exhausted, not being able to have intercourse more than twice a night. The girls in the countryside move differently from the ones in the city. The ones who move the most are the countryside girls (Sofala Province 1983).

> To have sex with an un-initiated woman is like sleeping with a dead body (Tete Province, 1983).

Mozambican men are devoted to – and dependent on – women, who have been adequately instructed, prepared and trained with specific reference to pleasurable sex.

Conclusion

My aim with this paper has been to present data material on female sexualities in Africa focused on pleasure, and at the same time to highlight shortcomings and limitations in conventional Western (including feminist) approaches and conceptualisations. The data material – partly from my own investigations of female initiation rituals in Mozambique and partly from other investigations in Mozambique and elsewhere in Africa – show the importance of pleasure as well as the central position of women. Often women seem to be the initiators and 'masters of ceremony' regarding erotic encounters; men seem to be depending on women for good sex – not the other way round. This kind of data invite to re-conceptualisations of conventional approaches to sexuality (and to studies of gender relations) which often take male dominance/female subordination for granted, seeing female sexuality as inherently passive, depending on male activity (Sigmund Freud) and which furthermore install an *apriori* separation between pleasure and desire, on the one hand, and fertility on the other (the Holy Bible).

The challenge is to *unlearn* such taken-for-granted notions and open the mind for different approaches or conceptualisations and ways of thinking about sexualities. Ifi Amadiume's point about 'shifting the focus from [the] man at the centre and in control to the primacy of the role of the mother/sister' is of importance here, as are Oyèrónké Oyewùmí's point about hierarchies of gender being less important than, for instance, hierarchies of seniority, as well as her critique of the Western primacy of vision over other senses: hearing, touch, smell – all of great significance in erotic play.

Concerning the writings by Nkiru Nzegwu and Bibi Bakare-Yusuf, one may talk about alternative logics in thinking about sexuality – one (dominant) logic being male-focused and characterised by particular distortions of thought introduced by Christianity, such as the separation of sexuality and fertility, and a general denial and excision of any kind of female sexual pleasure and desire. In contrast, an alternative logic – rooted in African sexual cultures, according to Nzegwu – is more open to female experience of sensuality, sexuality and childbirth as interconnected. The different logics also draw different borderlines between what is considered sexual and what is not – the policing of sexuality being fiercely undertaken in sexual cultures influenced by Christianity. In contexts of Christianity, sex is considered a moral issue; female sexuality should be under male control – if not, it is immediately condemned as immoral. Also, borderlines between heterosexuality and homosexuality are fiercely policed in the names of morality and religion.

Borderlines such as these have influenced conceptualisations of sexuality in Western contexts – but there are good reasons to ask about the implications. How do such conceptualisations influence thinking and politics? Bakare-Yusuf puts her finger at a key point: 'If female sexual pleasure and desire are highlighted, the supremacy of male desire, power and control is called into question' (Bakarssse-Yusuf 2013:35). This is what makes 'the erotic' an inherently subversive force, as asserted by Audre Lorde above (Lorde 1984).

A major problem – as also hinted at in the works quoted in this paper – is that approaches of the global (and extremely powerful) development machinery, even if ostensibly secular, are rooted in Christian lines of thinking regarding gender, sexuality and morality: male supremacy is taken for granted, women are perceived, either as passive victims in contexts of sexuality, or as active agents in contexts of economy – cf. the World Bank's focus on gender equality as 'smart economics' (World Development Report 2012).

Development discourse penetrates even the most remote areas of the African continent. By night, when initiation drums are beating, another logic (as seen by Nzegwu) may be a play. But by day, 'Church and health centres [have become] important interventions for reformulating African bodies, sexuality and moral codes' (Parikh 2005: 150). The challenge is to conceptualise sexuality more along the lines of such 'alternative logics'; of coining new concepts for analysis – and of using this alternative approach for investigating and understanding sexualities – in Africa and beyond.

Notes

1. Parts of this paper, first written as a contribution to the 2012 CODESRIA Gender Institute, were later lifted into an article in African Studies Review Forum on Women and Gender in Africa, ASR Vol 58, Issue 3, December 2015.
2. From 1980-1984 I lived in Mozambique, working as a sociologist in the OMM headquarters, Maputo.
3. The quotes marked with a location (a province) and a year are gathered during the OMM Extraordinary Conference preparation process, now in the OMM archives, Maputo.
4. A *capulana* is a piece of cotton cloth used as a skirt; ca 1.00 by 1.80 meters.
5. An article by Heidi Gengenbach 2003 is here an important exception, see also Arnfred 2015.

References

Adesina, Jimi, 2010, 'Reappropriating Matrifocality: Endogeneity and African Gender Scholarship', in *African Sociological Review* 14/1, Dakar: CODESRIA.

Arnfred, Signe, 2011, *Sexuality and Gender Politics in Mozambique*, Oxford: James Currey.

Arnfred, Signe, 2015, 'Female Sexuality as Capacity and Power? Reconceptualizing Sexualities in Africa', African Studies Review, Vol 58, No 3.

Amadiume, Ifi, 1987, *Male Daughters, Female Husbands*, London: Zed Books.

Amadiume, Ifi, 1997, *Reinventing Africa. Matriarchy, Religion and Culture*, London: Zed Books.

Bagnol Brigitte and Esmeralda Mariamo, 2011, 'Politics of Naming Sexual Practices', in S. Tamale, ed, *African Sexualities*, Cape Town, Dakar, Nairobi, Oxford: Pambazuka Press.

Bagnol, Brigitte and Esmeralda Mariano, 2012, *Gender, Sexuality and Vaginal Practices*, Maputo: DAA, FLCS, Universidade Eduardo Mondlane.

Bakare-Yusuf, Bibi, 2013, 'Thinking with Pleasure; Dander, Sexuality and Agency', in Jolly, Susie *et al.*, eds, *Women, Sexuality and the Political Power of Pleasure*, London: Zed Books.

Bergmann, Sunny, 2011, *Sexy Uganda*, documentary film, Viewpoint Production, VPRO.

Biaya, Tshikala K. and Steven Rendall, 2000, 'Crushing the Pistachio: Eroticism in Senegal and the Art of Ousmane Ndiaye Dago', *Public Culture,* Vol 12, No 3.

Diop, Cheikh Anta, 1959/1978, *The Cultural Unity of Black Africa: The Domains of Patriarchy and Matriarchy in Classical Antiquity*, Chigaco: Third World Press.

Gengenbach, Heidi, 2003, 'Boundaries of Beauty: Tattooed Secrets of Women's History in Magude District, Southern Mozambique', *Journal of Women's History*, Vol 14, No 4.

Epprecht, Marc, 2004, *Hungochani. The History of a Dissident Sexuality in Southern Africa,* Montreal: McGill-Queens University Press.

Groes-Green, Christian, 2011, 'Transgressive Sexualities. Reconfiguring Gender, Power and (Un)Safe Sexual Cultures in Urban Mozambique', PhD dissertation, Faculty of Health Sciences, University of Copenhagen.

Groes-Green, Christian, 2013, 'To Put Men in a Bottle': Eroticism, Kinship and Gendered Triads of Reciprocity in Maputo, Mozambique', *American Ethnologist* Vol 40, No 1.

Jolly, Susie *et al.*, eds, 2013, *Women, Sexuality and the Political Power of Pleasure*, London: Zed Books.

Kendall, 1999, 'Women in Lesotho and the (Western) Construction of Homophobia', in Evelyn Blackwood and Saskia Wieringa, eds, *Female Desires, Same-Sex Relations and Transgender Practices Across Cultures*, New York: Columbia University Press.

Lorde, Audre, 1984, *Sister, Outsider*, California: The Crossing Press.

Ly, Abdoulaye, 1999, 'Brief Notes on Eroticism among the Lawbe, Senegal', *CODESRIA Bulletin* 3&4, Dakar: CODESRIA.

McFadden, Patricia, 2003, 'Sexual Pleasure as Feminist Choice', in *Feminist Africa* 2, Cape Town.

Nyamnjoh, Francis, 2005, 'Fishing in Troubled Waters: *Disquettes* and *Thiofs* in Dakar', in *Africa*, Vol 75, No 3.

Nzegwu, Nkiru, 2010, 'Osunality' (or African eroticism), in S. Tamale, ed, *African Sexualities*, Cape Town, Dakar, Nairobi, Oxford: Pambazuka Press.

Oyewùmí, Oyèrónké, 1997, *The Invention of Women. Making an African Sense of Western Gender Discourses,* Minneapolis: University of Minnesota Press.

Oyewùmí, Oyèrónké, 2000, 'Family Bonds/Conceptual Binds: African Notes on Feminist Epistemologies, *Signs: Journal of Women in Culture and Society*, Vol. 25, No. 4.

Oyèrónke Oyéwùmí, 2002, 'Conceptualizing Gender: The Eurocentric Foundations of Feminist Concepts and the Challenge of African Epistemologies', *JENdA: A Journal of Culture and African Women's Studies* Vol. 2, No.1.

Parikh, Shanti A. 2005: 'From Auntie to Disco: The Bifurcation of Risk and Pleasure in Sex, in Adams, Vincanne and Stacy Leigh Pigg, eds, *Sex in Development*, Durham & London: Duke University Press.

Spronk, Rachel, 2012, *Ambiguous Pleasures. Sexuality & Middle Class Self-Perceptions in Nairobi*, Oxford & New York: Berghan Books.

Tamale, Sylvia, 2005, 'Eroticism, Sensuality and "Women's Secrets" among the Baganda: A Critical Analysis', *Feminist Africa*, Issue 5.

Tamale, Sylvia, ed, 2011: *African Sexualities. A Reader*, Cape Town, Dakar, Nairobi & Oxford: Pambazuka Press.

Tamale, Sylvia, 2011b, 'Researching and Theorizing Sexualities in Africa', in S. Tamale, ed, *African Sexualities*, Cape Town, Dakar, Nairobi & Oxford: Pambazuka Press.

Undie, Chi-Chi *et al.*, 2007, 'Metaphors We Love By: Conceptualizations of Sex among Young People in Malawi', in *African Journal of Reproductive Health,* Vol 11, No 3.

World Bank, 2012, *Gender Equality and Development*, World Development Report, Washington, D.C.: World Bank.

4

Rethinking Sex and Secrecy in Precolonial African History: A Focus on Kenya

Babere Kerata Chacha

Introduction

The selection of the theme *sex and secrecy* for this chapter was inspired by the IASSCS Conference that took place at the University of the Witwatersrand, Johannesburg, from 22-25 June 2003. It was the first time the conference would hold in Africa. Its aim was to break through the most kept secrets surrounding various forms of sexualities in different cultures across the world. Organised around the theme of 'Sex and Secrecy', the conference generated debate around a wide range of topics, from the politics of sexuality, sexuality and HIV & AIDS, histories of sexuality and prejudice, religion and sexuality, to gender-based violence, and so on.

As a historian, I was challenged then to reflect on the secrecy surrounding the so-called 'darkest' period in African history – the pre-colonial era. I believed that this is one of the periods that has been scandalously neglected in the study of African history. Interestingly, *both* African and Africanist scholars have paid scant attention to issues of gender and women studies in this period and, more so, they have ignored the role of sexuality in the context of African history. This silence, I believe, compromises the very analysis of African history. Though much has changed since and still much has to be written or is yet to be written on the subject. Therefore, I wonder whether certain silences and secrecy surrounding African sexuality affects how we produce historical works. On the other hand, there is the notion that Africans share a common sexual culture distinct from people elsewhere in the world. Is there anything like African sexuality? If so, is it different from other forms of sexualities? I think of Natasha Trethewey's conceptualisation of silences when she speaks to her incarcerated brother, Joe, in *Beyond Katrina: A Meditation on the Mississippi Gulf Coast*, 'I am keeping a silence to protect myself from knowing. So often this is what the silences – in families as well as in the public discourse of difficult events – are all about: *If something isn't spoken*, it isn't fully known, and we can absolve ourselves of the responsibility that knowing entails' (102).

Much of the available information on African sexuality is distorted often by research intended to support certain beliefs and stereotypes or racial agenda so that there are common misconceptions about a variety of sexual practices, such as the myths regarding polygamy, virginity, same-sex relationships, sexual parts and so on. In the eighteenth century, for instance, when African ethnic groups first began to be 'visited', extravagantly romantic views widely prevailed as to the simple and idyllic lives led by the said-to-be 'primitive' peoples. During the greater part of the nineteenth century, opinion tended in the opposite extreme, and it became usual to insist on the degraded and licentious morals of savages. For instance, the widespread custom of lending the wife under certain circumstances was especially regarded as indicating gross licentiousness. Moreover, even when intercourse was found to be free before marriage, scarcely any investigator sought to ascertain what amount of sexual intercourse this freedom involved. The reasons for such beliefs and stereotypes lie in the fact that African sexuality during this period was shrouded in mystery and often hidden from the public, thus making it difficult to collect narratives of sex for recording purposes.

While it is true that many cultures across the world have been pre-occupied with the regulation of sexuality in the past, this was much more evident in the Africa cultures. Discursive and practical control over cultural, political, economic and even psychological sexual politics was widespread, in myriad ways, and impacted of course on how people talk about sex: when, where, with whom and why.

Furthermore, matters of sexuality were commonly folded into social relations and their expression, carefully metred by custom, rituals and taboos. Different modalities of African cultures, however, structured sexuality through ritual secrecy – a high form of utopian male culture that produced sexual hierarchy and exaggerated gender differences. Such secrecy within ideas about 'African sexuality' thus became an object of European gaze. One can cite Marlow's story in *Heart of Darkness*. Set in the Belgian Congo, this work is regarded as the most notorious European colony in Africa for its greed and brutalisation of the 'native' people and depicts the monstrous wastefulness and casual cruelty of the colonial agents toward the African natives. However, there is no resistance to colonial rule from the 'natives' in the novel and there is no sense of their identity as people. It can be concluded then that constructions of the pre-colonial peoples of Africa are strongly influenced by Western phallocentric prejudice that defines 'native' as passive and subsidiary inferiors. A fundamentally racist mindset characterises a great deal of nineteenth- and twentieth-century writing on 'Africans' and their sexuality, and coupled with the reality of ritual secrecies within the fabric of many cultural approaches to questions of sex, gender, life, and death, this creates a complex ground from which to explore the meaning of 'sex and secrecy' in the twenty-first century.

Theorising Sex and Secrecy

As already noted, a very wide range of sexual experiences has been historically taboo in open and public communication in the African context. These range from those connected with sexual pleasure (such as homosexuality, 'adultery,' or public sex) to those identified as a form of violence (rape, paedophilia). Questions about pregnancy, abortion, initiation are also often shrouded in a sense of taboo and secrecy and, overall, it is widely believed that many people would not speak on these issues for the fear of exposure. Secrecy, therefore, can be said to be the scaffolding of the illusion of normalcy that reinforces the marginality and powerlessness of some and strengthens the power hold of others over them.

Critical questions in this analysis, therefore, revolve around many things: What power did secrecy have on the society? For instance, in rituals, secret knowledge and initiation, power is exercised over individuals because of the cultural imperative to maintain silence or secrecy. How, then, are people able to talk about sex, including those who compromise individual autonomy and disregard agency and bodily integrity, hidden codes and local rules? These matters form the intellectual pillars of sex and secrecy. Why are moments of secrecy and silences in Africa often less addressed? This gives rise to a number of questions. What are the silences, secrets, omissions and political consequences of such moments? What particular dilemmas and constraints do they represent or entail? What are their implications for research praxis? Are such moments always indicative of voicelessness or powerlessness?

Theorists of public morality have noticed that apparently private acts of vice, when they multiply and become widespread, can imperil vital public interests. This fact embarrasses philosophical efforts to draw a sharp line to distinguish a realm of 'private' morality that is not subject to law from a domain of public actions that may rightly be subjected to legal regulation.

Like in real life, sexuality as a field remains an underdeveloped domain in sub-Saharan Africa, with few scholars demonstrating keen interest in, and focus on, the subject. However, as Michael Gomez posits in *Exchanging Our Country Marks* (1998), 'Westerners label whatever they do not understand about non-Western societies and cultures as secretive and mystical; hence, the most important aspect of a phenomenon is its impenetrability or resistance to explication along conventional lines of analysis. While there are many secretive institutions in the

West, there are millions in Africa. Ironically, sexuality underlies numerous socio-economic and development challenges currently confronting sub-Saharan Africa. The challenges facing the region are numerous – most notably, perhaps, is the HIV & AIDS epidemic. The urgent need to stem the disease has necessitated an almost exclusive focus on behavioural change and, thus, the study of sexuality.

Consequently, in historical works, there have been myriads of stereotypical myths regarding the sexualities of 'Third World' peoples. The rootedness of the investigation of sexuality in the Victorian Age explains many of these legends (Leclerc-Madlala 2004). Unflattering portraits of sexuality in the developing world are legion, constructing this phenomenon as either 'exotic, mysterious, [and] uncivilized' (Jolly 2003:5), or as hypersexual (Geshekter 1995; Mama 1996; Elliston 2005). Several authors observe, however, that the beginnings of our knowledge about sexuality in Africa were shaped within conceptual schemes derived from colonial legacies and thought (e.g.: Mama 1996; Osha 2004). Indeed, scholars such as Arnfred (2004) and Leclerc-Madlala (2004) have indicated that contemporary conceptualisations of 'African sexuality' continue to be informed by earlier colonial and Western, Victorian-era imaginations. Within this conceptual framing, the portrait of sexuality in Africa that often emerges reflects 'the unbridled black female sexuality, excessive, threatening and contagious, carrying a deadly disease' (Arnfred 2004:67). In current research on sub-Saharan Africa – 'often donor-driven,' as Arnfred (2004:59) notes, not to mention programme-driven – the conceptualisation of sexuality has privileged a severely limited number of themes, including disease and reproduction. This should not come as a surprise, as much of what we have learned about sexuality in Africa has been stimulated by the HIV & AIDS epidemic. The content of this knowledge – drawn primarily from quantitative data in the population and public health fields – has not remained unquestioned, however (see, for example, Watkins 1993).

Kenya and 'Sexuality' under Colonial Anthropology

The pre-colonial history of Kenya emerged as a discipline in the University of Nairobi in the 1970s and since then, historical studies of Kenya have focused increasingly on African agency, reacting to both imperial and underdevelopment histories. While the former emphasised the progressive role of Europeans in Africa, the latter stressed the state-imposed structural obstacles to African progress that smothered earlier African initiatives. Like histories of other continents, there was very little on women, gender or even sexuality. Such deafening silence has reigned on these matters, as historians have preferred to tolerate and draw their resources from the harvest of anthropological sources rather than to cultivate their own fields. It is possible that inquisitive historians, naturally enough, have tried to avoid being tainted as 'promiscuous scholars' by the media paintbrushes or conservative historians, as might well befall them were they to admit publicly to such curiosity. The plain fact, though, is that the study of sexuality frightens historians. Most genuinely fear deviating from their own professional tradition, and many subconsciously fear what would gaze back at them from the subterranean depths of these stories were they to peer too intently into the well of history.

Indeed, the main pre-occupation of the early producers of Kenyan history in general was to prove that Africa had a history prior to its engagement with colonialism. This concern was heightened by the ranting of Hugh Trevor Roper who said the only history in Africa was that of Europeans in Africa. To him, Africa was indeed a 'Dark Continent' that deserved no studying, as darkness was not a subject of history:

> Perhaps in the future there will be some African history to teach. But at present there is none: there is only the history of the Europeans in Africa. The rest is darkness and darkness is not a subject of history. Please do not misunderstand me… I do not deny that life existed even in dark countries and dark centuries, nor that they had political life and culture, interesting to sociologists and anthropologists; but history, I do believe, is essentially a form of movement, and purposive movement too. It is not a mere phantasmagoria of changing shapes and costumes of battles and conquests, dynasties and usurpation, social forms and social disintegration.

So, according to this line of thinking, historians, anthropologists and sociologists described African societies as static, primitive, indigenous, native, or traditional. However, this stereotyping has many drawbacks. Perhaps one of the most important is that too large a proportion of its pages are still devoted to the 'East African invaders', to use Coupland's term, instead of to the East Africans themselves. But being the first to venture out into the unknown, the compilers of the volume were rather cautious in how they handled the new trend. To them, the whole undertaking was an experiment which could either succeed or fail.

The desire was to prove Trevor Roper wrong. Further impetus to work on pre-colonial Kenyan societies emanated from the 'winds of change' and African nationalism that was sweeping East Africa at the time. There was a need to prove to the world that Africans had civilisation and history prior to the arrival of Europeans and colonialism. Indeed, this also led to the formation of the committee of the UNESCO General History of Africa chaired by a prominent Kenyan historian, Bethwel Ogot.

Generally, therefore, before the establishment of the colonial period in Africa, and unfortunately even today, very little strides have been made in the study of pre-colonial history. Very few scholars dare take on this period because of methodological issues and problems with sources. It was in 1963 that Oliver and Matthew edited *History of East Africa, Volume One* as 'an experiment', to use their own language. As a book dealing with the pre-colonial history of East Africa, it was the first volume of its kind ever written with an attempt to put the African people, and not their European colonisers, in the foreground. It utterly neglected women sexuality and did not attempt any discussion on gender. Regrettably, this text formed the basis of further reconstruction of the history of Kenya.

Since the publication of *History of East Africa* in 1963, many more volumes dealing with pre-colonial history of East Africa have been written – a large number of them by African scholars themselves. They include such works as B. A. Ogot's *History of the Southern Luo*, G. S. Were's *History of the Abaluyia*, M. C. M. Kiwanuka's *A History of Buganda to 1900,'* R. S. Karugire's *A History of the Kingdom of Nkore in Western Uganda to 1896*, G. Muriuki's *A History of the Kikuyu to 1904*, and W. R. Ochieng's *A History of the Gusii of Western Kenya*, to mention just a few. Even though written in Western style, pointedly ignoring aspects of women, gender and sexuality, they were, at least, important in many respects.

First, these studies were carried out by emerging African historians who are genuinely interested in the history of their own people. This is very unlike the approach taken by colonial historians and anthropologists who studied African history as a way to understand the colonised people better but not with a genuine desire to study African history for its own sake. Coupland had given his view on this mindset of the coloniser when he concluded in his *East Africa and Its Invaders* that the only genuine African history was found along the coast where the indigenous population had come into contact with the outsiders such as the Europeans and Asians. He argued that there was only 'darkness' in the interior:

> Not many miles back from their [i.e. Europeans and Asians] settlements and ports and market-places [along the East African coast] a curtain falls, shrouding the vast interior of the continent in impenetrable darkness; where ignorant armies clash by night. But the reader should remember that the East Africans, though invisible, are always there, a great background to the comings and goings of brown men and white men on the coast. In the foreground, too. On the historical stage itself, the East Africans are always the great majority, dumb actors for the most part, doing nothing that seems important, so eclipsed by the protagonists that they are almost forgotten, and yet quite indispensable'.[10]

Equally, the famous explorer Speke, equated the Africans with the descendants of Ham, son of Noah (found in the Book of Genesis in the Bible), whom Noah condemned to be a servant of his brothers, Shem and Japhet. He writes:

> If the picture [of 'naked Africa'] be a dark one, we should, when contemplating these sons of Noah, try to carry our mind back to the time when our poor elder brother Ham was cursed by his father and condemned to be the slave of both Shem and Japhet...

With such attitudes, colonial historians could not be expected to write any reliable history of the African people. In effect, a number of African intellectuals sought tirelessly to offer an apt alternative of reconstructing African History after centuries of tainted images of the African continent. This school of Africanist historians, emerging around the mid-twentieth century, left an indelible mark in laying the foundation of African studies in various fields. Such foundation works, also referred to as canonical work, are referred to again and again, and have formed clear benchmarks in the reconstruction, reinterpretation and recompilation of intellectual realms of African history. The lives of authors of such foundation works have themselves become inspiring as they have emerged as heroes and heroines of the African cause. This has certainly changed with this crop of African historians into the scene. It, however, is worthy to note that African historians kept matters of family, sexuality, reproduction, marriage, divorce away from history, yet some of these discourses were the fabrics of which African history was made and produced. However, it was only the colonial anthologists that made a stride towards the study of African sexuality although not in its entirety.

In the 1920s, for instance, a new school of anthropologists came into existence. Named the functionalists, it was led by Malinowski and Radcliffe-Browne who mostly had an obsession with evolution, diffusion and racial theories. They approached studies of social change in the same way and with the same conjectural and confused consequences. They were interested in studying 'tribes without history'. Indeed, the tendency of functional anthropology was to assimilate indigenous history to the category of myth, which they considered it to be. They concentrated on marriage, circumcision, rituals and customs and not the depths of the anthropology of sex and sexual discourses.

On the other hand, whenever the functionalists showed any interest in problems of social change, the main concern was with the study of what they called 'culture contact' between 'tribal' and Western societies and the application of anthropological knowledge to the government of subject races. The British Government, for example, started from the 1930s to commission professional anthropologists to conduct surveys in their colonies. In Kenya, the field continued to be dominated during most of the inter-war period by amateur anthropologists. C. W. Hobley wrote his *Bantu Beliefs and Magic* in 1922 and G. J. Orde Browne published *The Vanishing Tribes of Kenya* in 1925. The latter had collected his material between 1909 and 1916 when he worked as Assistant Commissioner at various government posts in the Mount Kenya region. Another administrator, G. W. B. Huntingford, began his long academic associate with the Rift Valley region of Kenya with an article called 'The Social Organization of the Dorobo', which appeared in *African Studies* in 1942. Also, J. A. Maseam, another administrator, published *The Cliff Dwellers of Kenya* (1927), which was an ethnographical account of the Elgeyo. Perhaps the ablest of these amateur administrative anthropologists was H. E. Lambert, who was busy at this time assembling data on the Kikuyu that was to result later in two major works: *The Systems of Land Tenure in the Kikuyu Land Unit* (1950) and *Kikuyu Social and Political Institutions* (1956).

But the field was not entirely restricted to colonial anthropologists and the administrators. Some of the missionaries such as W. E. Owen decided to try their hand at anthropology. The most elaborate of such efforts was the book by Father Cagnolo of the Catholic Mission of the Consolata Fathers called *The Agikuyu – Their Customs, Traditions and Folklore* (1933). Despite the preponderance of the amateur anthropologists, it was during this period that the first works by professional anthropologists and historians on the peoples of Kenya appeared. The first three professional anthropological studies were: *The Akamba in British East Africa* (1920) by G. Lindblom, *The Social Institutions of the Kipsigis* (1939) written by J. G. Peristiany, and *Facing Mount Kenya* (1938) by Jomo Kenyatta. Although published much later, Glinter Wagner's *The Bantu of North Kavirondo* (Volume I, 1949, Volume II, 1956), A. H. J. Prins's *The Coastal Tribes of the North-Eastern Bantu* (1952) and *The Swahili Speaking Peoples of Zanzibar and the East African Coast* (1961), J. Stone's *Journal* (No. VII, 1949, pp. 24-40), belong essentially to the same scholarly tradition.

The concern of all these anthropologists was with social structure, which led to a disproportionate emphasis on kinship, law, government and cosmology. They all committed the fallacy of 'the ethnographic present', and the overriding concern was with the accumulation of data. It was further feared that as the unequal encounter with the West became more intense, the so-called primitive cultures would disappear. It, therefore, became imperative to mount a kind of rescue operation to retrieve the social 'facts' before all the 'primitives' disappeared. As Rivers put it, 'In many parts of the world, the death of every old man brings with it the loss of knowledge never to be replaced.'[11] A similar kind of concern was later to inspire the collection of oral traditions from the 1960s.

The anthropologists of the later 1960s, such as Walter Sangre's *Age Prayer and Politics in Tiriki, Kenya* (1966) or John Middleton's chapter in the Oxford *History of East Africa* Volume II (1965) dealing with 'Administration and Changes in African Life, 1912-45' or Kivuti Ndeti's *Elements of Akamba Life* (1972), are still basically tribal studies in the functional-structural tradition. Lest I give the impression that Kenyan historians have tackled the problem of social change more effectively than the anthropologists, I hasten to add that their position is only slightly better because they operated with a longer time-scale. Most of the works dealing with the precolonial history of Kenya, such as the writer's *History of the Southern Luo* (1967), Were's *A History of the Abaluhya of Western Kenya* (1967), Muriuki's *A History of the Kikuyu* (1974) and Ochieng's *A History of the Gusii* (1974), have adopted an organic and evolutionary approach which have more in common with the evolutionary school of anthropologists. The major difference in this set of works is that they are based on field work and not on armchair conjectural history. Unlike the works of the functionalists, these histories are not tribal studies despite their titles: they are regional studies.

And what about research on sexuality across these trajectories? I would argue that studies on the pre-colonial period, however murky, should be able to show a path in the re-thinking of modern African sexuality. To do this, one has to investigate inter-ethnic relations which, I believe, played a very significant role in African history. The migration and settlements of the Bantu and the Nilotes in the pre-colonial Kenya, for instance, shed further lights in the search for the sexual practices that existed during the period. It is, however, imperative to say that the Bantu were matrilineal while the Nilotes were patrilineal. In the contact between the two groups, Bantu shed off their cultures, allowing the Nilotic cultures to dominate the cultural history of Kenya until the beginning of colonial rule. As such, the Bantu are more liberal with discussions of sexuality than the Nilotes. More secrets are to be found in Nilotic sexual rites while, within Bantu traditions, they are often found in folklores and stories or even songs.

In Mbiti's philosophy, sex in African society was not entirely for biological purposes alone. It had religious and social uses too (Mbiti, 146). Sex was a solemn seal, a sacrament, a sacred action, with inward spiritual values. As such, it was deeply embedded in many socio-cultural relations. Consequently, among the Kuria Kisii, Meru and Taita, sexual fluids were considered dangerous to the family and kids. Washing after intercourse before the child is touched was required; sexual organs were regarded as gates of life. Therefore, naked exposure of these areas was strictly policed and often tabooed. In a few societies, sex was an expression of hospitality – this is typical for the Kisii and Maasai.

As a result of this strict regulation of sexuality, children had to be taught and guided on these matters but often in secrecy. Among the Gikuyu, a child had to be taught from childhood to develop the technique of self-control in matters of sex. Also, during early childhood, parents could talk freely to their children, explaining all matters connected with sexual taboos'. Curiously, pre-initiation masturbation was considered 'right and proper'; afterwards, it was said to be abandoned and referred to as a babyish habit. They were said to practice 'incomplete sex play' known as *ngwiko* after initiation at puberty (Ahlberg 1991: 61).

Girls in the same community were taught that masturbation was 'wrong' (p162). Formalised sex instruction was offered to girls in an initiation ceremony, including circumcision (Leakey 1931). Occasional infant and child betrothal was noted by (Routledge 1910: 124-5). Dundas (1915: 284) stated that infant betrothal was common. Usually, however, the betrothal is a girl's own affair. Sexual intercourse became part of initiation ceremonies of both boys and girls (Lambert 1956: 54-5; 34-5). For girls, it required full intercourse before nuptial age, 'to be wiped clean from the soot of the knife' (*kuhuuruo mbiro ya ruenji*).

It would take place before menarche (to avoid pregnancy), and should lead to defloration (but not wholly, since virginity was valued). Elders say that girls got rid of their 'initiation dirt' by intercourse with immature and uninitiated boys (a heinous offence on the part of an initiated girl except for this one purpose), who, not having reached the stage when sex was socially important, would not suffer from the taint.

Sexual intercourse before initiation was strictly forbidden. Any one who took advantage of the few opportunities for breaking the rule suffered severe beatings. Boys up to ages 14/15 were allowed to play at mutual masturbation and sexual intercourse with girls; afterwards, it was forbidden out of fear that they would abuse little girls. Big boys would have to settle for masturbation, sex with barren married women, or with goats or sheep, the latter both being tabooed. Most 14/15-year-olds build huts proudly announced as their *thingira* (men's hut), inviting boys and girls to 'play sexually in imitation of their initiated brothers and sisters. Today, Ahlberg *et al.* argue, circumcision still symbolises becoming a Kikuyu adult, but it is now performed in a clinic and no longer includes the ceremonies and open discourse that formerly conveyed sexual knowledge combined with strict social controls regulating sexual behaviour. The changes have resulted in 'numerous discrepancies between cognition and practice': although parents believe sexual intercourse should be restricted to marriage, they have employed 'a prohibitive silence' that is misinterpreted by youth who have little reliable knowledge about sexual matters.

According to the Luo of Kenya, young boys begin to experiment with sex when they are four to six years of age, but their behaviour is severely criticised and restricted. As mobility is limited, boys are first interested in girls who reside in the immediate vicinity, and due to residential patterns, these girls are close relatives Blount (1973:325). Sexual relations with them are incestuous, and although a young boy does not immediately understand this concept, he quickly learns that they are not 'available sex playmates'. If need be, a young boy will be sent to stay with a relative to remove him from the temptation of nearby female cousins or sisters. Only after a boy becomes a youth, at the approximate age of 13 to 15 years, is there opportunity for considerable contact with members of the opposite sex'. Luo boys are said to practice prenuptials conditioning at the age of 10 to 12 (Parkin 1973:335-6). The marital cycle 'proceeding' to the act of childbearing, is imitated (Ominde 1952). Genitals are compared, and 'something approaching a crude sexual intercourse' takes, place when older members of the family are absent. During the period when the crops are ripening, these older children, sometimes accompanied by younger ones who act as sentries, disappear into the cornfields to carry out this practice'.

Sexual instruction for girls took place within the swindhe, a form of communal living (Cohen and Odhiambo 1989). Child betrothal (p92) or marriage (p117) may take place (Wilson 1961), but this seems a peripheral custom. Child marriage (*nyar osiep*) includes marriage ceremonies without consummation (cf., Kyewalyanga 1977:24). The Kuria of Kenya approved of sexual relations only at night. The Kalenjin believed that sex during the day will cause thunderstorms and deadly lightning, leading to drowning of not only the offending couple but also of other innocent people. And the West African Bambara believed that a couple who engage in sex during the day will have an albino child.

Sex was prohibited in certain places and times. The Mende of West Africa forbade sexual intercourse in the bush, while the Semanga condemned sex within camp boundaries for fear that the supernatural will become angry. Among the Bambara, engaging in sexual relations outdoors will lead to the failure of crops. Pre-colonial Kenyan women, in particular, are noted for their innovative means of interlacing ideas of sexuality and pleasure into cloth design, music, and nuptial ceremonies. These could be found among the Taita, Swahili Khanga and Kuria.

On the other hand, colonial research notes that the Nilotic and some Bantu peoples practised female circumcision. It still continues widely among the Somali and Turkana, and surreptitiously among others. Some argue that its purpose is to reduce female sexual pleasure, and make women docile to their husbands and less likely to engage in adultery. Women not circumcised are referred to by traditionalists as 'unclean' or as 'prostitutes.' As a Kikuyu girls' circumcision song concludes, 'Now we can make love, for our sex is clean.' The Kikuyu, Maasai, and Meru only removed the clitoris (clitoridectomy) during initiation, at puberty. The Turkana and Somali practice pharaonic circumcision, removing the clitoris and the labia minora. The wound is then sutured (infibulation), leaving a tiny hole for menstrual flow. This is often inspected at betrothal as a sign of virginity. Pharaonic circumcision is performed on girls between the ages of 3 and 7. Administrators of the late colonial period as well as the missionary societies policed these behaviours. The Anglican Church, for example, strongly opposed female circumcision, and it has been illegal since the colonial period. The campaign reached a crisis point in 1929 when the Church of Scotland Mission made opposition to this practice a condition of employment and school entry. This politicised the question and gave rise to the Kikuyu resistance, and the independent church and school movements.

Conclusion

This brief kaleidoscope of what colonial anthropology offers us when thinking about the intersections of 'the Western document,' and questions of sex and secrecy shows that a very wide range of colonial writings have sought to describe and categorise diverse forms of sexual behaviour within a Kenyan past. We read of rumours, belief systems, practices, education, and surveillance at multiple levels and over all ages of people. It is very difficult to begin contemporary work on sex and sexuality within the continent without engaging these texts and their all-too imperialist gazes, especially as a historian. It is nonetheless imperative to do so, which does not mean ignoring them, but situating them with a politics of information.

References

Ahlberg, Beth, 1994, 'Is there a Distinct African Sexuality? A Critical Response to Caldwell *et al.*' *Africa* Vol. 64, pp.220-42.

Arnfred, Signe, 2004 'African Sexuality/Sexuality in Africa: Tales and Silences' in *Rethinking Sexualities in Africa*, Uppsala: Almqvist & Wiksell Tryckeri.

Caldwell, John, 1989 'The Social Context of AIDS in Sub-Saharan Africa.' *Population and Development Review* Vol. 15, pp.185-234.

Caldwell, John, 1991 'The African Sexual System: Reply to Le Blanc *et. al.*' *Population and Development Review* Vol. 17, No. 3: September, pp. 506-515.

Heald, Suzette, 1999 [1995] 'The Power of Sex: Reflections on Caldwell's 'African Sexuality' Thesis' in *Manhood and Morality: Sex, Violence and Ritual in Gisu Society*, London & New York: Routledge.

Le Blanc, Marie Nathalie *et al.*, 1991 'The African Sexual System: Comment on Caldwell *et al.*' *Population and Development Review* Vol. 17, No. 3: September, pp. 497-505.

5

The 'G-String' as a Space for Sexual and Political Imagination: Rethinking Discourses of Youth, Power and Globalisation in Kenya

Valerie Opiyo

Introduction

Not long ago, in his seminal presentation, 'Made in Riverwood': (Dis)locating Identities and Power through Kenyan Pop Music', Mbugua argued that there is a vast popular culture industry boiling up in Nairobi's prominent street, River Road, and that a dominant cultural form found in the metropoles in the form of hip-hop is hybridising and localising, producing new cultural matrices in urban Kenya (Mbugua 2008:10). Mobile phones, cyber cafes, sleek cars, women and sex are all integrated within the hip-hop ethos that gives voice to subcultureal discourses on youth, gender, and sexuality.[1] As a new and democratising cultural force, rap traverses the playing field, opening doors to new cultural players, 'circumventing the old guard' and 'corporate sharks', as Mbugua puts it.

In Kenyan cities, bill-board and television advertisements for Western commodities have increased, enlarging the marketplace and whetting youthful appetites for commodity consumption. As the speed of consumption increases, so does the lack of satisfaction, and thus the level of consumption (Howe and Strauss 1993:14). The consumption is endless, while the restlessness with what is actually being consumed is growing. Food is eaten quickly. 'Buy and toss' is turned into a consumption ideology. Everything is actually being consumed: lovers, marriages, friendships, foods, toys, clothing, furniture, homes, cities, towns and villages – everything (Wekesa 1999:19).

This chapter explores connections between consumerism, marketplace and the creation of youth subcultures through a focus on a literally, and perhaps, seemingly analytical negligible piece of clothing: G-string underwear. The exploration is grounded in questions about the emerging gender dynamics and power *and the politics of dress*; how do the youth deploy clothing as power, and how does the increasingly visible display of the *G-string* by young women offer them identities which simultaneously conform to gender-normative notions of heterosexuality and challenge notions of respectability?

Many researchers have written about certain products as indicators of communication or their users or about products as forms of nonverbal communication (Scheflen 1974:42). One of the earliest authors to assert that clothing consumption was more than for the mere protection of the body was Veblen who, in the fifties, developed a theory of fashion centring on the chattel status of those being required to wear the outrageous clothing of the times (e.g., women and servants) (Veblen 1953). Veblen's work undergirds major contemporary approaches to clothing use, specifically in his notion that clothing symbolises some of the core values of society.

Specifically, however, some works explicitly deal with particular cases and are also worth noting here. Stitziel's[2] book, for example, based on his dissertation, consists of seven chapters each of which treats the discourse on clothing and fashion in socialist East Germany; structures of the economic planning bureaucracy and the clothing industry in East Germany; difficulties that designers, magazine editors and most importantly the 'Fashion Institute' had in developing a high quality 'socialist' fashion not beholden to the West; prices and their impact on consumption patterns and especially the ever-present issue of quality and value of clothes; overproduction and overstocking (or 'glut') in the socialist planned economy; paradoxes associated with so-called boutique stores in Germany; and finally, attempts to get at ordinary East Germans' notions and attitudes towards fashion and clothing in Germany.

Fandy Mamounin, in his book, *Beyond Colonialism and Nationalism in North Africa*, looks at how the politics of dress in Egypt indicate the complexity of the country's society. This can be seen, in his argument that there is a glaring 'dynamism and flexibility of its citizens in choosing the kind of clothes to wear' (Fandy 1998). In Egypt, government employees usually wear Western clothes during working hours and Egyptian native dresses at home.

Jean Allman's *Fashioning Africa: Power and the Politics of Dress* is a collection exploring the 'ways in which power is represented, constituted, articulated, and contested through dress' in Africa and in the diaspora (p. 1). All the articles discuss clothing as an expression of identity. Clothing is a readily accessible, visible, and easily changeable indicator of individual 'identity, character, and status' which can facilitate the assertion of identity when people are living in heterogeneous or rapidly changing situations (Allman 2004:247). Thus, Fair describes women's use of clothing styles in early twentieth-century Zanzibar to express their 'new definitions of self' as free and cosmopolitan, and several authors note the role of clothing in proclaiming one's status as 'civilized' and literate (Holman 1980: 372-377).

Perhaps more politically significant is the role of clothing as an indicator of group identity and as a means of developing and strengthening ethnic, religious, or political solidarity. Several authors address the importance of clothing and fashion in creating solidarity within ethnic groups such as those in Zanzibar, Nigeria, Somalia and Ghana. Hay discusses the use of clothing for religious group identity by Mumboists and Christians in Kenya, and Akou discusses the problematic use of Islamic dress by Somali women in Minnesota to express their identity as Muslims, though specifically rejecting the full facial veil to avoid being identified as Arab in post-9/11 United States. Similarly, as Renne explains in her history of military vs. civilian regimes in Nigeria, clothing has been used in Africa both to announce one's political persuasion and to disguise or deny it.

African clothing is known for its colourful fabrics and distinctive designs. But few people take the time to examine the cultural or even political significance of African fashion. At various times in history, migration, and integration have spread African textiles to different regions of Africa and the world (Frances 1995: 74-97). In many ways, dress can be considered a visual language, an aesthetic code expressing ideas about status. Stylistic choices – such as material, texture, colour, cut – may send messages about the wearer's status, whether social, economic, political, occupational, religious or a combination of the above. At once inclusive and exclusive, dress establishes the wearer's membership in a certain group while distinguishing him from others (Ankomah 1995:38-41). As such, a man's clothing is an important vehicle through which power may be defined, sustained, negotiated or reinforced (Bawa 2000).

In Africa, power, politics and sexuality are represented, constituted, articulated, and contested through dress. Dress signifies a political language, comparable in eloquence and potency to the words of the most skilled orator or the writings of the most persuasive propagandist.[3] Quoting Gisele Aris:

> In Africa, dress provided a powerful arena for colonial relations to be enacted and challenged, and served as a method of cultural expression and resistance. Moreover, dress revealed dimensions of political and social transformations that could not be discerned through observed behavior or verbal and written articulations.

It is often not possible to generalise how each colonial power used clothing to assert domination, or how different African states employed the politics of dress in response. In Swaziland and South Africa, for example, Africans manipulated Western fabric to suit their own cultural agenda. No wonder, Sagarika Ghose argues that Winston Churchill may have called Gandhi a 'half-naked fakir' but the grand old man in a loin-cloth never changed his outfits to suit the demands of the audience.

It can also be said that African dress is dynamic and evolving with specific local histories that impact both form and meaning. Almost all the attires demonstrate some aspect of cross-cultural influence or aesthetic inventiveness, proving that novelty is not new. Some forms of dress, however, combine elements considered traditional with those signifying modernity in innovative ways that forge a distinctive, and powerful, identity. (Ankomah 1995:38-41). New materials and types of clothing often serve as creative stimulus for the transformation of local dress into novel forms of aesthetic expression, while traditional forms of dress may find new patrons or different contexts of use.

Consequently, therefore, the dress has historically been used as one of the most important and visually immediate markers of class, politics, status and ethnicity especially in East African coastal society. As one of many forms of expressive culture, clothing practice shaped and gave form to social bodies. Examining transformations in dress and fashion illustrates, however, that boundaries between theoretically distinctive social categories were often vague in practice (Mwai1997: 84-102). For instance, on the coast of Mombasa, dress is significantly used as a way to highlight women's roles in public and political domains, challenging the Western view that politics is a male domain. It represents the multilevel link between the personal and the public, linking the individual to the community and contemporary political currents; the simultaneity of tradition and modernity; and the contingency of fashion, so that the interpretation of a particular style may vary widely across locales, times, and political atmospheres. In Mombasa, therefore, dress (in general), and the wearing of kanga fabrics, in particular, offers women a means of communication in an image conscious and historically stratified society. It is argued that *kangas*[4] are still an integral part of ritual and social activities in Mombasa and that they shed light on the complex history of the Swahili coast. Placing the ethnography in a broader and contemporary context, it can be said that kangas contribute to the intangible heritage of Mombasa in their encapsulation of the island's oral history, art, social commentary and concepts of beauty (Lee 1999:10).

The Voice of the 'G-String' as 'African Clothing'

Having argued that African fabrics speak to the wearers and pass messages and codes to the external world, what, therefore, can be said of imported clothes? How do we begin to analyse the take-up of the garments of 'the North,' in terms of their integration into questions of identity and power, especially for young women? I want, in this chapter, to argue that the contemporary popularity of the G-string, as 'fashionable' clothing for young women is more than simply a version of commodity parasitism, where what is flaunted as 'contemporary' in the North is assumed to be desirable in an African city.

It is important to begin by suggesting that, in general, enquiries about underwear in Kenya are, as a legacy of British colonialism, considered both sexual and dirty. This dual association is seen in everyday social practices. In normal circumstances, Kenyans dry their clothes in open-garden cloth-lines, rocks and on fences but commonly dry their underwear in private and hidden places. In fact, recently, in the streets of London, an advertisement sponsored by the Oxfam Foundation read: 'Get Your Panties in a Bunch!' 'We Are Collecting Knickers for Africa, It read in part:

> What colour underwear are you wearing today? Seems like a simple (and rather nosy) question, right? We take things like underwear for granted and it's difficult to think of anyone having to live without basic things like knickers and bras. For many people, underwear is a luxury. We've decided to do our bit to help and make a difference to someone's life by donating Momiji pants to Knickers 4 Africa[sic]. They're a charity whose sole purpose is to donate underwear to people in Africa.

This was not to pass without condemnation from Kenyan political voices who termed the panties as dirty, and donating them was an abuse of Africa:[5]

> This is a shame! It may have good intentions, but it's completely undermined by the indecency and crudeness of sending these rural Kenyans used underwear. Labeling it 'pre-loved' is flat out offensive! They could easily go to a major brand of under garments and pitched the initiative as a Corporate Social Responsibility project.

Despite such views, however, urban street life in Nairobi is full of 'visible' underwear, worn by both young men and young women; fashionable young men may have their trousers hugging their hips, revealing lines of boxer shorts or other kinds of underwear, and the 'Y' of the G-string is clear above the back-lines of many young women's jeans as they walk along, or ride on the back of motorbikes. In Nairobi, as elsewhere, of course the type of clothes the youth wear sends signals of a particular meaning to the bystanders (Agechi 2008:1), the obvious being 'we are youth' but I am interested in whether – and how – this applies to the choice of a publicly visible G-string.

By the late 1980s, the G-string design had made its way into most of the Western world and became more and more popular through the 1990s. As of 2003, thong underwear is one of the fastest-selling styles among women and currently gaining popularity in African urban areas, particularly among young university students in Nairobi. I chose to explore this by interviewing young women in two universities to deepen my understanding of their choice of a form of clothing that was regarded by wealthy Kenyan women as garments for the poor ('the poa'), and marketed by Northern media in relation to notions of sexual independence and sexual pleasure. I interviewed over 20 young women and they gave a wide range of reasons for their choice.

Most of the respondents emphasised that they believed women's strength is within themselves and wearing a 'daring cloth' like the G-string, gives a woman the inner confidence and a sense of sexual and personal boldness. It also signifies an identity of being 'modern' and 'outspoken'. Most of them were clear that the underwear enhances their identity as sexual beings, and that it attracts young men. (In an interview with a young man, he said, 'Girls wear G-strings to grab a guy's attention! It turns us on![sic]…', suggesting that my women interviewees' analysis of their own desirability to men is dramatically enhanced by wearing a G-string.)

One woman, however, explicitly explained to me:

> I wear G-strings exclusively and I wouldn't say I do it just to grab guys' attention. In fact, most of the time, apart from my boyfriend, no guy would know I'm wearing one. I don't have it hanging out the back of my jeans, the only give away is that I have zero VPL (Visible Panty Line). The reasons I wear G-strings are numerous. Firstly, I do find them comfortable, they're so minimal they often feel like you're wearing nothing at all! Secondly I like the look, I think they are very feminine and sexy. The fact that boys love them is a bonus. Finally, they are the most practical form of underwear, especially as girls' clothing gets tighter and more revealing. If you don't want VPL a G-string is a must…

I found it interesting that my interviewees believed, overall, that G-string wearers were all senior students at the university and most of them had in one way participated in the student politics and or in club representation on campus. They also suggested that while many younger girls fear wearing the G-string, those who do are regarded as outrageous and they 'give no damn' in doing so. G-string wearers are understood as *'those that break the silence'*, those that go beyond the conventional norms and those that see customs as barriers to their progress. 'They are forward looking and full of hopes for future' 'They identify themselves with international models'

On the other hand, informants told me that G-string wearers can be regarded as immoral and 'bad girls' for wearing G-strings, 'they are considered to be "prostitutes" "cheap" and having many partners.' Some girls also agreed that the garment is not good enough to be worn by students as members of an elite class 'my goodness… G-strings… the worst undergarment ever invented… they make you feel like… uuuuugggggghhhhhhh… if you're going to wear a G-string… you might as well have no underwear on at all…'

As is the case with many commodities associated with pop culture, G-string underwear is not without its historical controversies as a product. In 2002, when the G-string made its entry into the Kenyan supermarkets, a certain shopping mall along the Muindi Mbingu Street, in Nairobi got into trouble with some churches which objected to its marketing, claiming they are too sexually suggestive. In April 2002, G-string underwear was at the centre of a media uproar after a headmistress of a school in Kakamega in western Kenya forced female students to lift their skirts before entering a school hall, in a so-called crackdown on G-string underwear.

In May 2003, the Head Teachers' Association meeting in Mombasa voiced concern that girl pupils were wearing thong underwear to school. This incident led to a media debate about the appropriateness of G-string underwear and the sexualisation of children. These actions are believed to have been prompted by both the deliberate and inadvertent exposure by young women of their G-string as well as a current trend at the time of men 'sagging', wearing their pants so low down that the pubis was exposed. According to my interviewees, G-strings have emerged as one of the ultimate symbols of 'the cool feeling' among Kenya's increasingly sophisticated youngsters, 'G-strings are cool,' 'They empower sexual freedom and choice.' Both young men and young women are invested in these notions, although from my interviews with young women, their meanings for 'being cool' involved aspirations towards independence that went beyond being heterosexually 'cool' and desirable to men. I found this very interesting as a way of making visible the complexity of the pull towards the G-string for women who want both 'independence' and 'men': the G-string gave my men interviewees simply a sense that for a woman to wear a G-string was to signal her 'cool sexual availability,' whereas the women acknowledged the sexual power of the G-string but claimed it as part of an independence that did not necessarily include 'attracting men.'

It must also be noted, that urban youth in African cities often place those in the movie and music industry on pedestals, vying to be like them in fashion and lifestyle. 'Many young people are emulating celebrity idols,' and these famous people have the power to determine what looks normal (Oliver 1999:9). 'It is partially through fashion that they begin to judge themselves and each other ... to continue to determine whether they are or are not the ideal image' (Oliver 1999:15). In this regard, the hip-hop and R&B music industry has also helped to promote the G-string, mostly under its American nomenclature of 'thong' by composing songs about it and featuring artists clad in them. Artists include Britney Spears, Christina Aguilera and Lil' Kim. One example of music that popularised this undergarment is the 'Thong Song' by Sisq which was released in 2000. In part the song goes:

This thing right here

Is lettin all the ladies know

What guys talk about

You know

The finer things in life

Hahaha

Check it out

Ooh dat dress so scandalous

And ya know another nigga couldn't handle it

See yashakin that thang like who's da ish

With a look in ya eye so devilish

The G-strings have thus become globalised icons of pop culture, and to many contemporary observers, this fashion trend for youth in Kenya gets 'sexier'. In Laikipia University, one student lamented that 'I feel like girls are overwhelmed with sexy images, and it makes us too obsessed with the way we look,' and popular magazines reinforce the idealisation of hyperfeminine sexiness.

In this chapter, I have argued that in Kenya today, collective identities of urban youth are shaped by – and expressed through – music, dance, fashion, art, and other cultural forms, and that this includes items of clothing as historically marginalised as women's underwear,[6] I have argued that the G-string, though considered 'dirty' by critics, constitutes a notion of future power for young men and for young women. Through dress, the 'secret underwear' is symbolically undermined by 'un-fixing' the classifications of representation, body, 'women' and 'problem'. Discourses of power, social activities and gender relations are regrouped by displacing the gaze from the fix of fashion to a statement about 'a new Kenyan woman'. This is not to argue that such clothes 'liberate' women, merely that the fashion is a discursive and representational response to, and intervention in, an ongoing struggle.

Notes

1. Just as ragtime, jazz, R&B, and other Black American musical idioms and forms entered mainstream culture earlier in the century; today it is hip-hop culture and its distinctive sound of rap music that is becoming an important form of music and cultural style throughout the globe. Hip-hop erupted from New York dance and party culture of the 1970s. Encompassing dance and performance, visual art, multimedia, fashion and attitude, hip-hop is the music and style for the new millennium. A highly protean and assimilative cultural ethos, it is here to stay, as it absorbs new influences, is appropriated throughout myriad cultural forms and forces across the globe, and has become a major mode of the global popular.

2. Judd Stitziel's study of the East German consumer economy, *Fashioning Socialism* (Berg 2007) acknowledges earlier on that the DDR never managed to create a distinctively socialist aesthetic – instead, via a series of misunderstandings and disavowed misappropriations of Western fashions and styles, there emerged such distinctive objects as the standardised dress, the plattenbauten apartment block and the Trabant.

3. Clothing research has attracted renewed interest in anthropology over the past two decades, experiencing a florescence that had been kept within bounds by reigning theoretical paradigms. The works have been influenced by general explanatory shifts in anthropology, which inform disparate bodies of clothing research that otherwise

have little unity. The most noticeable trend is a preoccupation with agency, practice, and performance that considers the dressed body as both subject in, and object of, dress practice. The turn to consumption as a site and process of meaning making is evident also in clothing research.

4. *Kanga* (sheet with printed words often worn on the waist) originated on the coast of East Africa in the mid 19th century. As the story goes, some stylish ladies in Zanzibar got the idea of buying printed kerchiefs in lengths of six, from the bolt of cotton cloth from which kerchiefs were usually cut off and sold singly. They then cut the six into two lengths of three, and sewed these together along one side to make 3-by-2 sheet; or bought different kinds of kerchiefs and sewed them back together to form very individualistic designs.

5. http://lovemomiji.com/momiji-pants-party visited on 12 March 2012

6. As we note below, hip hop is a broader cultural matrix that includes dance, performance, visual art, style, fashion, and a mode of life; rap is the form of musical idiom that articulates the ethos of hip-hop culture. On the relationship between hip-hop and rap and for various accounts of their historical genesis and significance, see Toop 1984; George 1988 and 1998; Gilroy 1991 and 1994; Dyson 1993 and 1996; Rose 1994; Lipsitz 1994; and Kellner 1995. This study was carried out as part of our forthcoming *The Postmodern Adventure*, which follows Best and Kellner 1991 and 1997.

References

Appadurai, Arjun, 1996, *Modernity at Large*. Minneapolis: University of Minnesota Press.

Agechi, Nathan Oyori, 2008, 'Sheng as a Youth Identity Marker: Reality Or Misconception?' in Njogu, Kimani, ed., *Culture, Performance and Identity: Paths of Communication in Kenya*, Nairobi: Twaweza Communications.

Allman, Jean, ed. 2004, *Fashioning Africa: Power and the Politics of Dress*, Bloomington: Indiana University Press, p. 247.

Anderson, Allan, 2005, *New African Initiated Pentecostalism and Charismatic in South Africa*. Leiden: Koninklijke Brill NV.

Barthes, Roland, 1967, *SystTme de la Mode*, Paris: Editions du Seuil.

Bickman, Leonard, 1971, 'The Effect of Social Status on the Honesty of Others', *The Journal of Social Psychology*, 85, pp. 87-92.

Bogatyrev, Petr, 1971, *The Functions of Folk Costume in Moravian Slovakia*, (translated by Richard G. Crum), The Hague: Mouton.

Buckley, Hilda Mayer and Roach, Mary Ellen, 1974, 'Clothing as a Nonverbal Communicator of Social and Political Attitudes,' *Home Economics Research Journal*, 3, pp. 94-102.

Carole, Collier Frick, 2002, *Dressing Renaissance Florence: Families, Fortunes, and Fine Clothing*, Baltimore: Johns Hopkins University Press, p. 347

Carole, Collier Frick, 2002.'The Globalisation of Pentecostalism.' Paper presented at the Churches' Commission on Mission, Annual Commission Meeting, Bangor, Wales.

Crawley, Alfred Ernest, 1931, *Dress, Drinks and Drums: Further Studies of Savages and Sex*, London: Methuen & Co., Ltd.

Cassell, Joan, 1974, 'Externalities of Change: Deference and Demeanor in Contemporary Feminism', *Human Organization*, 1, pp. 85-94.

Chitando, Ezra, 2002, *Singing Culture, A Study of Gospel Music in Zimbabwe*. Uppsala, Sweden: NordisticAfrikaInstitutet.

Comaroff, Jean and John Comaroff, 2005, 'Reflections on Youth: From the Past to the Postcolony', in Alcinda Honwana and Filip De Boeck, eds, *Makers and Breakers: Children and Youth in Postcolonial Africa*, Oxford: James Currey.

Apondo, Patricia Achieng, 2005, *The Politics of African Youth Identities in Post-Colonial Discourse*. Paper presented at the Codesria Child and Youth Studies Institute.

Aylward, Shorter and Njiru Joseph, 2001, *New Religious Movements in Africa*. Nairobi: Pauline Publishers.

Darley, John M. and Cooper, Joel, 1972, 'The "Clean for Gene" Phenomenon: The Effect of Students' Appearance on Political Campaigning,' *Journal of Applied Social Psychology*, 2, pp. 24-33.

Daugherty Sharon, 2006, *What Guys See That Girls Don't: Or Do They?*, Shippensburg, PA: Destiny Image Publishers.

Brown, Ray, 1978, 'Popular Culture: The World Around Us', in Jack Nachbar, Deborah Weiser and John L, Wright, eds, *The Popular Culture Reader*, Bowling Green, Ohio: Bowling Green University Press.

Droogers, André, 2001, 'Globalization and Pentecostal Success', in André Corten and Ruth Marshall-Fratani, eds, *Between Babel and Pentecost: Transnational Pentecostalism in Africa and Latin America*, London: Hurst, pp. 41-61.

Fandy, Mamoun, 1998, 'Political Science without clothes: The Politics of Dress Or Contesting the Spatiality of the State in Egypt', *Beyond Colonialism and Nationalism in North Africa*, in *Arab Studies Quarterly* (ASQ).

Lefkowitz, Monroe, Blake, Robert R., and Mouton, Jane Srygley, 1955, 'Status Factors in Pedestrian Violation of Traffic Signals,' *Journal of Abnormal and Social Psychology*, 51, pp. 704-706.

Kariuki, John, 2003, 'Which Way Gospel Music? Conservative and Liberal Christians Differ over Trends,' *Saturday Nation*, 23 July.

Jonaitis, Aldona, 1978, 'Reconciliation of Complementary Opposites: The Yakut Shaman Costume', *Anthropology*, 2, pp. 61-66.

Lasswell, Thomas E. and Parshall, Peter, F., 1961, 'The Perception of Social Class from Photographs', *Sociology and Social Research*, 45, pp. 407-414.

Manuel, Peter, 1988, *Popular Music of the Non-Western World: An Introductory Survey*. Oxford: Oxford University Press.

Manuel, Peter, 1988, 2004, 'Praise the Lord, Popular Cinema and Pentecostalite Style in Ghana's Public Sphere', *American Ethnologist* 1, pp. 92-110.

Ojo, Mathews, 1998, 'Indigenous Gospel Music and Social Reconstruction in Modern Nigeria.' *Missionalia* Vol. 26, No. 2, pp. 21-231.

Parsitau, Damaris, 2005, 'God in My Living Room: Pentecostal Televangelism and the Electronic Church Phenomena in Kenya', unpublished manuscript.

Paterson, Douglas B., 1995, 'Trends in Kenyan Popular Music'. Available at: http://hometown.aol.com/dpaterson/trends.htm

TerHaar, Gerrie, 1998, *Halfway to Paradise: African Christians in Europe*. Cardiff: Cardiff Academic Press.

Holland, D., &Eisenhart, M., 1991, *Educated in Romance*, Chicago: University of Chicago Press.

Hooks, B., 1989, *Talking Back: Thinking Feminist, Thinking Black*. Boston, MA: South End Press.

Kenny, L., 2000, *Daughters of Suburbia: Growing White, Middle Class and Female*. New Brunswick, NJ: Rutgers University Press.

Kilbourne, J., 1995, 'Beauty and the Beast of Advertising', in G. Dines & M. Humez, eds, *Gender, Race and Class in Media,* Thousand Oaks, CA: Sage Publications, pp. 121-125.

Kimmel, M., 2000, 'Introduction', in M. Kimmel & A. Aronson, eds, *The Gendered Society Reader*, New York: Oxford University Press, pp. 1-6.

Koza, J. E., 1994, 'Rap Music: The Cultural Politics of Official Representation' *The Review of Education/Pedagogy/Cultural Studies*, Vol. 16, No. 2, pp. 171-196.

Kumashiro, K., 1998, 'Reading Queer Asian American Masculinities and Sexualities in Elementary School',in J. Sears & W. Letts, eds, Teaching Cjueerly: Affirming Diversity In Elementary School, (???) Lanham, MD: Littlefield, pp. 61-70.

Lee, R., 1999, *Orientals: Asian Americans in Popular Culture*. Philadelphia: Temple University Press.

Lee, S., 200Ia, 'Transforming and Exploring the Landscape of Gender and Sexuality among American Teenaged Girls', *Race, Gender & Class*, Vol. 8, No. 2, pp. 35-46.

Lee, S., 200Ib, 'Learning America: Among American High School Students'. *Education and Urban Society*, Vol. 34, No. 2, pp. 233-246.

Lei, J., 2001, 'Claims to Belonging and Difference: Cultural Citizenship and Identity Construction in Schools', unpublished doctoral dissertation, University of Wisconsin, Madison.

Macdonald, M., 1995, *Representing Women: Myths of Femininity in the Popular Media,* London, UK: Edward Arnold.

Walt Disney Productions, 1998, *Mulan*, Burbank: Walt Disney Productions.

Nakayama, T., 1994, 'Show/Down Time: Race, Gender, Sexuality and Popular', *Critical Studies in Mass Communication*, 11, pp. 162-179.

Olsen, L., 1997, *Made in America: Immigrant Students in Our Public Schools*, New York: New Press.

Ong, A., 2000, 'Cultural Citizenship As Subject Making: Immigrants Negotiate Racial and Cultural Boundaries in the United States' in R. Torres, L. Miron, & J. Inda, eds, *Race, Identity and Citizenship: A Reader,* Maiden, MA: Blackwell, pp. 262-293.

Pyke, K., 2000, 'The Normal American Family As an Interpretive Structure of Family Life among Grown Children of Korean and Vietnamese Immigrants', *Journal of Marriage and the Family*, 62, pp. 240-255.

Silverstone, R., 1994, 'Television and Everyday Life: Towards an Anthropology of the Television Audience', in M. Ferguson, ed., *Public Communication: The New Imperatives*, New York: Routledge, pp. 173-189.

Tuan, M., 1998, *Forever Foreigners or Honorary Whites?The Asian Ethnic Experience Today.* Rutgers, NJ: Rutgers University Press.

Willis, P. E., 1977, *Learning to Labor: How Working Class Kids Get Working Class Jobs*, New York: Columbia University Press.

Khidekel, Marina, 2008, March, Cosmo Girl: *What is Sexy*, pp. 154-155.

La Ferla, R., 2006, 'An Impressionable Age', in New York Times, 10 August. Available at: www.nytimes.com/2006/08/10/fashion/10SCHOOL.html?_r=2 Retrieved 02/07/2008.

Norton, Leslie P., 2006, 'What's Cool at School', Retrieved 02/07/2008, from the ProQuest database.

O'Donnell, Jayne, 2007, 02, 21, 'And on This Floor, A Comeback'. Retrieved 03/23/2008 from USA Today.

Thelos, Philo, 2003, *Divine Sex: Liberating Sex from Religious Tradition*, Bloomington, Trafford Publishing.

Suedfeld, Peter, Bochner, Stephen, and Matas, Carol, 1971, 'Petitioner's Attire and Petition Signing by Peace Demonstrators: A Field Experiment,' *Journal of Applied Social Psychology*, 1, pp. 278-283.

Oliver, Kimberly L., 1999, 'Adolescent Girls' Body-Narrative: Learning to Desire and Create a "Fashionable" Image' .Retrieved 02, 16, 2008, from the ERIC database.

Schlecht, Christina, 2003, 'Celebrities' Impact on Branding'. Retrieved 02/16/2008 from http://www.globalbrands.org/academic/working/Celebrity_Branding.pdf .

Schlueter, Ingrid, 2007, 'It's 911 Time for Christian Girlhood'. Retrieved 02/16/2008, from http://www.christianworldviewnetwork.com/print.php?&ArticleID=1503

Tsai, Chia-Ching& Chang, Chih-Hsiang, 2007, 'The Effect of Physical Attractiveness of Models on Advertising Effectiveness' Research Library Core, Vol. 1, No.3: Winter.

Veblen, Thorstein, 1953, *The Theory of the Leisure Class*, New York: The New American Library.

6

'Daddy, Today we have a Match!' Women's Agentic Strategies in Initiating Sexual Intercourse in an Urban Ghanaian Community

Daniel Yaw Fiaveh

Introduction

The term agency signifies that a person is responsible for his or her own actions. Thus, agentic skills are those that individuals possess which enable them to make proactive self-reflecting choices (Collins 2000; Meyers 2002). Yet, in countries in Africa, men are perceived as sexually active while women are seen as passive in sex and less likely to initiate sexual intercourse compared to men (see Anarfi 2006; McFadden 2003) although in many African contexts, women are sexually expressive (Fiaveh *et al.* 2015a & 2015b; Pereira 2003; Tamale 2005). Using in-depth interviews with 20 women in Ghana aged 22 to 79 years, I provide evidence to suggest that women are not passive in terms of sexual relations and not as 'powerless' as popular knowledge makes them appear. Findings of the study have a potential to broaden our understanding on female agency and sexual practices in Africa.

Historically, the discussion of sexuality has been shaped by the continuing issue of whether sexual identity is biologically given or is socially constructed. From the perspective of essentialism, sexuality represents a biological drive, a natural given which forms the basis for sexual behaviour (Freud 1962). It argues that humans are biologically driven to seek sexual gratification (Boswell 1980).

Sexuality, from a biological perspective, therefore, encompasses the attribution of certain characteristics (e.g., sexual intercourse initiation) to a category, in ways that naturalise or seem to presume a homogenised group or reify what may be socially created or constructed (see Phillips 2010).

In contrast, the social constructionists (e.g., Berger & Luckmann 1966; Foucault 1978; Gagnon & Simon 1974) emphasize the constructivist nature of sexuality and argue that all human sexual behaviour is socially determined. By thinking of sexuality not merely as a reflection of biological drive but as a product of social knowledge, social constructionism sheds light on the fact that the ways in which sexual desire is conceptualized are always contingent upon specific social contexts and socially reinforced through education and culture (Foucault 1990; see also Bourdieu 1985).

Those who note the effect of human agency (e.g., some feminists and symbolic interactionists) on the construction of sexuality argue that humans make self-reflecting choices (Baldwin 1988; Blumer 1969; Bourdieu 1985 & 1990). Feminists (e.g., Adomako Ampofo & Prah 2009; Arnfred 2004; Bennett 2011; Oyewumi 2004; Pereira 2003; Tamale 2005 & 2010) have noted a more nuanced scenario of sexuality. They challenge the portrayal of African women as passively oppressed and visualise women as active agents of their own lives noting that sexual experiences, the desire for pleasure, sexual health, formal education, and exposure to the media, provide women space to wield sexual autonomy. Tamale (2010), for example argues that most of what is understood as culture in Africa is largely a product of misconceptions.

Studies in Ghana (e.g., Abotchie 1997; Adomako Ampofo & Prah 2009; Aidoo 1985; Akyeampong 1997; Sarpong 1977) and elsewhere in Africa (e.g., Dellenborg 2004; Diallo 2004; Tamale 2005) also indicate a more nuanced perspective of sexuality. For example, among the Akan of Ghana, women are said to have control over their sexuality and the sexual dissatisfaction of a woman could constitute grounds for divorce (Aidoo 1985; Akyeampong 1997; Sarpong 1977). Among the Anlo Ewe of Ghana, on the other hand, men are relatively stronger in sexual matters than women. Men use charms to restrict women's sexual activity (Abotchie 1997) although some women may also do same. Agency thus creates different kinds of lived experiences and social realities for different groups of people and an individual is able to make choices that contravene the cultural norms or values. How do women portray themselves as active agents of sexuality in their reflections on their own sexual desire? Drawing on the narratives of individual women's sexual practices in a suburb of Accra, Ghana, I illustrate how Ghanaian women engage in active responses to Ghanaian men in intimate sexual relations based on proactive self-reflecting choices.

Methodology

Data presented in this study was drawn from in-depth interviews with 20 women conducted from February 2012 to April 2012 in Madina, an urban community in Accra, Ghana. The study was undertaken as part of my PhD dissertation aimed at understanding sexuality, by interrogating sexual pleasure and the construction of masculinities and femininities in urban Ghana.

The study was exploratory in character. The population of interest consisted of Ghanaian women, 15 years and above, who had ever had sex, were residents of Madina, and were willing to participate in the study. The reason is because this population consists of the dominant age bracket of people who report being sexually active in Ghana (GDHS 2008). Within this population, interviewees were selected based on ethnicity, education, marital status, religion, and sexual activity. Interviewing these sub-groups also brought heterogeneity to the sample and diversity of beliefs and experiences in matters of sexuality.

Access to participants was in their homes and work places (based on appointment). Purposive and snowball sampling techniques were used. Purposive sampling was used because of its effectiveness in identifying specific interviewees (Bryman 2008). For example, there was the need to capture the experiences of different demographic groups such as the married and the unmarried, the employed and the unemployed, as well as variations in ethnicity, religion and sexual experiences. The interviewer approached potential interviewees (such as female artisans at work i.e., a seamstress) with the view of having a general discussion about young people's sexual behaviour. This approach was useful because in Ghana, adult women and men are willing to share their views on young people's sexuality, especially in relation to what they regard as the 'immoral' behaviour of the youth. I discovered that a good approach was for the interviewer to ask a female participant to share her views on young people's sexual behaviour and then redirect the conversation to focus on the participant's own sexual experiences.

I then employed snowballing to identify other interviewees who were willing to participate in the study (see Biernacki & Waldorf 1981). This method was appropriate because the study concerned a sensitive issue, sexual pleasure, for which I required the knowledge of persons who know those who would be willing to participate. I started each discussion with an oral vignette technique that problematised men's control over women's sexuality. For example,

> Please, I am Daniel, an Ewe man, but fluent in Twi, Ga, and Hausa [all these being major languages in Ghana]. I spent my childhood days and youth in Accra New-Town, Nima, Akotes, and Madina-UN. My experiences in these suburbs of Accra shows that women really have power, contrary to what some people think of them. To most people, men have total control over their women. I think this is not entirely true. In order to document this and to tell the story of women from their

own voices, I am undertaking this study. The study focuses on intimacy among men and women. Please, would you be willing to participate? What do you think? (Interviewer: man).

The stress on the ability to speak the local languages in the above quote serves as a means of building rapport with, and eliciting confidence and trust from the interviewees. It was also a means of helping interviewees feel free to discuss their sexuality in their native language without inhibition, especially in the case of those who had difficulty in expressing themselves in, or understanding, English.

In one instance, an interviewee, during the interview (tape recorded), introduced her friend who had been curious (i.e. eavesdropping) about what was going on. The interview was paused to ensure the confidentiality of the interviewee. She said *eh! meke faru nan?* [Hausa, what is happening here]. *Meh esa kun beri fera yendeh kun genni?* [Hausa, why have you two suddenly stopped chatting upon my entry?]. The friend remarked that *eh! menaadaa menua baa no oo, marima nka nokware* [Twi, make sure you do not deceive my sister for you men are liars]. The interviewee then requested that the interviewer talks with her friend afterwards, *mepa wo kyɛw sɛ yɛ wie a ɛne ono nso nkasa* [Twi, please when we finish, engage her as well]. All interviews were conducted by me, the author, and participants were assured of anonymity and confidentiality. The questions included: How often do you have sex… (probing for when was your last sexual intercourse, would you want to have sex the same way as your last sex)? How often do you initiate sex (probing for what factors influence decisions to have or not have sex)? How do you initiate sex (probing for who decides, when to have it, and how)?

The Institutional Review Board (IRB) of the Noguchi Memorial Institute for Medical Research, University of Ghana, granted ethical clearance (NMIMR-IRB CPN 048/11-12). Data was collected with informed consent and the names attributed to informants in this study are pseudonyms to ensure confidentiality. The age distribution shows that more than half of participants were under age 40, reflecting the comparatively youthful age structure of Accra. Eighteen had basic formal education while 2 did not. With the exception of two participants who were pursuing full-time formal education, the rest were working. Fifteen of the women were Christians while 5 were Muslims. Ten were married (Table 6.1). A greater number (16) of the women had their first experience of sex between ages 17 and 24 years. With the exception of a few women (8) who had their first sex to prove love to their partners, the rest (12) were forced into their first sexual encounter (sexually abused).

Table 6.1: Socio-Demographic Profiles

Res #	Pseudonym	Gender	Age	Marital Status	Duration of Relationship	Education	Religion	Occupation
R1	Sumaya	F	36	Never Married	1 year	Primary	Muslim	Seamstress
R2	Asantewaa	F	43	Married	8 Years	Middle School	Christian	Trader
R3	Memuna	F	35	Remarried	2 years	SSS/SHS	Muslim	Trader
R4	Naa	F	37	Remarried	3 months	Tertiary: Postgrad	Christian	Lecturer
R5	Sitsofe	F	31	Married	2 years	Tertiary: Postgrad	Christian	Teacher
R6	Dzidzor	F	38	Never Married	2 years	Vocational	Christian	Social Worker
R7	Aida	F	37	Married	11 Years	Tertiary: Postgrad	Christian	Lecturer
R8	Hajia	F	53	Married	26 years	Never attended any	Muslim	Trader
R9	Zu	F	26	Never Married	6 Months	Tertiary: Undergrad	Muslim	Student
R10	Akosua	F	32	Never Married	Not in relationship	Tertiary: Postgrad	Christian	Business Woman
R11	Anti Nurse	F	56	Divorced	10 years	Post Secondary	Christian	Nurse
R12	Koshie	F	36	Married	1 Year	Post Secondary	Christian	Admin Assistant
R13	Gyamfua	F	25	Never married	6 years	Tertiary: Postgrad	Christian	Student
R14	Akofa	F	30	Never married	2 years	Primary	Christian	Health assistant
R15	Adurowora	F	79	Widow	25 years	Never attended any	Not religious	Sells medicine
R 16	Oye-Mansa	F	22	Married	4 months	Tertiary: undergrad	Christian	Student
R17	Maame	F	30	Never married	5 months	Tertiary: Postgrad	Christian	Teaching Assistant
R 18	Adwoa	F	33	Married	10 years	Undergrad	Christian	Teacher
R19	Jun	F	31	Never married		Postgrad	Christian	Nurse
R20	Absu	F	42	Married	8 years	Postgrad	Christian	Administrator

*Senior Secondary School/Senior High School

Data Analysis

Audiotape interviews were transcribed verbatim using expert translators. All records (e.g., interviews and transcripts) were treated confidentially.

The transcripts were read three times. The first two readings were to understand the transcript and highlight emerging codes and themes. Notes were recorded for further use. In the final reading, a coding frame was made. The coding was carried out using a constructivist paradigm (i.e., in terms of socially constructed power relations), interviewees' lived experiences (i.e., in terms of personality), and personal lived experiences (including my interpretations of the quotes). The themes developed include sexual awareness and experiences, sexual 'silences', and sex initiation strategies. The first theme examines the sexual knowledge and experiences among women (i.e., the sources and nature of sexual knowledge and messages) and the link with individual ages, religion, marriage and sexuality. The second theme explores how women overcome their sexual 'silence'/challenges. In the third theme, I explore women's agency in initiating sexual intercourse and the factors that inhibit this agency. The segments with similar meanings were coded under one theme to avoid repetition of themes, i.e. new themes. New here means whatever I discovered that was unknown to me as a researcher and novel for existing theoretical and policy debates concerning women's negotiation skills in matters of sexuality.

I contacted all the interviewees three months after the interviews for a meeting or telephone conversation. In this conversation, I presented individuals with some preliminary findings and interpretations of their narratives, to seek confirmation and feedback regarding interpretations of the data. While I was not able to contact all interviewees (due to their work and busy schedules, relocation, travel, communication problems, and other reasons), the feedback from those contacted (6 women) is presented as part of the discussion. The interview extracts included in this study were the direct translation of the interviewees in their local languages and oral ('broken') English. This is to retain the faithfulness of the transcripts, and to project the interviewees' own voices.

Results

The women's ability to initiate sexual intercourse derives mainly from their sexual awareness (and experiences), especially with regard to interpretations of religious texts and access to the media, agency to overcome sexual 'silences', and the sex initiation strategies adopted.

Sexual Awareness/Experiences

The media (TV, radio, newspaper, and internet) and friends (hearsay) were the main sources of sexual messages for the majority of women. Given the proliferation of the media in Ghana and the fact that "sex sells" (i.e., the discussion of sexual matters have become necessary to gain media audiences), this comes as no surprise. Other sources of sexual knowledge include books (e.g., religious texts, fiction, and love stories) and personal experiences.

The women had access to the media. In particular, younger women patronized media messages that discussed sexual matters more than older women (those above 35 years). They patronized Telenovela films or Soap Operas and 'talk shows' (both local and foreign) that construct sexuality in relation to eroticism or romance or love. Others contain scenes of kissing and sexual messages that centre on 'real' men (e.g., loving and caring men/husbands, 'responsible' men, and 'good-looking' men). Messages also strengthened stereotypical sexual beliefs such as *men like too much sex and men lack sexual control.* A young woman had this to say:

> Ei! I think now I know more about sex, I've read more what you can do to enjoy sex. I remember watching a program on Adom TV [Cine Afrik], it's "Chocolate Factory" where the panel discussed about sex and how to go about it. They talked about communication and more romance. I'm still learning although not married. (Zu: 26 years, unmarried, Muslim).

The media messages also typify some stereotypical beliefs about women e.g., *women don't like too much sex, women like bold men, women are shy in sexual matters, good women do not discuss sex openly with men who are not their partners/strangers, good women exercise sexual restraints (are indirect to sex; not blunt), women who discuss sex openly are too difficult to please [in sex] and or too liberal to men's sexual overtures.*

In terms of the nature of sexual beliefs, women stressed that sex is about love, should ideally occur in marriage, and should be guarded. Thus, women had 'person-centred' beliefs regarding sex such as *I love him, I fell in love with him, or relational beliefs (we've been dating for long, he is my serious boyfriend, my parents [in most cases her mother] know him).* This suggests that the goal of a relationship for the women is to express emotional affection to a partner in a steady relationship.

Younger women indicated they had sexual intercourse as a means to express love for their partners than older women did. Women who had sex to prove their love for a partner indicated that intimacy is a deep feeling that means doing 'anything' for one's partner. Thus, sex is used to manifest and to reinforce love in their relationships. Younger and unmarried women compared to older and married women experienced a higher frequency of nonconsensual sex due to sexual intimacy blackmail (such as *prove your love, this relationship is over between us, you don't love me*) from young men. For elderly women (persons above age 49), sex is generally a matter of interest (*if I feel for it*) rather than to prove love. This is an extract from my discussion with *Adurowora*, a 79 year old widow:

Interviewer: Oh okay! okay. So at your age now, do you still have sex?

Adurowora: Oh, as for that one, if I feel for sex once in a while, I have sex [laughs]. "Enu dea yefa kuntu ase kakraa" [Akan proverb, as for that, we pass under the 'blanket' a little]. "Laughs", oh I had sex with a certain man, but that was long ago. But, at my age now, I don't like men [sex] except when I am conscious of it. You see when you are busy going about your business, sex wouldn't occur to you. "Or I lie?" [Is it not correct?] At old age, you are only thinking of afterdeath so you enjoy minimally if you can. (Widow, Not religious).

Agency Over Sexual 'Silences'

The findings showed that some women are able to discuss sexual matters and initiate sex with their male partners based on their sexual interest, partners attitude (e.g., liberal attitude towards sex), sexual experience (e.g., intimate violence or forced to have sex), moral justification and relationship dynamics (e.g., whether married or in steady/dating relationships).

The women were of the view that being in the right mood/condition or what some refer "right frame of mind" (e.g., mood for sex, sexual pleasure, pregnancy and menstrual issues, relationship stability, financial stability; for both parties, and general feelings of happiness/joyfulness) influence their interests in sex. This means that a bad mood signifies no desire and a poor attitude towards sex. The bad mood is context-specific and includes petty quarrels and misunderstanding between partners and especially partners' show of disrespect and refusal to show remorse. According to one respondent:

> You see, when your partner makes you angry and you are having sex with him, if he doesn't apologize for your heart to be at peace you won't feel anything. Me that is how I am, me when you annoy me, and you are having sex with me I don't even feel your presence unless my heart is appeased (Gyamfua: 25 years, unmarried, Christian).

These women had a conservative attitude towards some sexual practices. This was mainly about exercising sexual restraint in engaging in sexual practices through expressions such as "my religion forbids that" and "it's not good". Among the women, even the desire for sex is linked to their menstrual cycle with some indicating that they were not stimulated to have sex during their menstrual period compared to some other days (especially during ovulation) when they experience heightened sexual stimulation.

> Mmm, you know, I am very careful in having sex if I'm not safe or I have my visitor [menstruation]. My religion forbids that [having sex in menstrual moments] (Sitsofe: 31 years, married, Christian).

The attitude of partners also creates the opportunity for both parties, especially women, to communicate their sexual concerns in sexual relations. They were of the view that some men are "close minded" (i.e. not liberal towards sex), which makes it difficult to discuss sex with them. The women indicated that if some male partners do not "judge" their women (for instance as being too exposed to sex), then, women would easily discuss their sexual concerns with men, including asking for sex when appropriate.

The women also discussed issues relating to 'moral and religious rights'. A woman, for example, cites the Hadith to support her view of the rights of women to initiate sex. Her religion plays a very important role in her sexual behaviour and perception about sex as she strives to live by the tenets of her faith. She suggests that regardless of the situation, partners should not deny each other sex or refuse to satisfy each other sexually, especially in marital context.

> It is not good [to deny wife sex] because according to the Hadith the Prophet Mohammed says you must not deny partner sex or even the man you don't have to deny your wife sex. If you do that, me if I'm married to you I will leave [divorce] you (Sumaya: 36 years, unmarried, Muslim).

The women were of the view that since marriage offers them the legitimate context to sexual intercourse, it is incumbent upon all women to create the sexual space for intimacy and sexual intercourse with their partners. This also points to the fact that while religion places some limitations on women's sexuality (based on the interpretations of texts), it also affords women the space.

However, there was a limit to women's sex initiation. Some were shy to initiate sex while others stated that their inability to directly express sexual desires was due to their past forced sexual experiences. Older women did not give direct answers to questions about their personal sexual experiences probably due to the gender of the interviewer (i.e. a male researcher) and the moral standards expected of them (e.g., in Ghana, it is considered careless for adults to discuss their sexuality either with or in the presence of the young). They preferred using indirect expressions in responding to the question. Hence, it was difficult to extract exactly the meanings they attached to those expressions although some of the imports of the expressions were symbolic to understand. For instance, responses to some probing questions (e.g., some people believe that older women are not active in bed, what do you think?) were: *oh, ok you mean that? Oh, you should know; ah we too we are human beings, we have feelings*; and so on. *Hajia*, Muslim woman aged 53 years had her own wiliness about the questions asked:

Interviewer: Could you please share with me how you initiate sex with your partner?

Hajia: Oh! You get closer to him.

Interviewer: How do you get closer?

Hajia: [Laughs] oh! You should understand what I mean.

Interviewer: Could you give me some examples?

Hajia: Oh! As for that one I can't tell you. My husband understands. (Married).

Besides, elderly women responded to some questions (such as preference for sexual positions) with interesting phrases and comics – oh, *ɛno nsoso hia* [Twi, meaning they are also important]. They did not give any direct responses. That said, this does not mean that older women do not have an active sexual life. Rather, some felt that the interviewer was invading their privacy. In my view, the indirect responses had significant meanings. For example, *Hajia* responded to my question on how she initiates sex with oh! *You get closer to him*. This in itself is an affirmation that she has an active sexual life. She laughed and said, Oh! *You should understand*, based on further probes regarding what she meant by that expression. In Ghana, the expression "oh", though context specific, is a symbolic expression that a party to a conversation expects the other party to know what he or she is talking about.

Additionally, the experience of any past abuse (verbal, emotional, or physical) also contributed to a negative sexual reception and women's ability to discuss sexual matters with their partners. Women in relationships who had never experienced forced sex (e.g., through rape or verbal assault) had a positive attitude towards sex, such as discussing their own sexual spaces with their partners, compared to those who had experienced forced sex. To those who had experienced forced sex, discussing sexual matters is a re-visitation of the ordeals they suffered, events they do not want to recount.

> My aunt's child raped me, so I don't like visiting it [the rape incidence]. I cannot forget although he asked his adult friend even to plead. I am sorry, but talking about sexual experiences, even with my current fiancé, I really feel uncomfortable. He forces me *aaaa* [so many times] before (Sumaya: 36 years, unmarried, Muslim).

> At the least provocation, he wants to throw his hand [to be violent]. You can't even tell when he is in the mood for that (talking sex). If he doesn't have money or something goes bad [wrong] in the office "dieer" worse. So you have to be careful [with partner]. Ei, but if he is in the mood [for sex or financial matters become stable] everything is fine (Koshie: 36 years, married, Christian).

That said, women have sexual options and find ways to discuss sex and initiate sex with their partners provided they have a mood and the appearance and disposition (especially in terms of liberal attitude and relationship dynamics) and personal experiences allow them to discuss issues with ease.

Sex Initiation Strategies

The findings from this study show that women employ several agentic skills including direct and indirect strategies to obtain sexual contact with their partners. The indirect strategies used were mainly romance (i.e., wearing specific [erotic] clothes or perfumes or style/posture/way of walking). The women indicated that while a woman's sexuality is largely explained by both aural and visual arousal (sweet talk, melodic music, personal hygiene e.g., partner smelling good, and romantic movies), those of men depended on visual arousal and 'beauty' (i.e., erotic exposure of the breasts, buttocks, and thighs). They claimed that the problem of men is with their penis, i.e., they get sexually aroused because the penis 'controls their mind'. Hence, women use their beauty to entice their men for sex.

The direct strategies were direct/verbal communication and physical contact. Direct communication included text messaging or phone calls or the use of special language 'codes' (concealed) such as *Charlie ha wɔ gbu fio* [Ga for Charlie lets "dig" small], *daddy["daa"] today we have a match, Alhaj, yau dey mun jey Cannan oo* [Hausa, meaning Alhaji today we will go to Canaan].

> Yes, sometimes you can say it or sometimes you can go and lie on the person or just rub [massage] the person or use gestures. But, I think that if you have reached that level of communication, you can call the person over the phone and you are like, "where are you? I feel this way or that way and the person will [also] go like, you too where are you" [both laugh]. Me, it's simple, I call him, "daddy today we have a match?" [Daddy we need to have sexual contact today]. But if you really are at the point, you should be able to talk about it or just drop a text message or send an email or something, you see. (Koshie: woman, 36 years, married, Christian).

The women also reported the use of deliberate/romanticizing appellations including *"me wura" (Fanti, meaning my Lord), my husband, sweetheart, "sweedie"* [sweetie], *"baiby"* [baby], *"masoyana"* (Hausa, my heart), *"me dɔfo pa"* (Twi, my dearest love), "daa" [Twi, daddy]. Demographic profiles (age, marriage, and religion), sexual experience (ever been sexually abused), and partners' liberal attitude were found to influence women's ability and inability to initiate sex. For instance, the choice of appellations depended on relationship dynamics, age and level of sexual awareness. Thus, while those in a marital relationship were likely to adopt appellations that relate to a 'good' husband, those in dating relationship were more likely to opt for sweetheart or "sweedie" [sweetie] or "baiby" [baby] as a 'fine' or lovely boyfriend/fiancé or husband-to-be. Below is an example of the agentic skills recounted by a female interviewee in a marital relationship:

> I call him "Masoyana" [Hausa, my sweetheart], Charlie I miss you paa! [a lot] What do you think of it, are you ok? He would say I am ok or not. All these things I'm talking about I could not do while I was with my former husband. Because I had somebody who was much closed-minded [not liberal to sex]. But, the person I'm currently married to is very open and we can talk about anything. With him, you don't feel like he is judging you or picking on you. (Memuna: 35 years, married, "secondary education", Muslim).

Others used physical contacts such as caressing partners' sexual organs or 'sensitive' parts of the body (e.g., nipples). Some women also indicated that they "hold a partner down" after *"an unsatisfactory round [first round] of sex"*. The women indicated that they explore all possible means at their disposal to ensure sexual contact, including the use of physical threat, or ending a relationship or emotional manipulation or force. As pointed out by a respondent:

Asantewaa: Me, if I haven't enjoyed [it], I won't be fine kroaa [at all]. I will worry you "aaaa" until you yourself… hmm [laughter] "*Hwε*" [Twi, you don't know].

Interviewer: So how would you worry him [partner] aaaa?

Asantewaa: Asantewaa: Oh! That one "*deε*" [as for that]. Maybe I will frown for no reason. He will ask [me]: "why you are looking like this?" Then we take it up from there. Or "*me foroso na me maye madea*" [Akan, I climb [go on top] him and do my own thing] (43 years, married, Christian).

Another woman, *Memuna*, was very assertive and vocal about sex. She is able to express her sexual feelings although her assertiveness depends on certain circumstances such as partner's open-mindedness. For instance, she was unable to express her sexual feelings or wants with her former partner (husband), who she claims was *lousy in bed* and was not willing to abide by her sexual terms. She divorced her partner because she claims he was very opinionated and not open-minded. She has remarried. According to her, the current partner listens to her and is willing to engage her in sexual negotiations. Therefore, it is easier for her to initiate sex and to resist some positions, techniques or forms. Thus, a partner's tolerance and liberal approach to sex is important in helping women to express their sexual desires and sexual contact.

Discussion

In this chapter, I have explored women's ability in negotiating intimate sexual relations drawing on the narratives of 20 women in urban Ghana. The findings raise three key issues that point to promising directions for advancing the discourse on women's sexual agency. Participation in the study was response driven and purposive, using qualitative data gathered through in-depth interviews with women in an urban settlement in Madina, Accra, Ghana. Therefore, caution is exercised not to oversimplify sexuality beyond the interpretations given to the responses of the interviewees at Madina. The choice of Madina was based on convenience; the cosmopolitan nature of the area offers varied contexts from which sexuality was understood among different categories of women. The interviews were conducted by a male researcher, who was discussing culturally sensitive issue such as sexuality with female respondents. There is a possibility that some respondents were inhibited in their answers or simply provided what was perceived to be culturally acceptable answers.

First, the media remain key sources of sexual awareness on sexual practices among women in Africa (Bennett 2011; Fiaveh et al 2015a & 2015b; Tenkorang 2012). The media have equipped women with the knowledge to define their own sexuality and to foster the space for women's sexual practices and sexual agency. The evidence presented suggests that although perceptions on the quality of sexual relationships (such as marriage and steady dating relationship) were associated with the extent to which women exercise sexual agency with regard to initiation of sex, women have sexual choices.

Second, differences in socio-demographic factors (such as age and religion/culture), forced sexual experience, partners' understanding, and individual factors (such as protection of privacy, being in a bad mood and menstrual cycle) create different barriers as well as enhancers to sex initiation amongst different categories of women. The most common reason women gave for initiating sex was to receive "love", intimacy, and sexual pleasure. Married women like those in non-relationships negotiate their sexual spaces. Compared with older women, younger women initiate sex with their partners, and hold low commitment to moral and religious values. For older women, in addition to sexual privacy, moral and religious inhibitions posed some barriers to initiation of sexual contact with partners.

A third important concept is about women's agentic skills. Women exercise differential agentic skills in initiating sexual contact. Although differences in socio-demographic profile, sexual experience, and a partner create different barriers to sex initiation, generally, women are not powerless. The women find ways (including use of force) to seek sexual contact. As the findings show, women employ sexual negotiations as a means to have sex with a partner; in other situations women resist sex based on moral/religious consciousness. Morality or religion in this sense is an agentic strategy and not a coercive social structure on women's sexuality in a negative way. The findings, thus, lend credence to discourse that point to a more nuanced perspective of sexuality including the interplay of agency and structure (such as Bourdieu 1985 & 1990; Fiaveh *et al.* 2015a & 2015b; McFadden 2003; Pereira 2003; Tamale 2005 & 2010) as a central concept.

To conclude, the findings show that female sexual experiences and behaviours are nuanced and multifaceted, at least from the Ghanaian context. Thus, in addition to the views espoused by Anarfi (2006) that ascribe cultural explanations as the primary reason for women's sexual 'silence', the findings in this study show that the silences surrounding sexuality, particularly among women, are because of a complex blend of factors, i.e., demographic profiles, sexual interests, sexual dissatisfaction, partners' attitudes, moral and religious persuasions, mood for sex, menstrual issues, and forced sex. However, women have sexual agency pointing to the need to deconstruct misconceptions associated with female sexuality organised around masculine ideals. Work aiming to support women's sexuality needs to pay attention to their sexual negotiation skills.

References

Abotchie, C.K., 1997, *Social Control in Traditional Southern Eweland of Ghana: relevance for modern crime prevention*, Accra: Ghana Universities Press, pp. 10-145.

Adomako Ampofo, A., & Prah, M., 2009, 'You may beat your wife, but not too much: The cultural context of violence in Ghana', in Cusack, K., & Manuh, T., ed., *The Architecture for Violence Against Women in Ghana*. Accra: The Gender Centre.

Aidoo, A. K., 1985, 'Women in the History and Culture of Ghana'. *Research Review*, Vol. 1, No. 1, pp. 14-51.

Akyeampong, E., 1997, 'Sexuality and Prostitution among the Akan of the Gold Coast c. 1650-1950'. *Past and Present*, Vol. 156, pp. 144-173.

Anarfi, J. K., 2006, Talking and Deciding about Sex and Contraception in Ashanti Towns, in Oppong C., M.Y. Oppong, & I. Odotei, ed., *Sex and Gender in an Era of AIDS: Ghana at the Turn of the Millennium*, Accra: Sub Saharan Publishers, pp. 169-172.

Arnfred, S., 2004, 'African Sexuality'/Sexuality in Africa: Tales and Silences, in Arnfred, S., ed., *Re-thinking Sexualities in Africa*, Uppsala: Nordic Africa Institute, pp. 1-188.

Baldwin, J.D., 1988, 'Habit, Emotion, and Self-Conscious Action'. *Sociological Perspectives*, Vol. 31, No. 1, pp. 35-57.

Bennett, J., 2011, Subversion and resistance: Activist Initiatives, in Tamale, S., ed., *African Sexualities: a Reader*, Cape Town: Pambazuka Press, pp. 79-100.

Berger, P. L., & Luckmann, T., 1966, *The Social Construction of Reality: A Treatise in the Sociology of Knowledge*. New York: Anchor Books.

Biernacki, P., & Waldorf, D., 1981, 'Snowballing Sampling: Problems and Techniques of Chain Referral Sampling'. *Sociological Methods and Research*, Vol. 10, pp. 141-163.

Blumer, H., 1969, Symbolic interactionism. Englewood Cliffs, NJ: Prentice-Hall.

Boswell, J., 1980, *Christianity, Social Tolerance, and Homosexuality: Gay People in Western Europe from the Beginning of the Christian era to the Fourteenth Century*, Chicago: Chicago University Press.

Bourdieu, P., 1985, 'The Gensis of the Concepts of "Habitus" and "Field"'. *Sociocriticism*, Vol. 2, No. 2, pp. 11-24.

Bourdieu, P., 1990, *The Logic of Practice*. Stanford University Press.

Bryman A., 3rd ed., 2008, *Social Research Methods*. New York: Oxford University Press.

Collins, P.H., 2nd ed., 2000, *Black Feminist Thought: Knowledge, consciousness, and the politics of empowerment*, NY: Rutledge, pp. 2-299.

Dellenborg, L., 2004, A Reflection on the Cultural Meanings of Female Circumcision: Experiences from fieldwork in Casamance, southern Senegal, in Arnfred, S., ed., *Re-thinking Sexualities in Africa*, Uppsala: Nordic Africa Institute, pp. 79-94.

Diallo, A.,2004, Paradoxes of Female Sexuality in Mali: on the practices of magonmaka and bolokoli-kela, in Arnfred, S., ed., *Re-thinking Sexualities in Africa*, Uppsala: Nordic Africa Institute, pp. 173-189.

Fiaveh, D.Y., Izugbara C.O., Okyerefo, M.P.K., Reysoo, F., & Fayorsey, C.K., 2015a. 'Constructions Of Masculinity And Femininity and Sexual Risk Negotiation Practices among Women in Urban Ghana'. *Culture, Health & Sexuality*, Vol. 17, No. 5, pp. 650-662.

Fiaveh, D.Y., Okyerefo, M.P.K., & Fayorsey, C.K., 2015b. 'Women's Experiences of Sexual Pleasure in Ghana'. *Culture and Sexuality*, Vol. 19, No. 4, pp. 697–714.

Foucault, M., 1978, *The History of Sexuality, volume 1: An introduction*, New York: Pantheon Books, pp. 75-160.

Foucault, M., 1990, *The History of Sexuality: The Use of Pleasure (Vol. II)*, New York: Vintage Books.

Freud, S., 1962, *Three Essays on the Theory of Sexuality*, New York: Harper/Colophon Books.

Gagnon, J.H. and Simon, H., 1974, *Sexual Conduct: the social sources of human sexuality*, London: Hutchinson.

McFadden, P., 2003, 'Sexual Pleasure as Feminist Choice', *Feminist Africa*, Vol. 2, pp. 50-60.

Meyers, D.T., 2002, *Gender in the Mirror: Cultural Imagery & Women's Agency*, Oxford: Oxford University Press.

Oyewumi, O., 2004, Conceptualising Gender: Eurocentric foundations of feminist concepts and the challenge of African epistemologies, in Arnfred, S., ed., *African Gender Scholarship: concepts, methodologies, and paradigms*, Dakar: CODESRIA, pp. 1-8.

Pereira, C., 2003, 'Where Angels Fear to Tread? Some thoughts on Patricia McFadden's Sexual Pleasure as Feminist Choice', *Feminist Africa*, Vol. 2, pp. 61-65.

Phillips, A., 2010, 'What's Wrong with Essentialism?' Distinktion: Scandinavian journal of social theory, Vol. 11, No. 1, pp. 47-60.

Sarpong, P., 1977, *Girls' Nubility Rites in Ashanti*. Tema: Ghana Publishing Corporation.

Tamale, S., 2005, 'Eroticism, sensuality and "Women's Secrets" among the Baganda: A Critical Analysis', *Feminist Africa*, Vol. 5, pp. 9-36.

Tamale, S., 2010, The right to Culture and the Culture of Rights: A Critical Perspective on Women's Sexual Rights in Africa, in Izugbara, C.O, Undie, C.C., Khamasi, J.W., eds., *Old Wineskins, New Wine: Readings in Sexuality in Sub-Saharan Africa*, USA: Nova Science Publishers Inc. pp. 53-69.

Tenkorang, E.Y., 2012, 'Negotiating Safer Sex among Married Women in Ghana'. *Archives of Sexual Behavior*, Vol. 41: 1353-1362.

7

Construction of Social Identity in the Erotic Juju Song-poetry of Saint Janet

Adebayo Mosobalaje

Introduction

Erotic music has been described by different scholars using various names that range from song of banter, song of abuse to lewd song (Peek 1982:62). All the descriptions point to constant references to sex. Often, the song is considered raw, vulgar, and obscene and fit for condemnation by all civilised associations of the contemporary Yoruba people. The general reaction to people who play erotic music is contempt and a total dismissal of the song as being lowly and banal.

It, however, must be said that the Yoruba abhor sexual promiscuity or the licentious as instances abound in indigenous societies that point to sexual morality and uprightness. Virginity was usually celebrated during traditional weddings as a symbol of dignity (Olajubu 1972:152). This is because the bride would be deemed to have let honour remain in her homestead if she preserved her virginity. The parents of the bride and the groom always prayed that the nuptial cloth would be stained with blood as a symbol of the purity of the young bride.

Having said this, we should also state that the Yoruba engage in erotic song because, to them, obscenity does not belong in the realm of the words of the mouth but in the actual actions that may serve as a direct material manifestation of the contents of the song (Ojoade 1983:201). Erotic music is a language game, in the manner of literature, which could be gentle at times, as well as bitter and subversive at other times. As an oral form, performers are not confined to men but include women who fall for the lure of the art form or crave for the therapeutic pleasures it gives to the senses. Occasionally, children also constitute a sizeable part of the production regime, especially during festivals. Oral artistes enjoy poetic license and could freely sing about the genitalia during festivals and life-cycle events such as naming ceremony, house warming and burial rite for the departed. Artistes wield their poetic power without endangering the moral sensibility of the listeners.

Erotic songs or what, in some other quarters is referred to as indecent talk, has varied and communally sanctioned socio-cultural values. Erotic performances could be used to pay homage or *ijuba*. Homage could be rendered to people of different cadres ranging from the old to the young, men and women across the age grades. Artistes pay homage to fellow artistes or masters in the art. Fundamentally, homage in Yoruba-land is paid to *Olodumare* (God), then Yoruba divinities and the earth mothers referred to in Yoruba as *awon iya mi*, translated as our mothers or witches. It is believed that the earth mothers could make and unmake performances and even tamper with the fortune of oral artistes. Thus, homage is paid by praising the invincibility of the genitalia of the earth mothers.

Normally, erotic song is well suited to satiric performances. Usually in moonlight performances that would wind to the early hours of the morning, artistes would sing satiric vibes. Occasionally, the songs would be sung to shame perpetuators of vices of various forms. This would be done in front of the homestead of the subject of attack, reeling out his misdeeds with impunity (Isola 1992:19). Lewd songs served multiple purposes, including describing physical attributes, passing on instructions, educating and entertainment (Peek 1982:63). Oral artistes wished to thrill their audiences and tantalise their emotions. The utility value attached to this was the harmless discharge of the pent-up and dangerous emotions in a socially acceptable way.

As mentioned above, indigenous Yoruba women partook actively in the erotic sub-genre of folk music. They formed a sizeable segment of the performers of a satirical performance known as *efe* and the core performers of *oriki* (panegyric) genre that extensively uses erotic songs (Mosobalaje 2008:110). The advent, and wide spread of Christianity in Yoruba-land in the latter part of nineteenth century put paid to the performance of erotic music which the religion considered immoral, heathen and lowly. As a result, the oral form was, for long, submerged until the breakaway of some daring male performance poets and singers at the turn of the twentieth century in the spirit of cultural rebellion.

The late 1990s witnessed the outburst of the most volatile women singers of erotic music and the consequent subjugating reaction of the male religious superstructure to this female art form. Interestingly, the return of the male performance poets and singers was not greeted with stiff opposition while that of women singers was condemned, as confirmed by Saint Janet's interview below:

> I am not saying anything that has not been said before by the likes of Sir Shina Peters, Grace Jones, Millie Jackson, Madonna, Lady Gaga, Obesere and King Sunny Ade. The entire hip-hop generation of today is about sex and they are sometimes very explicit about it. So what have I done wrong? Is it because I am a woman? Women are the ones who are used as mere toys for sexual appeasement of the male in many musical videos, why does anyone not see anything wrong in that? I am fighting for women (*This Day*, 16 December 2012).

By Christian male world ignoring the performance of men's aberrant masculinities while chastising women to preserve their purity and virtue, the Christian male world exhibited hypocritical righteousness. The colonial religious gaze was upheld not only by contemporary Yoruba men but also by women.

The artiste and the erotic *juju* music under study which came up in the early 2000s are examined against the backdrop of music-making as an art of subversion of the contemporary Yoruba dominant male cultural hegemony endorsed by Christian hypocrisy.

Saint Janet's erotic *juju* is a commercialised vocal musical genre with percussive instrumental accompaniments and Western musical gadgets. The erotic *juju* is purely social music that celebrates pleasurable issues or what the Yoruba regard as *faaji* and has nothing to do with the term 'black magic' or its connotations. Unlike other variants of *juju*, and *fuji* music, widely practised by Moslems, hers does not engage the Yoruba *oriki* (panegyric) genre wholesale but sparingly and even then only using the stylistic resources of the erotic *juju*. Moreover, her kind of music does not dwell on anti-establishment politics such as Fela Anikulapo Kuti's Afrobeat music (Collins 1977:60). The politics and activism in her music, however, can be situated elsewhere in the realm of *faaji* that has gender implications and contends with male hegemonic power. For this, she describes herself as 'Mama Yabis' from the Pidgin English word 'yab', a reduction of the English word 'yap', which she may have borrowed from Fela Anikulapo Kuti who always asked in his songs 'Make I yab them?' each time he was about to attack the government. The protest in her own music is largely in the socio-political realm and thus her erotic *juju* is music of defiance vigorously contending the male socio-cultural space (Labinjoh 1982:128). Within the context of the socio-political erotic *juju*, Saint Janet entertains, instructs and satirises.

The composition of her band is unique; Saint Janet leads the band while men play supporting roles including her husband who is a guitarist in an era when women usually play the second fiddle in popular music and gender relation (James 1992: 237). The structure thus removes social distinction in terms of gender implications (Waterman 1990:373). Her band, therefore, is an alternative society that the Yoruba society should strive to emulate in terms of democratic distribution of roles.

Reflections on Erotic Music

As a potential change agent, erotic music by urban underclass women challenges the socio-cultural stratagem of the male religious world. The agency, therefore, is feminist and in clinical opposition to the Christian exclusion of women from the erotic sub-genre of Yoruba popular music. The theoretical approach that I propose for the study is a coinage that I describe as Phallic Feminism.

And what do we mean by phallic feminism? Phallic feminism differs from the Western conception of feminism which places women in an antipodal relation to the men folk. It is closer to the African womanism in its celebration of complementarity. In the framework of African womanism, complementarity approaches men and women as complementary partners for the common good of humanity and frowns at advocacies for breakaway of women from men. While not objecting to other socio-cultural dimensions of complementarity between men and women, phallic feminism focuses solely on the mutual complementarity that exists between male and female genitalia and the boisterous celebration that goes with the mutual dependency. Beyond the point of complementarity, phallic feminism is anchored upon the belief that the male and female genitalia are natural companions for the preservation of the human species. Arising from the foregoing, phallic feminism thus foregrounds heteronormativity and a dialectical power nexus between men and women.

The task of scholars of phallic feminism, while studying literary texts or other art forms such as popular music, is to draw out the aesthetic strategies of the feminist concept vis-à-vis its vision and mode of revolt (Brustein 1962:10). The vision would undoubtedly determine the nature of characterisation, language and style and the atmospheric setting of the feminist art or music. Realised in any cultural performances or literary works, the vision of phallic feminism is that of revolution. The mode of the revolt is contained in the sexualisation of the art form or popular music and its consequent performance as a counter-discourse to the dominant male religious strictures and gaze.

The freedom to express the deepest feelings of women in real life or creatively would always amount to a loss of the grip of a male-controlled domain of sexuality of women which men have for long been suppressing politically. The realisation of the power of the erotic and the creative expression of it is the fountain of humanity of women, the fall of their subjugation by external forces and the assumption of agency as argued thus by Lorde Audre (1984:2):

> When I speak of the erotic, then, I speak of it as an assertion of the lifeforce of women; of that creative energy empowered, the knowledge and use of which we are now reclaiming in our language, our history, our dancing, our work, our lives.

The struggle for the reclamation of the deepest feelings of women and the right to engage them within their whims and caprices through popular music as done by Saint Janet are targeted at a retrieval of the selfhood of women and a challenge to the male power gaze. It is this creative reclamation, without inhibitions, and the power and tension it generated in the process of thwarting the oppression and hegemony constantly raised and enjoyed by the male world that earned Saint Janet the *asa* identity. The persona and vision of character of phallic feminist works and discourse are always imbued with authentic and powerful reclamative creative energies in the cause of wrestling, mediating and dialoguing with power.

Phallic feminism is appropriately suited for the study of the erotic *juju* sub-genre of popular music of Saint Janet wildly practised for the enjoyment of the contemporary Yoruba people. It is a useful conceptual paradigm to theorise a women's war – that creatively uses the penis and vagina as weapons in contemporary Christian male-dominated Yoruba society to assert humanity.

Strategies of Representation of Identity and Sexual Diversity

It would be rewarding to start this section with a brief look at the social context of erotic music of Saint Janet. She was largely influenced by the palm-wine music culture mostly found in the Nigerian higher institutions of learning. We must hasten to distinguish this from the palm-wine music popularised by the Kru sailors from Liberia (Alaja-Browne 1989:233; Collins 1989:222). Unlike the sort popularised by the Kru sailors in the coastal area which later permeated the cities of Lagos and Accra, the one in Nigerian higher institutions of learning was popularised by Nigerian students through what they call the *Kegite* Club. The club is a composition of university youths all over the country who are devotees of the palm-wine keg. Sitting around their palm-wine keg during *tappings/gyrations* (performance meetings), Nigerian students have evolved a special genre of music known as *kegito songito* or gyration music. The *Kegite* Club, along with its music, has succeeded in forging a life-long social identity for the university youths. The club is noted for impacting on chains of networks long after university life. The music of Saint Janet is undoubtedly a spin-off of *kegito songito*. She considers her musical performance context as a *kegite* shrine which she describes as Sinner's Chapel or St. Bottle's Cathedral in which she is the General Overseer, perhaps, to mock the ridiculous proliferation of churches and general overseerism in Nigeria.

Her music and 'cathedral' also double as advertorial agency for the local strong liquor depots that sell various concoctions of herbal syrup. Herbal liquor depot, also known as *jedi* depot, is usually a roadside liquor shack and may have emerged as a direct offshoot of palm-wine depot. *Jedi* depot is a haven for the gathering of mainly jobless *lumpen* proletariat and low-income earners who cannot patronise high-class beer parlours in most Yoruba cities and states for relaxation and company. The *jedi* seller is usually a woman whose supplies consist of *jedi* or *opa eyin* or *ale* (herbal liquor concoctions) for the cure of piles and for penis turgidity, and other items such as cigarettes, marijuana and *kain-kain* (distilled liquor of usually around 80 per cent potency). The specialties of the matron of the *jedi* depot, among others, are penis turgidity and proper erectile functioning, and her prescribed drug is the herbal liquor concoction. Saint Janet's music is woven around the depot and devoted to the praise of the effects of the interplay between the herbal liquor concoction and sexual intercourse. Drawing from the larger social context, her erotic *juju* is also filled with numerous free borrowings from *kegito songito* which she must have learnt as a student member while at Moshood Abiola Polytechnic in Abeokuta.

Influenced by the foregoing contexts, the music has explored changing identities and the social contexts that inform them. If the performance context of her music sometimes suddenly becomes a church and what they deal in there are herbal liquor and sex, then the music can be appropriately described as erotic gospel. The foregoing nature of the social context and mission of the music are adequately encapsulated in this song from *Faaji Plus*:

Eyin boys	You boys
So sin le?	Is it becoming turgid?
To ban le	If it is becoming turgid
E nawo so ke	Raise your hands
Bi o ba le	If it is not becoming turgid
Ewari mi	Come and see me
Leyin isin	After service
Elere ta jedi	Musician sells concoction for piles
Ale wa	There is one for penis turgidity
E tun le test e	And you can actually test it

The song above quickly takes us to the issue of social identity or the character construction of the persona of the phallic feminist discourse that is the central concern of the paper. People who engage in erotic song in Yoruba after the advent of the two foreign religions are generally referred to as *asa* or someone who has no moral scruple. The word *asa* is not a contemporary coinage but its political context is. The contemporary Yoruba society tolerates and reserves the identity configuration for a few aberrant males but considers it undesirable, in totality, for women. It is one of the subtle criteria that men consider before choosing women as wives. Therefore, it is a social stigma for a woman to be an *asa*. No 'big' woman in Yoruba could afford the *asa* identity. While the *asa* trait could be condoned with respect to aberrant male popular musicians, it is purely unworthy for women to engage in such music making. Engaging in such would, therefore, be challenging not only to the male religious superstructure but also to women who have been completely frozen by the internalisation of the religious strictures of the male world. Saint Janet has thus, with the erotic gospel, moved out of the socially and culturally acceptable identity configuration created for women in Yoruba society to that of the *asa* identified in the phallic feminist discourse by singing a type of music that is deafening to the hearing of the male religious world. This is when, according to Lipsitz in Averill, (1996: 177) musical practices become 'strategies of signification and grammars of opposition' to deterritorialise the totalising and grand narratives of Christianity.

By singing erotic *juju* music, Saint Janet has deconstructed the music as the male preserve and assumed the *asa* identity reserved only for the daring male musicians. The *asa* identity wielder thus deploys aesthetic resources of phallic feminism appropriate to her revolt. This chapter discusses three aesthetic resources identified in the music for the analysis of the *asa* identity. They are audio pornography, erotic gospel and signifying the subaltern sex. What these resources do is subvert the genre of the erotic performance poetry beyond the artistic imagination of the male religious world. We shall begin our analysis, under this segment, on the use of audio pornography.

Audio Pornography

Audio pornography is another way of describing obscene words. Pornography, in this sense, means audio pictures that use visual, kinetic and olfactory imageries. One such example is drawn from Faaji Plus in which Saint Janet accounts for different structures of foreplay and actual coitus:

Towo mi bawa loyan re	*If my hand is on your breast*
Tenu mi bawa lenu re	*And my mouth is in your own mouth*
Ti something mi wani sale	*And my something is in between your thighs*
Sa roju duro ma yedi	*Just endure and do not move your hips*
Duro	*Wait*
Roju duro ma yedi	*Endure and do not move your hips*
Duro o duro	*Wait o wait*

Meek and submissive women do not use the language in the song above. One of the subtle arguments of the religious male world is that it is not befitting for mothers who are culturally saddled with the responsibility of protecting morals both within the home and the society to be singing lewd songs. When asked if she could allow her children to listen to the music, Saint Janet explained that she plays all kinds of music and that *Faaji Plus* was meant for a select audience. Her child is not yet an adult but she feels that her children could listen to her music. One of the fans of Saint Janet interviewed in this study said Saint Janet is a beautiful musician and is, therefore, happy that women are beginning to participate actively and publicly in erotic song that is usually shared privately among them.

The ability to arrest the male public space constitutes some empowerment or performance of power to a number of her fans. One of the means of achieving this is through intertextuality. Saint Janet, using a song text of hers, could engage a dialogue with erotic song texts composed by male musicians. A typical example is the following composed by Saint Janet in *Faaji Plus* which is a slight variation of the original by Akande Obesere:

Eyin Obinrin	*You ladies*
Isan te ba fa ti o ba le	*A caressed muscle that does not become turgid*
E gbe senu	*Put it in your mouth*
Eyin Okunrin	*You men*
Awo te ba naa ti o baro	*A well-beaten leather that does not turn soft*
E won mi si	*Sprinkle water on it*
Amen, amen	*Amen, amen*
Somebody shout Alleluyah	*Somebody shout Halleluiah*
The Lord is good	*The Lord is good*
All the time	*All the time*

Among the contemporary youths in Yoruba cities, *isan* (muscle) and *awo* mean penis and vagina, respectively. Still with them, a coital act means a thorough drilling of a piece of leather until it becomes exceedingly soft when it can actually be said that a man has done a good job satisfactory to his lady companion. A penis that refuses to rise up, perhaps after a round or two, should be roused through fellatio. The pornographic content is realised within the context of songs of service in the Sinners' Chapel by Saint Janet whose praise epithet is *omo ti o dese ri* (a child who has never sinned). The structure of the song text is reflective of the ironic contrast that imbues the church compared to the Nigerian orthodox churches. The last four lines of the above song text mark the difference between the version of Akande Obesere and that of Saint Janet. The celebratory and possessive contents of the audio pornography actually lead Saint Janet to intone and open the last four lines with 'Amen' and the word 'lord' which she actually pronounces to suggest 'rod'. It is within the same church that a young lady has been calling a brother frantically as shown in the following from Stress Tonic:

Boda, mofe mu bura yin	*Brother, I want to suck your penis*
Ani mofe mu bura yin	*I said I want to suck your penis*

The Erotic Gospel

The aesthetic strategy of phallic feminist discourse as drawn up by Saint Janet for the *asa* identity representation which irks the male religious world more than any other is the use of the Christian hymnal composition and rhythms. The experiment of identity configuration within the context of erotic gospel reinscribes and marks the gospel and erotic kinds of music as two different sites of vibrant dynamism and meaning making. Saint Janet has immensely appropriated the rhetorical resources of the Christian evangelical services, hymnal tunes and choruses for her erotic music in order to poignantly foreground her subversive counter-discourse. On the other way round, her gospel music has been enriched by the themes and usual tropes of the erotic music. Through the masterful experiment of Saint Janet, we have been able to observe a beautiful artistic expertise, hybridity and collaboration between the gospel and the erotic. The aesthetic collaboration is possible given the mode of oral composition which is always eclectic and collage because of spontaneous improvisation within the context of performance. More important in this regard is the fact that there is a porous boundary between the profane and the sacred in Yoruba spiritual cosmology (Barber 1991:261-276). This allows for free intermingling among the forces of liquor, sex and spirituality in Janet's Sinners' Chapel. What the chapel has undergone in the hands of Saint Janet is a 'Yoruba indigenisation.' And beyond the point of indigenisation, for whom are churches meant, if not meant for sinners?

The resource of erotic gospel is built by two main features. The first is the structure of contrast and the second consists of artistic grafting. Structure of contrast means that erotic songs are produced within gospel song in the manner of story within a story in dramatic composition. Saint Janet achieves this through the use of one of the techniques of oral chanters known as opening and closing glees. The opening glee usually contains *ijuba* known as homage before the performance proper and after which the closing glee would wrap up the performance. In record after record, Saint Janet features *ijuba* prominently in both the opening and closing glees. A fresh listening to her music may be confusing and would juggle one's ear drum, wondering what genre it belongs to . Here is an opening glee from the furor-provoking record Faaji Plus:

Heavenly Lord
Your name is wonderful
Your name is excellent
Your name is beautiful
We worship you Lord
For you are mighty
You got the whole world
In your hand
You got the whole world
In your hand

What normally comes after the *ijuba* is the contrasting blast of the erotic music and it is realised through artistic grafting. Grafting is borrowed from the register of agriculture. It is a process whereby a part of a living plant is cut and attached to another plant, most likely a damaged one. Grafting is also used mostly in the medical practice. In the parlance of art, it is a technique through which a piece of song is attached to or parlayed upon another rhythm. In the case of Saint Janet, she removes the Christian sacred texts and grafts the profane erotic texts on hymnal rhythms. The experiment is revolutionary not only in terms of aesthetics but also in terms of ideology. The revolution is proportional to the radical strength of the *asa* identity wielder so envisaged in phallic feminist discourse. We would be citing, for convenience of analysis in the study, both the Christians hymns and the rendition of Saint Janet:

Otito Jesu fun agbara wenumo?	*Have you been to Jesus for the cleansing power?*
A we o ninu eje odo aguntan	*Are you washed in the blood of the Lamb?*
Iwo a gbeokan le ore ofe re	*Are your garments spotless, are they white as snow?*
Awe o, ninu eje	*Are you washed, in the blood*
Ninu eje odo aguntan	*In the blood of the lamb?*

Below is the erotic adaptation as found in American Swagger.

Omo kekere to loun o gboko nla	*Little girl who has refused to take big phallus*
Itura n be ninu epon mi	*There is warmth in my scrotum*
Ma run e	*I will squeeze you*
Ma gun e	*I will pinch you*
Ma wo e	*I will rail down on you*
Inu e a yobombo	*And your stomach will turn rotund*
Wa wa gba wipe super wa lepon mi	*You will then believe that my scrotum is superb*

The common occurrence in intertexual dialogue or grafting is cannibalisation. The sacred evocation in the hymnal song is silenced or rather submerged within the wail of the profane. Various songs of praise to Jesus and the Almighty God that Yoruba people dance to with all energy and high spirit in expression of heartfelt gratitude for endearing accomplishments are adapted artistically for a new sort of dance, reason and sub-cultural group. Another example is a chorus from the Christian songs of service 'Mo tin Roba'.

Mo ti n roba	*I have been seeing kings*
Mo riru Jesu yi	*I have never seen a king like Jesus*
Ko yipo pada	*He changeth not*
O joba titi aye	*He reigneth for ever*
Ajinde ati iye	*The resurrection and the life*
Lo ni gbogbo ogo	*Has all the glory*
Mo ti n roba	*I have been seeing kings*
Mi o riru Jesu yiri	*I have never seen a king like Jesus*

The following is the rendition of the above song by St. Bottles' Cathedral from Faaji Plus:

E ti n somo	You have been having sex with type girls
E o riru elele yi ri	You have never seen this type before
To baka tan soke	If you raise one of her legs
A tun sumo e peki	She will jerk her buttocks close to you
Ti kini e bawo sale	If your thing enters her
A ni bobo e mo wowa	She would yell, 'Paddy, bring your arm'
E tin somo	You have been having sex with girls
E o riru elele yiri	You have never seen this babe before

While the reason for the praise of the Lord Jesus in the orthodox rendition is His invincibility, contained in the praise of the St. Bottles' rendition is the power of the herbal liquor for sex enhancement. Still on the power of liquor or quality sex performance, the following chorus 'Oyin Ni' from the songs of service is recast for the pleasure of the Sinners' Chapel.

Oyin ni	It is honey
Oruko Jesu Oyin ni	The name of Jesus is honey
O wonu aye mi	It has entered my life
Ko tun soro ekun mo	There is no cause for tears again
O wonu aye mi	It has entered my life
Ko tun soro ibanuje	There is no cause for sadness anymore
Oyin ni	It is honey
Oruko Jesu oyin ni	The name of Jesus is honey

Below is the St. Bottles' rendition in Faaji Plus:

Oyin ni	It is honey
Kinni abe re oyin	The thing between your thighs is honey
O fi ne sisi yen ko tun mona ile mo	You have lavished it on that babe and she cannot find her way home again
Oyin ni	It is honey
Kinni abe re	The thing between your thighs
Oyin ni	It is honey

In the closing glee, as found in *Faaji Plus* but varied in other records, we have a repeat of the *ijuba* and she closes, by asking all the band boys to stand up waving their hands in silence, with a hymn which she intones without the full musical accompaniment:

Ma joba lo Oluwa	Keep reigning Lord
Ma joba lo Oluwa	Keep reigning Lord
Oba ta ko le roloye	The king that cannot be dethroned
Alagbara ta ko le segun ni	The powerful one that cannot be defeated
Ijoba re dun yeye o	Your kingdom is blissful
Ma joba lo Oluwa	Reign forever Lord

Just like the opening glee, the closing glee has no St. Bottles' rendition.

The Subaltern Sex

Signifying the subaltern sexual self of women is well achieved in the erotic *juju* of Saint Janet. Still in keeping with the identity configuration of the good woman which could find a place under the umbrella term of good character known as *omoluwabi*, Yoruba people run away from being tagged *asa* which, as indicated earlier, constitutes a big social stigma. For the simple reason of not wanting to be stigmatised and earn the *asa* label, Yoruba women submerge their sexual self and identity. A great majority of women, in the contemporary Yoruba society, who have cool and vibrant appetite for sex, would simply prefer to redirect the appetite to other socially acceptable engagements lest they are tagged as prostitutes. Quite a few of the womenfolk are now waking up to the need to talk freely about the reality of their sexual self and identity. They have a strong feeling to state, within moral and social bounds, the needs of their bodies to their spouses without being misread just as men are free to tell the world both their moderate and extreme sexual feelings. As a phallic feminist art, the erotic *juju* provides a public forum for the engagement of the subaltern self and sexuality of women. A good number of Saint Janet's lyrics are devoted to signifying the sexual self, but we shall limit ourselves to the ones in her record *American Swagger*:

> *If you marry Ekiti lady*
> *Make you fuck am well well*
> *If you no fuck am well well*
> *She go run away*
> *If you marry Edo lady*
> *Make you fuck am well well*
> *If you no fuck am well well*
> *She go run away*
> *If you marry Ibadan lady*
> *Make you fuck am well well*
> *If you no fuck am well well*
> *She go run away*

There is a popular gossip surrounding the sexual identity of Nigerian women as captured in different ethnic social cognomen. Some ethnic groups regard the women of other ethnic groups as being more sexually demanding than others in an attempt to categorise them as being wayward. Within the Yoruba ethnic group, some tend to spread the gossip that women of Ondo town are more sexually demanding. The song above clearly, by selecting sample cities in Yoruba land, calls attention to the principal role of adequate and fulfilling sex in the stabilisation of the home. Sexual desire serves biological, physiological and cultural needs for women and vibrant demand for it is not townspecific.

Moreover, Saint Janet deconstructs the *asa* identity and *asakasa* (indecent act) with the issue of infidelity. She probes the political context of *asakasa*, and establishes its strength as being pure ruse which the male religious superstructure uses to sustain cultural hegemony. She warns that men should be loyal to their wives or be prepared to witness the inner sexual self of women which they may have repressed. She warns:

To ba ngba awo egbe	*If you love having sex with random ladies*
To ba lo yawo e loju e	*And they mate with your wife*
Le lelelele	*Lelelelele*

The yell of hilarity 'le lelelele' signifies and identifies with the just return of the communally sanctioned repression of the female sexuality in Yoruba-land for the purpose of the stability of the home. It is a precious warning to the Yoruba men folk who think that men are biologically and naturally polygynous. Saint Janet seems to be saying that women can also partake in the natural quota of polygyny or polyandry.

Another song from *American Swagger* also details a contemporary social fad belonging to young girls in post-secondary and university institutions. Through their choice of attire, they have broken away from the generation of women who cover their entire bodies even when the weather is exceedingly hot in keeping with the religious strictures prescribing the character profile of the good woman. Going by the exposure of the young girls in this cadre to foreign films, musical videos and novels, a thriving subculture of dressing has come to displace the old one. Young girls now wear skimpy miniskirts, sleeveless tops, body hugs and G-string panties to flaunt attractive parts of the bodies. Moving out of the old regime of dressing has precipitated a new mode of quality response to the female body. The following lyrics capture the social fad and the desired implications it has for the female body:

Gbogbo awon omoge iwoyi	*All the young girls of nowadays*
Ti won ba wa mura	*If they dress*
Pelu miniskirt ni	*It is with miniskirt*
Won o gbodo bere rara	*They must not bend down*
Nkan o gbodo jabo labe won	*Something must not fall from them*
Ti won bafe bere	*If they must bend to pick an item*
Won a fa go slow repete	*They will cause serious commotion*
Iyen la muse ya	*That makes the exercise faster*
Yeye ye	*Yeye ye*
Miniskirt lo gbode	*Miniskirt has taken over*

While probing the social context of her music, Saint Janet states the crucial therapeutic and socio-cultural ends the erotic *juju* has achieved. According to her, the music is an invaluable stress reduction tool in a Nigeria nation that is filled with so many broken dreams and hopes. Through the music, emotional weight is shed (Olajubu 1972:154). More than the above, the music serves as a mouthpiece that unknots the submerged social and sexual identity of women. She teases out, in the song text below from American Swagger, as being normal and permissible what the average Yoruba woman considers an asakasa to give flamboyant expression to thrilling coital pleasure:

Mi o se ru e mo	*I don't do such a thing anymore*
Mi o se ru e mo	*I don't do such a thing anymore*
Ka fi somolomo ni furo	*To penetrate a woman's anus*
Ko ma sede ti o daa	*So that she begins to jabber*
Ede ti o da bi 'ouch-ch-ch'	*Foul language like 'ouch-ch-ch-chhhh'*
Awon ede bi 'O yeah'	*Language like 'O yeah!'*
'Stop it, I like it'	*'Stop it, I like it'*
Mi o se ru e mo	*I don't do such a thing anymore.*

The signification of the subaltern sexual identity of women is one of the ideological projects of phallic feminism which aims at a full representation of the sexual yearnings and the authentic emotional being and self of women without inhibition. The commitment of this music to the foregoing ideology, therefore, marks the social identity of the music itself as a female art and the singer as championing the cause of women, whether consciously or not. The *asa* identity is ambivalent, steeped in politics but phallic feminist discourse partakes, celebrates and transvalues the politics.

Agency and the Contradiction of the Yoruba Society

The Christian male gaze popularises the binary opposition between the *asa* identity and the *obinrin rere* (good woman) that all the faithful must strive to emulate as a paragon of moral virtue. Enlisted in the enforcement of the male gaze are the clergies and dedicated Christian faithful across the Yoruba-land. The clergies along with the teeming Christian soldiers, therefore, constitute the surveillance network of the male religious gaze. The agency of erotic juju is firmly established in its capacity to shake up the cultural hegemony and reinscribe the male verbal space of erotic music. What this means is that the artiste has moved away from the meek and submissive Christian 'good woman' whose voice must not be heard in the church to an independent and self-assertive woman in the Sinners' Chapel in perfect keeping with the character persona of phallic feminist discourse. The syncretic fusion of the Christian hymn with the lyrics of the erotic has created a hybrid personality that could be aptly described as a variant of the new and contemporary urban Yoruba-Christian social identity forged by the forces of contemporary culture and economics. Saint Janet, through the use of the aesthetic tropes of phallic feminism, has transvalued the Christian male gaze and put male surveillance mechanisms in check.

Despite the immunity that the traditional oral chanters enjoyed, the domain of political music and writing has always been that of terror (Osofisan 1998:83). Saint Janet's music of defiance and her challenge of the male hegemony turned her to an enemy of the male religious world and their female sympathisers. Thus, she became guilty of war. Irked by the handiwork of the devil known as the erotic *juju* of Saint Janet, religious leaders, both Moslem and Christian, joined forces, condemned the music and vigorously resisted its advancement (*Sunday Tribune*, 22 July 2012). The Christian and Moslem religious male world sought the overwhelming support of the state against the subversive erotic gospel. The following were the responses to Saint Janet and her music:

> St. Janet has in the past weeks been vehemently criticised due to the lyrics of her song purported to be 'immoral'. The Music Advertising Association of Nigeria (MAAN) and the leadership of Performing Musicians Association of Nigeria (PMAN) placed a ban on the album in a dissipation of energy which the two bodies should have committed to fighting piracy and hunting for talents towards developing the industry (Sahara Reporters, 24 February 2010).

> The Lagos State House of Assembly on Thursday adopted a motion to ban the music album of St. Janet, titled *Faaji Plus*, from being played in public places and broadcast stations on the grounds that it promotes obscenity. The motion, which was moved by Sanai Agunbiade, representing Ikorodu I, was widely accepted by the lawmakers because they said the album's popularity is 'spreading like wildfire.' The album, which was released into the market about three months ago and marketed by Omu Iyadun Music, is sung entirely in Yoruba. According to the lawmakers, the album was filled with lewd lyrics craftily composed around gospel chorus tunes. A music critic, Ayeni Adekunle, the Chief Executive of Black House Media, said 'it is good that the government is making attempt to protect all of us, especially our children'. (Nairaland Forum, 30 January 2010)

Although the state ban was issued by, and for, Lagos State only, no radio or television station that we know of in the entire Yoruba-land, which comprises about five other states, airs her music. Despite the ban and threats of arrest, Saint Janet has not fled the country like other artistes of the General Babangida Must Go era (Haynes 2003:84), and her records have forever thereafter kept on selling like wildfire.

The persecution of her art, undoubtedly confirms the active agency of her socio-political music. It thus deepens interest in the contradiction of Yoruba society. The contradiction lies in the society that can produce but must not listen to its products. All art is a product of society in terms of form and contents.

The artistes are also a product of society through a thorough consumption of all the noetic formulae of all the genres in existence within such society. What artistes do is recycle with emblematic freshness, which we often describe as artistic innovation. The ethos of creative composition in Yoruba performances, as submitted earlier, favours improvisation within the context of performance. In performance, therefore, popular artistes borrow freely from master chanters or from the repertoire of texts of the society. There are erotic folk songs produced by Yoruba society which are very handy for oral artistes. The Freudian return of the repressed has brought back the erotic songs onto the contemporary popular music scene and the question of which society must produce and must not listen to or consume its product comes to the fore. One of such is the following erotic folk song, as presented, found in the folklore or produced by the indigenous Yoruba society in one of its lighthearted moments:

O do mi do mi la tana	*He has been having passionate sex with me since yesterday*
Ko ma je n sun o	*He would not let me sleep*
Oba mimo wo run obo mi	*Holy God, check my pubic hairs*
Meta loku	*Only three remain*

She now presents a less vulgar one by replacing the word obo (vagina) with isale (underneath) in the example below:

O do mi do mi la tana	*He has been having passionate sex with me since yesterday*
Ko ma je n sun o	*He would not let me sleep*
Oba mimo wo run isale mi	*Holy God, check my hairs underneath*
Meta loku	*Only three remain*

Often, she pokes fun at the gamut of the contemporary male religious hypocrisy each time she mentions the word *obo* (vagina) or *oko* (penis) so pointedly by quickly and derisively saying 'sorry' as if to withdraw what has been said deliberately. This is because a sizeable number of the members of the legislature who have placed a ban on her music are also her fans till tomorrow.

> But the banning of my CD made me popular. Now, virtually everybody knows Saint Janet. The same government officials that banned my songs listen to my music. I don't want to mention names but I play for them. They invite me to private parties and I perform there *(The Punch,* 23 March 2013).

In effect, we want to state that the crime of the character persona of the phallic feminist discourse, Saint Janet, lies in giving back to the society, rather publicly, what she has taken from society, very privately.

Conclusion

In the chapter, we have tried to examine the erotic music of Saint Janet in contemporary Yoruba society within the context of the politics of the male religious world that considers the art form as a male preserve for the daring and aberrant

Yoruba oral artistes. Through the use of phallic feminism as a theoretical approach to study selected audio records of Saint Janet, we have observed that her music is a subversion of the Christian male cultural hegemony in spite of the watchful eyes of the religious clerics and the devoted among the faithful who constitute the army of soldiers that monitor traces of disobedience to the religious strictures.

With the return of women singers of erotic music joining their male 'renegades', the religious leaders have observed the collapse of the male religious surveillance superstructures and thereby sought the assistance of their political male allies who introduced the repressive state apparatus in the *fatwa* ban on the music of Saint Janet and subsequent threats of arrests in order to muffle the erotic creative prowess. The agency of the erotic *juju* of Saint Janet is, undoubtedly, marked by its impact on the entire society and how the forces of the society, the religious leaders and the Lagos State Government have risen in war against the musician who wants to completely subvert the male religious world from the centre stage of power and identity creation.

The study reveals that the erotic *juju* is a product of syncretic social contexts that range from Christian choir practice to palm-wine and *jedi* depots and, of course, the *Kegite Club*. The social contexts have shaped and given the artiste the appropriate rhetorical grammars of defiance which irk the male religious superstructure. Indeed, the *Kegite Club* contributed in no small measure to the shaping of the revolutionary spirit and ideology of Saint Janet.

The study also shows the erotic music as an authentic female art by serving not only as a podium of economic empowerment for women but also as a domain of the performance of power or social empowerment by popularising socio-cultural trends that, in turn, entrench fundamental identities of women in terms of sexual diversity. By attending to the socio-economic and cultural needs of women, both private and public, and the politics surrounding the body of women, the erotic *juju* sub-genre has become a powerful social and economic agent of the urban underclass women who may ascend the social ladder to the elite group.

Finally, the music itself theorises in its celebration of the mutual dependency that exists between the male and female genitalia as a major weapon in a deep socio-political war against the male religious world in a contemporary Yoruba society. The erotic *juju* is a veritable site of contestation of meaning, negotiation of identities and, thus, political struggle.

References

Alaja-Browne, A., 1989, 'A Diachronic Study of Change in Juju Music' *Popular Music*, Vol. 8, No. 3, pp. 231-242.

Averill, G., 1996, 'Dangerous Crossroads: Popular Music, Postmodernism and the Poetics of Place by George Lipsitz' *Contemporary Sociology*, Vol. 25, No. 1, pp. 116-177.

Barber, K., 1991, *I Could Speak Until Tomorrow*. Edinburgh: Edinburgh University Press.

Brustein, R., 1962, *Theatre of Revolt: An Approach to the Modern Drama*. Boston-Toronto: Little, Brown and Company Limited

Collins, E.J., 1977, 'Post-War Popular Band Music in West Africa' *African Arts*, Vol. 10, No. 3, pp. 53-60.

Collins, E.J., 1989, 'The Early History of West African Highlife Music' *Popular Music*, Vol. 8, No. 3, pp. 221-230.

Haynes, J., 2003, 'Mobilising Yoruba Popular Culture: Babangida Must Go' *Africa: Journal of the International African Institute*, Vol. 73, No. 1, pp. 77-87.

Isola, A., 1992, 'The African Writer's Tongue' *Research in African Literature*, Vol. 23, No. 1, pp. 17-26.

James, D., 1992, 'African Popular Music: Performers and Regional Styles' *Current Anthropology*, Vol. 33, No. 2, 235-238.

Labinjoh, J.,1982,'Fela Anikulapo-Kuti: Protest Music and Social Processes in Nigeria' *Journal of Black Studies*, Vol. 13, No. 1, pp. 119-134.

Lorde, Audre, 1984, 'Uses of the Erotic: The Erotic as Power' *Sister Outsider: Essays and Speeches*. New York: The Crossing Press.

Mosobalaje, A., 2008, 'The Return of a Landowner: Islamic Strictures and the Emergence of a Female Art' *Journal of African Symposium*,Vol.8, No. 1.

Ojoade, J.O., 1983, 'African Sexual Proverbs: Some Yoruba Examples' *Folklore*, Vol. 94, No. 2, pp. 201-213.

Olajubu, Oludare, 1972, 'References to Sex in Yoruba Oral Literature' *The Journal of American Folklore*, Vol. 85, No. 336, pp. 152-166.

Osofisan, Femi, 1998, 'Reflections of Theatre Practice in Nigeria' *African Affairs*, Vol. 97, pp. 81-89.

Peek, P.M., 1982, 'Sexual References in Southern Nigerian Verbal Art Forms', *African Arts*, Vol. 15, No. 2, pp. 62-63.

Waterman, C.A., 1990, *Juju: A Social History and Ethnography of an African Popular Music*. Chicago and London: University of Chicago Press,.

Nigerian Newspapers

Nairaland Forum 30 January 2010.
Sunday Tribune, 22 July 2012.
Sahara Reporters, 24 February 2010.
ThisDay, 16 December 2012.
The Punch, 23 March 2013.

8

Language, Sex and Power Relations: An Analysis of Shona Sexual Expressions

Pauline Mateveke

Introduction

The subject of human sexuality has attracted a lot of scholarly engagement. Sexuality as a system ... of mutually constituted ideologies, practices and identities that give socio-political meaning to the body as an eroticised and/or reproductive site' (Hall and Bucholtz 2004), has also found itself at the centre of African studies. Questions of sexuality are imbued with political contestations (Weeks 1985; Evans 1993; Bennett 2011), and when working within African contexts, there is a need for researchers to be wary of colonial discursive influences on the meaning of concepts we deploy for analysis and exploration. In Arnfred's *Re-thinking Sexualities in Africa* (2004), some writers argue that debates on African sexualities remain, even in the twenty-first century, undermined by the 'dark continent discourse' which either exoticises or pathologises perceptions of the African world (see Jungar and Onias, Ratele in Arnfred 2004). Arnfred advocates for a reconceptualisation of African sexualities that transcends stereotypical colonial and even postcolonial European imaginations and states that, '... rethinking necessitates a double move of de-construction and re-construction... through a critique of previous conceptualisations, attempts are made to approach new materials in new ways, coming up with alternative lines of thinking' (2004:7). Arnfred's position is that rethinking African sexualities creates new knowledge and hopefully new levels of consciousness or awareness of a liberating kind.

Sylvia Tamale's *African Sexualities: A Reader* (2011) reiterates and expands on the ideas echoed in Arnfred (2004), advocating for the study of African sexualities from the recognition of multiple 'sexualities' as '… there are no uniform or monolithic ways of experiencing sexualities within one culture or community or even among individuals' (2011:12). Central to Tamale's insights is the need to do away with homogenised assumptions about African sexualities as these would only result in stereotypes and renewed essentialism.

Tamale and Arnfred's projects both provided this study with critical ideas and methods through which to explore my own research interests in Zimbabweans' language expresses issues concerned with sex and sexuality. Overall, I am interested in trying to make a connection between the language that is used to communicate sex and sexuality and the continued disempowerment of Africans as a race. The study is an attempt to push for Africans [in this case Zimbabweans] to reconsider the way we engage language within our sexual communication and I plan to make a bold assertion, based on my research on Shona terminology and usage, that sometimes this language can be clearly shown to be shaped within a culture of domination.

I argue that 'African' sexualities continue to be entangled in stereotypical discourses and that further research can be done to address the discrepancies between notions of equality/respect and notions of 'sex-as-dirty/women-as-dirty' that are inherent in such discourses. Essentialist depictions of African sexuality as exotic, immoral and irrational continue to supply the world with a ready-made grammar of negative social attitudes towards Africans. My study seeks to answer the following questions:

- What are the Shona speakers' attitudes towards Shona words that express sex and sexuality?
- What are the dominant ideologies behind Shona speakers' attitudes towards Shona words that express sex and sexuality?
- And, what are the implications of these language attitudes?

Studies on human sexuality have made connections between language and sexuality and have revealed the multiple ways in which language constructs sexuality. Hall and Bucholtz (2004) stress the importance of identity in the linguistic study of social and cultural practices such as human sexuality. Language, as the most powerful, definitional or representational medium available to humans, shapes our understanding of what we are doing when we are doing sex (Cameron and Kulik 2003). Cameron and Kulik further argue that the language that we have access to in a particular time and place for representing sex and sexuality exerts a significant influence on what we take to be possible, normal and desirable. Cameron and Kulik further argue that there is a relationship between the linguistic representation of sex or sexuality with power relations, and language serves as an important element in the political struggles around sexuality. These insights from Cameron and Kulik serve as a reference point to this study as it endeavours to explore how sex and sexuality are linguistically represented in the Shona language.

Language, as a reflection of a people's culture and the manner in which the people perceive themselves as well as others, is an important dimension to the study of human sexuality because the language that is used to express sex and sexuality also reveals how people perceive their sexuality. One of the issues of concern to this study is the relationship between colonial languages and those which belong, by history and ancestry, to people. There are many debates on the ways in which different African nations, post colonialism, organised the relationship between the coloniser's language (often embedded in education and government) and other languages of the people, and Manyonga argues that some have accepted the notion that indigenous languages are 'inferior and uncivilised' (Manyonga 2002).

Adegbija (1994) also recognises the disproportionate attitudes of superiority towards European languages in sub-Saharan Africa. Adegbija argues that there are attitudes of low self-esteem and inferiority towards indigenous African languages, and thus African languages end up being excluded from important spheres of communication. Because European languages carry with them a tide of cultural imperialism (Phillison 1992), the exclusion of African languages also has devastating political consequences.

There has not been much research on the daily language that communicates engagement with sex and sexuality in African contexts, and Tamale (2011) suggests that research on African sexualities needs to hone distinctive techniques and methods that unearth invisible, silenced and repressed knowledges. The study thus argues that studying African sexualities through the lens of the ordinary (and non-colonial) language that is being used to talk about sex offers a ground-breaking entry point .

This study explores Shona terms that express sex and sexuality and asks questions about the ways such terms are deployed, and about why certain concepts concerning gender and sexuality are rendered in Shona rather than in the colonial language, English.

Approach to the Study

Burgess (1993) asserts that there is not one best method of conducting social research. Instead, researchers need to consider the kind of research question they wish to pose and the most appropriate methods of research and techniques of data collection. For the purposes of this research, predominantly qualitative methods were used in recognition of their ability to '…reflect and capitalise upon the special character of people as objects of inquiry' (Bryman 1988:3). Bryman further argues that the most fundamental characteristic of qualitative research is its express commitment to viewing events, action, norms and values from the perspective of the people who are being studied. In the twenty-first century, this includes thinking of social media sites as a 'field' for ethnographic exploration and I chose to conduct an in-depth Facebook analysis of the ways in which Shona-speaking men and women talked about their sexual experiences. I would argue that Social Networking Websites (SNWs) have offered Zimbabwean women space in which to exercise their agency without the boundaries that exist in real life networks and that often people in SNWs share ideas and speak differently because they are more comfortable to talk about issues that may be hard to discuss in real life networks.

The study also interacted with quantitative methods of research so as to complement the qualitative analysis. A total of 60 survey questionnaires were administered to 30 urban-based women and 30 urban-based men. The participants were also purposively selected on the basis of their age [they had to be 18 years and above]. The selected sample of men and women were randomly selected from different economic and educational backgrounds, but such a method cannot guarantee any version of class or background representativity. I was interested in exploring my ideas, and thus a small sample sufficed to initiate the research. The questionnaires were administered in both English and Shona so as to suit the literacy levels of the participants. The questionnaires consisted of both closed and open-ended questions. The closed questions requested the participants' information pertaining to their age, sex, marital status, religion, place of residence, highest level of education and whether they had had sex before or not. These closed questions were necessary because they are '…precoded and are quick for the researcher to analyse and for the respondent to complete' (Burgess 1993:57). The open ended questions requested information on the respondents' general language use in public and private communication, their preferred language for use when communicating issues of a sexual nature, their preferred language for use during sex. Respondents were also requested to explain these preferences. The respondents were also asked to list a few expressions that they preferred to use during sex and those which would make them uncomfortable to use during sex and to explain what compelled them to use or not to use the mentioned expressions. The data was qualitatively analysed and reviewed for themes by the researcher.

Because the study endeavours to analyse Zimbabwean Shona speakers' language attitudes towards some Shona words that express sex and sexuality, the researcher selected some of the words mentioned by the respondents and subjected them to Critical Discourse Analysis (CDA). CDA is concerned with the study and analysis of words used in discourse so as to reveal the source of power, abuse, dominance, inequality and bias and how these sources are initiated, maintained, reproduced and transformed within specific, social, economic, political and historical contexts (VanDijk 1988). CDA will be suitable in analysing these discourses in order to find the hidden meanings within them. CDA is not restricted to the description of the linguistic forms but it is also aware of the purposes or functions which the linguistic forms are designed and serve in human life (Brown and Yule 1983).

Uncovering the Connections between Shona Language

Use, Gender, and Notions About Sex

This chapter analyses the open-ended questions and addresses four themes linked to the research. The question requesting to know the participants' language of choice in public and private communication sought to identify the participants' perceptions about the English language versus their vernacular Shona language. The general opinion of the respondents was that Shona was more comfortable to use in both public and private communication because it came 'naturally'. However all the respondents that had a University degree confirmed that they mixed Shona and English depending on the situation. They also affirmed that there were situations in which they had to stick to the use of English such as at work or in a work-space meeting. The use of English was constructed around notions of prestige with one respondent arguing that it was 'unprofessional' to use Shona at work.

On the question of their preferred language of use in communicating issues of a sexual nature, both the male and female respondents replied that they found it easy to use Shona when they were communicating with their friends, but it was difficult to use Shona with 'respectable people'. One respondent answered '*Shona inonakidza kana uchitaura neshamwari dzako but haidi pane vanyarikani*' [Shona is fun to use when you are with your friends but it is not appropriate when there are respectable people]. However only two respondents admitted that they used Shona when discussing matters of a sexual nature. It did not matter whether they are with friends or with other people. What is interesting about these two respondents is that they had the least educational qualifications. Those who argued that Shona was not appropriate to use when there were 'respectable' people generally explained that Shona '*inonyadzisa*' [is embarrassing]. One respondent asserted that 'Shona is too deep' to use when talking issues of a sexual nature.

The third question pertained to their choice of language during sex. It was interesting to note that the women generally had different views from the men. Of all the women that responded to the question, only two admitted to using Shona during sex. They both suggested that they got 'turned on' by the 'dirtiness' of Shona words. Only one respondent admitted that they did not say anything during sex, and it was her husband who liked talking but most of the time the things he said were unintelligible. The other respondents' general view was that they did not use Shona during sex and instead preferred to use English. They explained this choice on the basis of the 'crudeness' of the Shona language. Some suggested that Shona was not romantic enough. Responses ranged from '*Chirungu hachinyadzisi*' [English is not embarrassing], or 'Its easier to use English because it is a second language so most of the heavy connotations in Shona are lost when translated into English', or 'Shona is too backward, so it's not as romantic as languages like English, Spanish, French and Italian'. Another respondent was very vehement about her disgust with the use of Shona during sex, she said 'Shona just puts me off, it is raw and when my husband says he wants to come in Shona [ndoda kutunda], I cannot help feeling like he is dumping shit or garbage into me. I prefer more sexy and romantic expressions, like if he says, 'Babe, I'm coming' or something like that. Plus I like being complemented in English, e.g., 'Babe, you turn me on', etc. The same respondent, however, admitted that her husband liked using Shona during sex so she has to concede and use it as well because it turns him on 'If I use Shona, he comes'. Another respondent admitted that she did not like using English during sex even though she also felt that Shona was too vulgar; hence, she and her husband resorted to the use of a personal register or idiolects. For example, if her husband says 'half time' it means he wants to have another round of sex, if he says 'ndakugohwesa' [I'm scoring], it means that he is about to ejaculate. They also formed their own words to communicate sex. For example, 'gambi' means vagina, 'la li la' means having sex.

On the other hand, all the male respondents suggested that they preferred to use Shona during sex and they explained that Shona just 'came naturally' to them during sex with women. One respondent argued that 'English forces you to think but during sex there is no time to think'. Another respondent argued that Shona was 'exciting'. Noteworthy is the fact that they all viewed Shona as 'dirty' and 'vulgar but suggested that it is precisely this 'vulgar' and 'dirtiness' that was exciting to them.

The questionnaire also required the respondents to identify some of the words or expressions that they preferred to use during sex and those that made them uncomfortable. A bulk of English expressions found themselves on the preferred list eg 'I want to make love to you', 'You are so sexy', 'I'm coming', 'You are hot'. They regarded Shona expressions in similar circumstances as too vulgar and uncomfortable, e.g., 'kusviira' [having sex], 'kutunda' [ejaculating], 'mboro' [penis], 'matako' [buttocks], 'mboro yangu yamira' [I have an erection].

On a superficial level, the results collected so far may lead one to conclude that Zimbabweans are still being influenced by colonial discourses '...of dubious and often harmful value' (Onyewumi 2003). This is because it is the indigenous, ancestral language, Shona, that is regarded as 'too dirty' for 'respectability,' and that while men deploy such 'dirtiness' as part and parcel of erotic pleasure, women are bothered by the link between their own sexuality and any celebration of 'vulgarity.' Shona's 'sexual crudity' is thus both gendered and colonial.

The facebook discussion on the issue of language use during sex also reveals that women are disgusted and appalled by their 'own' language when it is used to describe sexual desire and sexual experiences. I plan to do more analysis of this part of the research, but am willing to suggest that on the basis of initial facebook page analysis and the analysis of the questionnaires, Western cultural imperialism seems to permeate Africans' everyday lived experiences, including experiences as private as the sexual act. The preliminary results confirm the researcher's suspicion that 'colonial education' can be implicated in the Shona speakers' negative attitudes towards Shona words that express sex and sexuality. All except one woman respondent admitted that they feel 'ashamed' and 'embarrassed' to use Shona sexual words (the one respondent who does not feel this way has only achieved Grade 7 education and, thus, it could be said that she is not literate enough to speak English and so Shona is the only language available to her). Most of the women respondents have a university degree and these are the ones who view Shona sexual words as dirty and vulgar. The irony is that the same respondents readily agree that Shona is generally easy to use in everyday conversations, although they sometimes mix it with English. Although the male respondents enjoy using Shona sexual expressions, they still concede that these expressions are 'dirty'.

I argue that this study, even though it is introductory, suggests a critical problem: what do such attitudes towards one's native language mean for Shona-speaking Zimbabweans? Bennett (2011) warns against the effects of European colonialisms when exploring issues of sexuality. The researcher argues that the negative perceptions towards Shona sexual expressions inhere from '…homogenised assumptions about African sexualities' (Tamale 2011). Tamale further argues that the language of Western colonialists has dominated sexuality discourses and this has resulted in the shape and construction of meanings and definitions of such concepts reflecting the realities and experiences outside Africa. Since language is an important vehicle in the transmission of cultural beliefs and values, I would argue that the choice to make 'respectable' love using English (and 'dirty' love using Shona) profoundly affects African realities. Prevailing research on African sexualities have remained stereotypical and demeaning. Africans have been regarded as sexually depraved and unrestrained. The rejection of Shona sexual words by the participants, especially by the women, may reflect a subconscious need to distance themselves from the 'immoral, lascivious and primitive' frameworks that they connote.

However a more sophisticated analysis of the results is required to appreciate the underlying socio-cultural intricacies that may be at play. It would be naïve and simplistic to conclude that the negative attitudes towards Shona sexual expressions can only be explained in terms of the Zimbabweans' interior colonialism. Moore (2012) defines sexuality as an identity as well as a social location that structures individuals' lives alongside race, gender and class. In this definition, Moore points her finger on the intersecting social categories that may shape and determine one's identity. Hill-Collins (2000) reiterates Moore's insights and takes them further by arguing that sexuality is an entity that is manipulated within distinctive systems of oppression such as race, class, nation and gender. Hill-Collins further posits that sexuality is a social location and conceptual glue that binds intersecting oppression together and helps to demonstrate how oppression converges. The insights from Moore and Hill-Collins have helped in trying to comprehend the results that I got from the research. The women respondents from the Facebook forum and those that responded to my questionnaire [except one], condemn the use of Shona during sex, while the male respondents seem to enjoy it. This result makes for an interesting binary. Santaemilia (2008) posits that sex-related language is without a doubt a highly gendered type of language which, through socialisation and power conflicts, constructs people as complex 'sexual' and gendered beings. I thus choose to locate the female respondents' reluctance to use Shona within Santaemilia's arguments. I argue that their refusal to use Shona sexual expressions may in fact be deeply embedded in a need to reject being categorised as passive objects in the sexual act. Chimhundu (1995) shows how the actions of the transitive verbs that indicate love making can only be performed by males as subjects. For example the words 'kusviira' or 'kuisa' which when loosely translated refer to the act of inserting and only a man can 'insert' and the woman becomes the one to be inserted 'kiuswa'. Chimhundu's work, therefore, shows what he refers to as the built-in sex differentials in everyday language that are reflective of basic assumptions about status, roles, responsibilities and even capabilities, sometimes. Shona sexual expressions tend to position men in a dominating position while the woman is the one to be dominated. Could it be argued that far from desiring 'respectable English,' the heterosexual women were interested in 'liberated/undominated sexual subjectivity' (regardless of the language in which this was articulated)?

It is necessary, therefore, to take the debate further in order to have a balanced understanding of these women's refusal to use Shona during sex. I would also argue that femininity, sexuality and culture are interwoven in a complicated fashion and Christianity may also have a bearing on the negative attitudes towards Shona sexual word. Given that the rejection of Christianity has, in some parts of the struggle against colonialism, been very important, can we explore men's preference for Sona terminology for sex as, in fact, 'anti-colonial' rather than as evidence of a 'depraved masculine heterosexuality'?

And, finally, less adventurously, perhaps the men's acceptance of Shona sexual expressions may also be explained within Shona cultural dynamics that control women's sexuality: while men have always been sexually liberated and were at liberty to use the sexual expressions during sex; for most women; it was a controlled discourse and she could not easily say these words, instead she had to use metaphorical language. One of the participants on the Facebook discussion attested to using metaphorical language during sex such as found in Shona love poetry because she could not get herself to use the sexual expressions directly.

I conclude by freely asserting that while my exploratory research into the links between the use of Shona, sexuality, and questions of colonialism has raised interesting questions, the results of my analysis are not conclusive but tantalising. I plan to continue the work, and expect to create new arguments in my next piece of writing.

Bibliography

Arnfred, S., ed, 2004, *Re-thinking Sexualities in Africa*. Uppsala: Nordiska Afrikainstitutet.

Bennett, J., 2011, 'Subversion and Resistance: Activist Initiatives', in Sylvia Tamale, ed., *African Sexualities: A Reader,* Capetown: Pambazuka Press.

Cameron, D. and Kulik, D., eds, 2006, *The Language and Sexuality Reader,* Oxon: Routledge.

Cameron, D. and Kulik, D., 2003),*Language and Sexuality*. Cambridge: Cambridge University Press.

Chimhundu, H., 1995, 'Sexuality and Socialisation in Shona Praises and Lyrics' in Liz Gunner and Graham Furniss, eds, *Power Marginality and African Oral Literature.* Cambridge: Cambridge University Pres,.

Chitauro- Mawema, M., 2002, 'Gender Sensitivity in Shona Language Use: A Lexicographic and Corpus Based Study of Words in Context'. A dissertation submitted in partial fulfilment of the requirements for the PhD degree to the faculty of Arts University of Zimbabwe in collaboration with the Faculty of Arts of the University of Oslo.

Collins, P., 2000, *Black Feminist Thought: Knowledge Consciousness and the Politics of Empowerment 2nd Edition*, New York: Routledge.

Evans, T., 1993, *Sexual Citizenship: The Material Construction of Sexualities,* London: Routledge.

Fairclough, N., 1989, *Language and Power,* New York.Longman Inc,

Foucault, M., 1978, *The History of Sexuality: An Introduction*, Translated by R. Hurley. New York.: Harmondsworth.

Hall, K. and Bucholtz, M., 2004, 'Theorising Identity in Language and Sexuality Research', *Language in Society* 33, p. 469-515.

Janguar, K. and Onias, E., 2004, 'Preventing HIV?: Medical Discourses and Invisible Women', in Arnfred (2004) ibid

Machera, M., 2011, 'Opening a Can of Worms: A Debate on Female Sexuality in the Lecture Theatre', in Arnfred (2004) ibid

Moore, M.R., 2012, 'Intersectionality and the Study of Black, Sexual Minority Women', *Gender and Society* Vol. 26, 33.

Moto, F., 2004, 'Towards a Study of the Lexicon of Sex', *Nordic Journal of African Studies* Vol. 13, No. 3, pp. 343-362.

Santaemilia, J., 2008, 'Gender, Sex and Language in Valencia: Attitudes towards Sex Related Language among Spanish and Catalan Speakers', *International Journal of the Sociology of Language* Vol 2008, Issue 190.

Tamale, S., ed., 2011, *African Sexualities: A Reader,* Capetown: Pambazuka Press.

Internet Source

http://www.astroconsulting.com/SDU/feminine_sexual_repression.html

9

Feminism: How Women in Uganda are Shaping the Way we Think about Sex and Politics

Prince Karakire Guma

Introduction

For long, hegemonic masculinity, which is 'a central element in a gender order', has exerted a controlling effect over all men and all women in Africa (Vale de Almeida 1997). Throughout its history, patriarchal and patrilineal practices that shaped and perpetuated gender inequality and striped women of any form of control over their sexuality were prominently justified and widely promoted. Tasks and roles were clearly divided along gender lines, and although there are some exceptions to the rules, most Africans understood those rules within their specific community context and began to identify them as norms (Bwakili 2001). It turns out, therefore, that the African history is one largely dominated by men – not that women have always accommodated the deeply patriarchal nature of society. A cursory review of some of the available literature reveals that one of the most significant features in the lives of women in Africa in general has always been the urge for self-reliance, wealth creation, and economic independence. Women have always found ways of resisting patriarchy using the institution of motherhood, access to political power, religious authority, autonomous institutions, etc. (Amadiume 1988; Davies and Graves 1986).

But over the last three decades, gendered and democratic politics and practices have taken a significant leap in Africa with women exerting pressure on governments by challenging the status quo. While the specific events which triggered the mobilisation of contemporary feminism differ in each African country, the Ugandan movement was the response to the post-1980s crises which galvanised networks into spontaneous action in a new direction. During this time, fashion, slogans, banners and symbols of identification were quite typically frequently used to create feminist group identity during this period of mobilisation. In particular, Museveni's NRM has been commended for strengthening the feminist movement in Uganda and bringing many progressive changes into the country's affairs through affirmative action and policies; financial assistance for strengthening women agricultural activities; promoting gender equity through women empowerment; and supporting girl-child education at tertiary level (see Nansubuga 2008). The outcome of this kind of arrangement has apparently changed the original system which allowed men to hold social power and enjoy a sense of unconscious political entitlement by virtue of their sex.

My interest, however, transcends such dynamics. My main argument is that these dynamics would not have occurred in their form or context in the absence of a concerted and focused impetus from women. It is in this regard that I attempt to connect the critical issue of femininity to the equally burning questions of sexuality and political reform, by providing theoretical, political and action-oriented pointers and frameworks for a gendered analysis of contemporary feminism in the context of a present-day modern state.

While I acknowledge that 'feminism' is best approached as a movement of some kind, I simply define it as a commitment to achieving the equality of both sexes (Tuana 1994). I choose this approach in the attempt to avoid variations that would lead to confusion over what 'feminism' is all about. My opinion is that the approach that I choose to adopt makes feminism a more ideal concept of application since it is very easy to locate 'in the country's historical realities of marginalisation, oppression and domination brought about by slavery, colonialism, racism, neo-colonialism and globalisation' (Butegwa 1997). It (feminism) places this study in a clear ideological position that is imperative in examining women as political actors influencing a new generation of policies advancing women's rights and liberal democracy in the context of contemporary Africa.

The rest of this paper is subdivided into four sections. Immediately following this introduction is an ideological attempt to frame the debate by examining feminism in relation to change. The third section pulls from secondary souces on feminism and change, in raising debate on how – and how much – women have been able to frame thought, debate, and perception on sex and politics in the context of post-colonial sub-Saharan Africa. The aim is to evoke a rich image of how women shape and orient the way we think about these issues, by examining specific 'processes' women have used (and are still using) to mobilise and unite in broad coalitions on the basis of their identity and belonging to demand for change. The last section draws especially on primary sources to provide reflections on the achievements of the feminist movement in its effort to construct social change and democratic transition in Uganda.

Framing the Debate

Feminism in the Global South, Uganda inclusive, surged forward during the modernisation and liberalisation era. Because it was born as both a part of, and an answer to, modernity, 'it criticised the old paradigms of action and knowledge, while at the same time being influenced by them' (Virginia 1992:198). And while economic growth – according to the modernisation theory – 'enabled the expansion of opportunities for women, ...it was the liberalisation of politics that helped women obtain positions in the political decision-making' (Zamfirache 2010). These trends were able to generate social and political streams and symbolic spaces upon which women capitalised to shape the way we think about sex and politics. This study, which is an ideological attempt to frame this debate, is grounded upon a feminist praxis – *the interplay of feminist ideas and practice.*

Inspiration for a feminist praxis derives from the misconstrual of the notion 'feminism' which some writers still use to refer to a historically specific political movement in the US and Europe, women's activism from the late 19th century, and also as attack on men. Arndt, (2002:1-3), for instance, cites Chinweizu, a Nigerian African cultural scholar and theoretist of decolonisation who says:

> Feminism is a movement of bored matriarchists, frustrated tomboys and natural termagants; each of these types has its reasons for being discontented in the matriarchist paradise that is women's traditional world ... feminism is a revolt in paradise; and the feminist rebels jeopardize the ancient matriarchist privileges of all women.

Of course, other writers have urgued that African wo/men who sympathise with feminism are 'blind copycats of Western European feminists' who have allied themselves with the western outsider (Arndt 2002). Such accusations usually come with 'the insinuation that feminists deny their African identity, their history and their specific problems, and are victims of the colonisation of thought and consciousness' (Arndt 2002).

Consequently, it is not unusual to find women activists quite occasionally avoiding reffering to themselves as feminists. In fact, some would rather describe themselves as 'gender activists' rather than 'feminist activists.' For them, gender is safe, feminism is threatening; and while gender can be accommodated and tolerated by the status quo, feminism challenges the status quo (Tripp 2000: 13-16). Khan (1999) cites a scenario where at a conference in 1998, a woman stood up proudly to announce, 'I have moved beyond feminism to gender'. Khan (1999), argues that while this might not apparently be wrong, the problem with the notion of 'gender' is that it can mean both men and women or either man or woman and largely ignores the specificity of women's oppression. This, thus, makes feminism a more ideal concept of application since it is 'located in the country's historical realities of marginalisation, oppression and domination brought about by slavery, colonialism, racism, neo-colonialism and globalisation' (Butegwa 1997). Besides, choosing to name oneself a 'feminist' places one in a clear ideological position that is imperative for achieving the movement's political motives, since as Tripp (2000) argues, the work of fighting for women's rights is deeply a political one, too.

Notwithstanding, I adopt the concept feminism in such a manner that is less flawlessly and more suitably in consonance with the apparent dynamics. As such, I do not seek to respond to the apparent complex and shifting realities in which classic, modern or radical 'feminism' is manifested. Rather, I start from the premise that there is generally a level of consistency in the overall assumptions of what feminism is about and what feminists are doing – a different point of departure: one based on an acknowledgement of the apparent ambiguity and problematic status of the notion 'feminism'. My assumption, in agreement with Mbire-Barungi (1999), is that although feminist concerns cannot be generalised, fundamental commonalities can be found by looking beyond political rhetoric and focusing on the reality of women's lived experiences.

A feminist perspective to how women are shaping the way we think about sex and politics has two major implications. The first concerns the feminist vision for 'ending all forms of discrimination against women and, specifically, those forms that impede women's human rights and foster sexual and gender-based violence.' The second has to do with the urge for a holistic analysis that acknowledges and builds on the women's struggles for social change and political reform. What follows is an assessment of the radical strategies that women have adopted in their struggles for change in regards to the way we think about sex and politics.

Research Methods

This undertaking is methodologically grounded in feminist praxis. It was pursued by means of a case study analysis of Uganda. The national site, has been chosen because of its political, social and economic systems and trends over the recent decades. Recently, Uganda has been praised as a model country in relation to women's numerical participation in politics, specifically in relation to its place in political parties and government, that have seen the institution of affirmative action for women at all levels of the political structure. It is widely accepted, within feminist literature, that the feminist experience in one country can provide lessons for feminists elsewhere. In contemporary times, the feminist movement in Uganda has shared an influential early literature, and therefore, my approach is neither to develop a general theory, nor to aspire to develop a general explanation, but to contribute to our understanding of this problem from a contemporary dimension.

My methodology is journalistic in nature and drew heavily upon a systematic analysis of newspaper articles (both in print and online) and websites, Ugandan media reports, newsletters, pamphlets, and other unpublished documents, in addition to the growing secondary literature available on the subject. I frequently use the words, 'Ugandan women' or 'Ugandans' or 'Women' to designate the people who expressed their views through the print and electronic media. Although it was difficult to locate key figures of the Ugandan feminist movement because of time and financial constraints, I was able to conduct sit-down and phone interviews with the aid of a master list of questions for a deeper analysis and examination of the problem. The interviews were mostly conversations with participants that allowed me to accumulate an array of differing opinions on matters relating to the subject. My data about the perspectives of Ugandan women therefore is derived from interviews given in the press, published in both private and government-owned newspapers.

Women, Sex and Politics in Uganda

The impact of women in Uganda is still generating serious debate among scholars and commentators of different ideological persuasions. A cursory review of such literature indicates how celebrated Uganda was in the early 1990s into the 2000s as a model country in the bourgeois political science literature and among neo-liberal 'development' agencies, in particular for its unique experience in relation to how, and how much women were able to shape the way we think about sex and politics. There was general agreement during this time on the impact of women's professional organisations, religious associations, non-governmental development organisations, rural self-help groups, and feminist policy advocacy groups. However, while the emergent feminist social and political pursuits during the NRM times undeniably played out in many forms leading to dramatic changes, initial relative enthusiasm in women activism dates back to colonial times. The subsequent sub-sections are revelations of the impact of women and their mobilisations, organisations, institutions and structures to this end.

Emplacing Trends in Historical Perspective

During the early years of colonial rule, the entire Ugandan populace was disenfranchised. Only three Ugandans were formally incorporated into the colonial Legislative Council (LEGCO) for the first time. Ugandan women were not only initially barred from being voted into public office, but also marginalised as voters (Kanyeihamba 1975:20). According to Nassali, women in the first nationwide LEGCO elections in 1957 were effectively denied the right to vote on account of franchise restrictions, such as property, income and employment pre-qualification (1998). This meant that Ugandan women, the majority of whom were engaged in unpaid and invisible subsistence work, were disqualified from voting, or any form of participation through such efforts as co-opt and control.

This notion of women as 'minors' when it came to elections and other broader political processes was sustained in the post-independence period. For instance, the regime that inherited the colonial state at independence was almost entirely consisted of men. Uganda's first independent parliament consisted of 88 men and only two women (Matembe 2000: 43). The country's first Constitution contained no references to gender equality or any specific provisions to ensure women's rights (Republic of Uganda 1962). This Constitution was suspended in 1966 by Prime Minister Milton Obote, and the subsequent dictatorial regimes and coups d'état in the 1970s and early 1980s, while destructive for nearly every sector of Ugandan society, were especially disastrous for women.

Neither the Uganda People's Congress (UPC) nor the Democratic Party (DP) had the commitment to advance women's interests in politics, though the UPC did support a number of 'Women in Development' initiatives which were beginning to attract foreign funding in the first half of the 1980s (Rubongoya 2006). Neither party challenged conservative ethnic and religious conventions about women's social, economic or political rights and roles. Both parties had women's wings through which women party members were expected to provide a 'hostessing' service for leaders. But there were also some prominent women politicians, such as Cecilia Ogwal and Mary Okwa Okol in the UPC, and Maria Mutagamba and Juliet Rainer Kafire in the DP. These were not 'token' representatives of women, but hard-core party activists who had made it up through the ranks (Goetz 2002).

While these women did not see themselves as representing women's interests in politics and never took a feminist stance in policy debates, they played a key role in shaping perceptions on sex and politics at the time. It is perhaps not surprising that their frustration with sclerotic leadership and the slavish sycophancy of the middle ranks of their political parties prompted some of them – such as Ogwal in the UPC and Maria Mutagamba in the DP – to struggle for internal party reform in the post-1986 period, and eventually either form breakaway factions, or leave their parties altogether and join Museveni's NRM (Goetz 2002). In other words, the historical lack of interest that parties showed in promoting women's interests led many women and feminists inside and outside Uganda to give a cautiously positive reception to the NRM's 'temporary' suspension of party competition when it came to power in 1986 (Rubongoya 2006; Goetz 2002).

Paradoxically, however, most scholars argue that Museveni's NRM government was not immediately receptive to gender equity and equality. It was rather the product of the resilience and energy of women in civil society in Uganda that a small group of urban women's organisations mobilised to lobby Museveni soon after his take-over. They demanded that women be appointed to leadership positions, arguing that women's support for the NRA during the 1981-86 guerilla war justified this through urban feminist associations such as Action for

Development (ACFODE), a small group of professional women (Tripp 2000: 70). Other women's organisations such as the International Federation of Women Lawyers (FIDA), Katosi Women Development Trust (KWDT), Isis Women International Cross Cultural Exchange (Isis-WICCE), Council for Economic Empowerment of Uganda in Africa, Uganda Chapter (CEEWA-U), Disabled Women's Network and Resource Organisation (DWNRO), Uganda Women's Network (UWONET), Forum for Women in Democracy (FOWODE), among others, were established as autonomous spaces, further strengthening and elevating women in their fight for the right to be seen, heard and counted.

It is not surprising, therefore, that Museveni made quick political capital with the urban women by appointing some of them who were strong NRM supporters to very prominent positions. For a starter, Museveni appointed Joyce Mpanga Minister for Women and Development in 1987. By 1989, there were two women serving as ministers and three serving as deputy ministers in the NRM cabinet. Gertrude Njuba, a high-level combatant in the NRA, was appointed deputy minister of industry, Betty Bigombe was given the vital task of leading the project of pacification of the North, and Victoria Sekitoleko became minister of agriculture. Museveni appointed two women lawyers, Miria Matembe and Mary Maitum, to the Constitutional Commission, created a Ministry of Women in Development, and conceded to the demand to create a seat for a woman at all levels of the now five-tier – village to district level – Resistance Council system (Tripp 2000; Goetz 2002). In addition to appointing high-profile figures to important posts in the public administration and the judiciary, Museveni also appointed Wandera Specioza Kazibwe as the first female Vice-President in an African country in 1994 (Matembe 2000). During this time, women became very active, and did play an integral role in the process of drafting the 1995 Ugandan Constitution, which guarantees women's rights to equality, freedom and security of the person, freedom from violence, the right to make decisions concerning reproduction, and the right to security and control over one's own body.

Feminist Achievements into the Late 2000s

One of the many achievements realised by the feminist movement in Uganda in the late 1990s was the internationally-applauded increase in the numbers of women in representative politics through affirmative action (Ahikire 2009; Tripp 2000; Goetz 2002; Goetz and Hassim 2003). It was widely acknowledged that no other group was as organised and cohesive as women's organisations when it came to making a concerted effort to influence the Constitution-writing process (Tripp 2002). Women's organisations wrote more memoranda submitted to the Constitutional Commission than any other sector of society. They also took part in a countrywide effort to educate women about the purpose of a Constitution and to gather views into memoranda (Tripp 2002). Their role in improving women's legal status was rather impressive as they increased mobilisation by pushing to pass or amend laws to improve women's legal status. The main issues that emerged had to do with property rights, land rights, inheritance laws, citizenship laws, domestic violence, rape and defilement – rape of girls under the age of consent. The 1995 Constitution thus guarantees explicit provisions for the protection and promotion of the rights of women, thanks to women's movements, advocacy, analysis, research and institution building.

The women's struggle against corruption was also quite a significant feature of the feminist movement at the time. Because of past gender-based exclusions from formal political and economic life, women, like other politically marginalised groups, have often had less at stake in maintaining the old order and subsequently have the potential for greater openness to adopting new incentive structures. It was, therefore, no accident that women like Winnie Byanyima emerged among the fiercest opponents of corruption and patronage politics (Budlender 2000; Tripp 2002). Along with the anti-corruption stance, it is striking how often one found women politicians adopting an anti-sectarian position where others had politicised ethnicity, race, or religion. One of the reasons many women politicians sought non-sectarian support had to do with their bases of support. At the national level, the common cause of women's rights had united many women of diverse backgrounds. Women had found that it was impossible to mount an effective struggle around legislation affecting women without building a broad-based movement (Tripp 2002).

In 2006 Uganda reformed its system for reserving seats for women by raising the number of women district representatives from 69 to 80 (Waring, 2010). In addition to these, women won 14 constituency seats, and held a number of appointed seats: one each of the youth and disabled representatives, and two representatives from both the workers, and Ugandan People's Defence Forces – resulting in 99 women taking their place in the 332-seat Ugandan parliament. At the moment, right from the national legislature down through all five tiers of local government, women have numerous opportunities to participate in politics and influence democracy. Uganda has a female Speaker – Rebecca Kadaga – in a Parliament of which 35 per cent of the seats are occupied by women. The political mobilisation of Ugandan women hs been largely successful. Women constitute more than half of the population and turn up in largest numbers every election year to vote (Mukangara and Koda 1997; Mukama and Murindwa-Rutanga 2005). This way, they are able to progressively get their views on the policy agenda, while the state and processes of governance are being reconstructed to promote democracy and good governance through advocacy (Asiimwe-Mwesige 2006).

During this time, more spaces sprung up, popular political culture gradually became more accepting of female politicians, while new female faces and voices increasingly became seen and heard. Even more so, female bids for power set an important precedent for the country. Feminist scholarship, advocacy, and activism indeed provided a major force for change precisely by influencing a number of social and political spaces, including the political systems of power and domestic discourses on gender and sexuality. It constituted, according to Tripp (2000:23-25), 'one of the strongest mobilised societal forces in Uganda,' and 'one of the strongest women's movements in Africa'. Indeed, this era dramatically led to the disappearance of the patriarchal and hegemonic structures that existed within the original culture and to the gradual decline of men's rights and consequent demand to keep their power. Women quickly rose onto the political scene and engaged in fundamental struggles against patriarchal control and exclusion. In so doing, they confronted national and international economic, religious, social and political orders; persistently challenging the inherent sexism, discrimination and devaluing of women; while taking ownership of their society, with the aim of changing it.

Today, women are no longer required to be chaste, decent or modest, to restrict their sphere of activity to the home, or even to realise their properly feminine destiny in maternity. The aspirations and opportunities available to women have dramatically increased, while their political participation and engagement is fast expanding with women forging far more established links with their active involvement in public affairs and mobilising wide coalitions.

Even men, however grudgingly, are beginning to allow lee way for women's rights into the public sphere, as older forms of domination and the tendency to constantly disregard women in the political arena are continuously being eroded. In one of the *Observer's* cover stories, for instance, Patience Akumu writes:

> I have met men who stand for the women cause before [sic]. Most of them have a sophisticated knowledge, an understanding cool and empathy [sic] towards women and their rights.

The story which highlights David Butema Ndikabona – a High Court Registrar and lecturer at Makerere University's Gender Department – as a 'proud feminist', quotes him assaying;

> We have trained many judges, police officers, probation officers and civil servants and they have understood ... have you met [Professor] Oloka Onyango or Arthur Larok (Action Aid Country Director)? These are men who also work hard for the rights of women.

All these are signs of new forms that are indeed arising, spreading, and becoming even more consolidated. And while such triumphs and victories may apparently seem scattered, together they play a significant role in challenging the barriers created by colonisation and dictatorships and, thus, a great role in shaping thought and perception on sex and politics.

The Contemporary Spectrum – Resistance and Resignation

While the Ugandan feminist movement achieved quite a lot over the years, in its heydays it was indeed vibrant, socially influential and politically powerful. It played an integral role in achieving dramatic accomplishments, specifically the NRM's enthronement of competitive multi-party democracy, liberalisation of the political space, accommodation of ethno-regional diversities, and political expression., It is still left to be said whether this legacy has been sustained with the same vigour and robustness. Concrete and theoretical questions surrounding this are becoming more prevalent in social and political spaces.

One common account is that the gains achieved by the feminist movement are turning out to be short-lived since the political shift to multi-party dispensation in 2005. The sceptics believe that the movement has not achieved much since and has rather become laid-back. Indeed, while one of the major achievements of the feminist movement of the late 1980s and early 1990s was the achievement of gender balance, particularly the propagaton of the Affirmative Action, such achievements were not in themselves sustainable. According to a report by Akina Mama wa Africa (2008), the Affirmative Action had no clear institutional structures, or levels through which to measure success along the target set by the Beijing Platform, for instance. Not only has it obliged women to settle for less, it has also increased laziness as women work with less passion and vigour, waiting for mere tokens of positions from the NRM regime that they do not merit. As such, women have yet to realise substantial pay-offs from such measures and efforts one could argue merely represented 'cosmetic' rather than 'deep' transformation.

As Rubongoya (2006) argued, although the NRM's central drive was to consolidate, legitimise and entrench its power by appealing to women's groups, the no-party era seems to have been a pivotal period in the women's movement – a period during which gains were made that would have been impossible to contemplate in a multi-party system. According to him, since the multi-party dispensation began in 2005, emphasis on women's rights and empowerment began to wane, the NRM shifted into co-optive mode, and the autonomy that had previously been given to women's associational organisations in the mid-1980s which enabled them to push for legislative initiatives such as the Land Bill began to be compromised. And President Museveni once declared that no other Ugandan but himself has the 'vision' to run the country – a condescending attitude that has led to the repression of women leaders. Such tendencies have further weakened the feminist movement's spirit and those of the other civic groups which apparently are unable to assert enough pressure on the country's leadership as was the case before the multi-party dispensation.

In view of these developments, it is not surprising that the feminist movement seems to have hit a snag with less achievement over the last 20 or so years. Indeed, 'no change' has been Museveni's NRM party's slogan ever since its inception as a political party in 2005. Such tendencies as these should have given women more reason to actively participate in building a 'better' state. The feminist scholars and activists in Uganda should have drawn more inspiration from these experiences rather than be deterred. But this, apparently, has not been the case.

What is increasingly becoming prevalent is not just the threat of the achievements turning out to be short-lived but also the increased disappearance of optimism that has led to even more perceived resignation over the last decade or so. For instance, in the parliament where women were active and visible in the 1980s, 1990s, and early 2000s, they have difficulty in being taken seriously today, or even being listened to. Quite surprisingly, not many of their suggestions nowadays are taken on board either by government or even the budding opposition political parties.

A case in point is the horrendous Anti-Homosexuality Bill – referred to by many as the 'Kill the Gays' Bill – that proposes criminalise homosexuality, which is still progressing through the house despite wide and fervent opposition from international and national (especially the queer) feminists that align themselves with the feminist and sexual rights movements. While feminist women, as a group might rightly consider the Bill to be synonymous with neo-colonialist opposition to sexual rights and freedoms in Uganda, state institutions remain relentless in excluding their opinions and suggestions. This is somewhat surprising, given the impact women had had as voters, leaders, and activists on politics in Uganda, especially during the last two decades.

In the same vein, the Domestic Relations Bill remains the longest running legislation in Parliament and has recently been shelved now for nearly two decades. Its most vocal advocates, like Miria Matembe, have spent their entire careers in politics pushing for the passage of this Bill, but it is still not guaranteed. Similarly, the Marriage and Divorce Bill (which has been on the agenda for the last 47 years) which sought reforms and consolidation of all laws relating to equal rights and protection in marriage and divorce hit a snag at the beginning of 2013. The proposed Bill sought to legalise cohabitation and sharing of property, and to provide for recognised types of marriages, marital rights and duties, and divorce (Bill No. 19, 2009). Beyond the details of the various versions of the Bill, however, the rhetoric both for and against the Bill is symbolic of a deep concern about the apparent state of the nation in regards to the way we think about sex.

From a broader perspective, the manner in which such Bills are treated is reflective of a contemporary defiance of the feminist movement, particularly in the political sphere. But even outside the political sphere, most women organisations, movements, and activities operate on the margins of clientelistic networks, while others run on a shoestring budget; are heavily donor-dependent and – driven; and lack the necessary mechanism and capacity to sustain long-term activities for sustained growth and development (Budlender 2000; Tripp 2002:13-14).

But with increasing panic regarding the short-lived successes, the fading optimism, and perceived resignation of the feminist movement, has been the reappearance of feminist bashing – both within the political and social spheres. Contemporary and budding feminists are increasingly subjected to ridicule, some of which is expressed through local media. One of the dailies for instance wrote:

> 'Apparently absolutely nothing was right or good before feminism came into the picture. Feminists and some of their advocates have questioned (and asked for change in) various aspects of a woman's life and, when you consider these demands, you realize that religion, culture, family life and common sense were all 'wrong'. Because feminism, femininity and all corresponding variables are, by their very nature, incomprehensible...'

In some cases, feminists even receive threats to their lives, and are frequently subjected to humiliating stereotypes and derogatory remarks (Tamale 1999). They are often called 'frustrated', 'miserable spinsters', 'castrators', 'home wreckers' and many other epithets (Ekwee 2006). Such things are often said to discredit 'those lost, polluted women, who want to cause trouble with our women who are happy where they are' (Ekwee 2006). Spontaneously, prohibitive attitudes and perceptions that women's 'proper' place is in the home rather than in public sphere are increasingly re-emerging.

Even institutions of state that ought to know better how best to protect rights and freedoms of citizens are increasingly tending towards patriarchal and unrelenting tendencies in their defiance particularly of women's rights and issues. A case in point occurred when the Minister of Ethics and Integrity, Simon Lokodo, re-tabled the Anti-Pornographic Bill in Parliament early in 2013. The Bill sought to restrict a range of practices and activities, including the wearing of certain items of clothing. Indeed, that the Bill was nicknamed the 'Mini-skirt Bill' almost immediately goes a long way to show why most Ugandans became more concerned about the *unsaid* rather than what was actually stated in the articles and clauses of the Bill. But also, that a whole public institution such as the Parliament should be debating what women ought to (or not) wear consistently signals one thing: the wide belief (albeit, somewhat unconscious) that women's bodies are not their own. It is this unconscious belief and attitude, a design of a patriarchal system, which is often overlooked and yet extensively portrayed when parliamentarians and the public, through social and electronic media, deliberate upon whether to ban 'mini-skirts' in public spaces.

It, therefore, becomes apparent that such a Bill is most certainly a blatant attempt to suppress women's assertion of their sexual rights and freedoms. Of course it calls into question the NRM government's commitment to women empowerment. But it could also in itself be the result of counteraction to women's 'increased independence' – which would make a logical argument since the more women are determined to demand sexual independence, the bigger the backlash against them is expected. But that this is happening today, at the time when the movement's heyday is way past it, makes such an assertion quite questionable. Nevertheless, it goes a long way to show that for as long as Ugandan feminists continue to push for their sexual and political rights and freedoms, one can expect even more structural sexist attacks in retaliation. This would imply, therefore, a need for women to re-examine conventional (and even contemporary) efforts for better results.

What the Women Say

Women, during the study, expressed concern over the fate of the feminist movement and wondered if it has achieved the kind of change it always intended to achieve. Issues raised varied. But they mostly include the fact that gender equality is still not yet achieved: many women continue to earn, on average less than men; they are mostly concentrated in low-paying jobs; are sexually abused in workplaces; and are always much more likely than men to be poor. Also, violence against women in their homes is still widespread. It's such concerns that explain the widespread pessimism apparent today as was expressed by one Irene Mirembe, a human and women's rights activist, in Kampala:

> Women haven't won, yet. Even now, we are losing our hard-won rights. The men still own everything. Wherever you look – be it representation of women in politics, or engagement at senior levels of government or the civil service, or rates of pay at the workplaces, women remain in a vulnerable state. And that is not progressive posturing, it's simply a fact. Those in power are legislating away women's rights, dictating what they should wear – like how they can't wear miniskirts, criminalising their identities, and maintaining a status quo in which half the population are invisible and hopeless. But that's not because men are failing us. It's because women are. We are failing our own selves.

But while such a landscape concerns women in Uganda today, what concerns them even more is the fact that there exists almost no signs of concerted hope and vibrant efforts for change in the status quo. As an article in a local daily that cited a group of 'girls, many of them corporates drawn from different career pools in their mid 20s', (NOT CLEAR) noted:

> ...a group of vibrant, almost elite Kampala women actually think the feminism movement has lost track. They think it is time to start posing the hard questions, if only to salvage the original woman, who they argue gets lost in the emancipation labyrinth.'

I addition, others believe that some feminists used (and continue to use) feminism as a vehicle for achieving their own ends. The belief is that women used progressive reform in the 1990s not as a stepping stone to more pervasive change in society and politics, but for their own selfish ends. A few women are concerned that many womens' equality organisations that once existed as women's organisations with large partnerships have become shrewd bureaucratic structures run by paid staff.

In tandem with this percption is the widely held belief that feminist activism, which was once vibrant and provocative, has totally lost concern with women's conditions and has now become largely 'pretentious' and 'fake'. According to one scholar and researcher from Makerere University:

> Today's feminism, in today's clothes, is all about how weak and helpless women are. It is all about what we cannot possibly achieve on our own. A number of younger self-styled 'feminists' are emerging and turning back the clock, declaring themselves 'victims' over and over again. This, is for us [women], a disappointment. For them [young feminists], am afraid, it might yet be a self-fulfilling prophesy.

But not all agree to this line of thought. Some women contend that while the feminist movement may seem to be losing it's grip, it is only that unlike today, women in the early 1990s organised as politicians, within political organisations. During the first two decades of the NRM regime, women organised as politicians and within conduits of their political party organisations which allowed a cohesive voice. In other words, the feminist movement of the 1990s that permeated Ugandan politics for years was a distinctive characteristic of a locally-driven, and internally motivated drive for political reform within the NRM regime. This is contrary to the present times where feminist activism has become more dynamic and versatile, especially since Uganda's transition to a multi-party dispensation. This era saw key elements in the feminist movement, such as Maria Matembe and Winnie Byanyima, dropping out of the NRM party institutions to either form different political parties, or leave active politics altogether. This, in a way, affected the feminist movement's agenda as it lost the cohesive voice it once had.

But women argue that developments such as the emergence of female wings under political party structures, and campaign groups over new media networks such as twitter and facebook, can only lead to growth in scale on which young women are actively getting involved. Indeed, media debates have played a key role toward this end. On facebook for instance, a number of pages offer interesting space for such debates. A few remarks that were posted on a freethinkers' group about feminism in Uganda on July 23rd for instance, are important to overview:

> 'Such sites in this country is integral for the resurgence of feminism – especially considering that the word remains largely bad and forbidden forbidden even. It is so encouraging to see dynamic conversations happening everywhere... The Internet is opening up better channels for us. We are not isolated from one other. We are able to understand each others' lives and support ourselves through sites like this, which for me is the heart of feminism.'

> 'In the 90s they didn't have what we have now [developments in technology and structural organizations with PR]. These developments today are enabling activism to thrive even over the social networks. What we have today has the potential of mobilising resurgences of grassroots feminist activism both on-line and on the streets.'

Although this trend may not necessarily have led to the mobilisation of resurgences of grassroots feminist activism, it has facilitated the emergence of a newly exuberant and dynamic generation of feminist activism in Uganda. This was mostly witnessed in the first decade of the 21st century. Reminiscent in some ways in its liveliness of the Ugandan feminist movement of the 1990s and 2000s, this new movement appears to be occurring above all among young women and in relation specifically to politics.

This movement is part of a broader emergence of new forms of feminist 'activism' that emerged in the 21st Century. Recently, there is a growing movement of budding feminists who are leading a sea of change in informal politics through the civil society sector in creative and flexible ways. In such cases, women feminists and activists do not necessarily belong to a political organisation than was the case in the past. Over the years, despite the odds stacked against them, women show admireable resilience and engage in struggles to keep their families together. Women form the majority of members in community organisations and social movements, and have developed a rich store of institutional knowledge over the years within the contexts in which they work. Often times, they will be seen organising as grassroots activists, feminists, defenders of women's rights, academics and policy-makers to design the best strategic response to issues in real time. Some projects are designed to raise awareness of a certain issue in activist, funder, and policy circles, such as pan Akina Mama Wa Africa; others are designed to bring activists and policy-makers together to create policy change, such as the Uganda Feminist Forum.

The other common respose was that feminism has even crossed to the academy. Indeed, through scholars such as Sylvia Tamale, Jackie Asiimwe-Mwesige, Josephine Ahikiire, Stella Ssali, and so on, feminism in the academy is now becoming more entrenched, acclaimed and legitimate within institutional structures of the academia, independent of national political struggle, and of its community roots. Academic feminists have played a key role in reconceptualising core concepts of sex and politics while uncovering new empirical knowledge concerning the feminist discourse within the Ugandan context. They have studied specific empirical situations to deduce explanatory and ethical theories and conceptualisations grounded in the local context; and also written on specific feminist dilemmas. In other words, they have introduced theoretical content and empirical applications of feminist theory to 'real' local situations in regional politics. However, the challenge lies in bridging the gap between feminist theory and activism. As Flax suggests, 'Feminist theory is the foundation of action and there is no pretense that theory can be neutral. Within feminist theory is a commitment to change oppressive structures and to connect abstract ideas with concrete problems for political action. There has to be a commitment to do something about the situation of women' (Arndt 2002).

Conclusion

This paper sought to trace feminist influence in shaping gender equality and political reform. It highlights varied developments that justify the emerging visibility of women as political and social actors; the recent adoption of a new generation of policies advancing women and political rights; and their relative enthusiasm into the early times of the 21st century. Notably, the findings reveal that while the feminist movement in the late 1990s had a visible and audacious development – particularly nourished by initiatives and networks of themes and actions that united the strength of women all over the country – the gains then do not seem to be taking root now. Besides, the movement has for the last decade or so displayed signs of weakness, vagueness and ambiguity. Consequently, 'modern' feminist efforts encounter numerous obstacles and are likely to encounter even more challenges in the decades to come. The patterns of intimidation, harassment, and resistance to women's assertion of their sexual and political rights and freedoms are bound to persist. As such, women need to be persistent in their opposition to patriarchal and even sexist systems, but also to change their tools in their fight for change.

References

Ahikire, J., 2009, 'Towards Women's Effective Participation in Electoral Processes: A Review of the Ugandan Experience'. A paper drafted as part of the CODESRIA Multinational Working Group on Gender and National Politics.

Ahikire, J., 2009, 'Women's Engagement with Political Parties in Contemporary Africa: Reflections on Uganda's Experience', *Policy Brief* 65, Centre for Policy Studies.

Ahikire, J. 2001. 'Gender Equity and Local Democracy in Contemporary Uganda: Addressing the Challenge of Women's Political Effectiveness in Local Government', *Working Paper* 58, Kampala: Centre for Basic Research.

Akina, Mama wa Afrika Women, 2008, 'Peace and Security Lessons in Domesticating UN Resolution 1325 in Africa, *Leaders Journal*, July 2007 - July 2008.

Amadiume, I., 1988, *Male Daughters, Female Husbands*, London: Zed Press.

Arndt, S., 2002, *The Dynamics of African Feminism: Defining and Classifying African Feminist Literatures,* Asmara: Africa World Press.

Bartky, S.L., 1997, 'Foucault, Femininity, and the Modernization of Patriarchal Power', in Katie Conboy, Nadia Medina, and Sarah Stanbury, eds, *Writing on the Body: Female Embodiment and Feminist Theory,* New York: Columbia UP, pp. 122-81.

Bauer, G. and Britton, H., 2005, *Women in African Parliaments*, Boulder, CO: Lynne Rienner Publishers.

Basu, A. ed., 1995, *The Challenge of Local Feminisms: Women's Movements in Global Perspective.* Boulder, CO: Westview.

Bwakili, D.J., 2001, Gender Inequality in Africa: Contemporary, *Women Review* Vol. 279, No. 163, pp. 270-272.Chiroro, B., 2000, 'Representation of Women in Politics', *SAPEM*, 13, 6.

Davies, C.B. and Graves, A.A., 1986, eds, *Ngambika: Studies of Women in African Literature,* Lawrenceville, NJ: Africa World Press.

Diamond, L. and Plattner, M. F., 1996, *The Global Resurgence of Democracy,* Baltimore and London: The Johns Hopkins Press.

Ekwee, B., 2006, 'The Transition to Multi-party Democracy and Legal Changes: Impact on Civil Society Work Activism and Networking At Sub-National Level'. Paper Presented at a Round-table for District Networks in Eastern Uganda, Mbale.

Fallon, K., 2008, *Democracy and the Rise of Women's Movements in Sub-Saharan Africa,* Baltimore: Johns Hopkins Press, Ch. 6.

Geisler, G., 2004, *Women and the Remaking of Politics in Southern Africa: Negotiating Autonomy, Incorporation, and Representation,* Uppsala: Nordiska Afrikainstitutet, Ch. 2.

Goetz, A. M., 2002, 'No Shortcuts to Power: Constraints on Women's Political Effectiveness in Uganda', *Journal of Modern African Studies,* 40:4, pp. 549-575.

Goetz, A. M. and Hassim S., eds, 2003. *No Shortcuts to Power: African Women in Politics and Policy Making,* London and New York/Cape Town: Zed Books/David Philip.

Hale, S., 1997, 'The Soldier and the State – Post-Liberation Women: The Case of Eritrea', Draft Monograph, Anthropology Department, University of California, Los Angeles.

HURIDA, 2013. *90% Of Ugandan Women Sexually Harassed At Work,* Kampala: Uganda Human Rights Defenders Association. Hannah, B., 2005, *Women in the South African Parliament; From Resistance to Governance,* Urbana: University of Illinois Press.

Hassim, S., 2006, *Women's Organizations and Democracy in South Africa: Contesting Authority,* Madison: University of Wisconsin Press.

Kambarami, M., 2006, 'Femininity, Sexuality and Culture: Patriarchy and Female Subordination in Zimbabwe,' Understanding Human Sexuality Seminar Series, a Collaborative work between Africa Regional Sexuality Resource Centre and the Health Systems Trust, South Africa.

Kuypers, A. J., ed., 1999, *Men and Power,* Halifax: Fernwood Books, pp. 59-83. Mbire-Barungi, B., 1999, Ugandan Feminism: Political Rhetoric Or Reality? *Women's Studies International Forum,* Vol. 22, No. 4, pp. 435-439.

Mukama, R. and Murindwa-Rutanga, 2005, *Confronting Twenty-First Century Challenges: Analyses and Re-directions by National and International Scholars,* Kampala: Makerere University Printery.

Mukangara, F. and Koda, B., 1997, *Beyond Inequalities: Women in Tanzania.* Harare: Southern Africa Research and Documentation Center (SARDC).

Nansubuga, I., 2008, 'Feminism in Uganda'. Available at: http://www.nawey.net/

Nassali, L., 1998, 'Gender Inequality in Africa,' Contemporary Review: 270–272. From: Men, Feminism, and Men's Contradictory Experiences of Power, Michael Kaufman (In Brod, H., & Kaufman, eds, 1994, Theorising masculinities (Vol 50) Sage Publications, London).

Matembe, M., 2000, *Miria Matembe: Gender, Politics, and Constitution Making in Uganda.* Kampala: Fountain Publishers.

Mikkola, M., 2012, *Feminist Perspectives on Sex and Gender,* The Stanford Encyclopedia of Philosophy, Edward N. Zalta (ed.). Available at http://plato.stanford.edu/archives/fall2012/entries/feminism-gender. Accessed on 29 June 2013.

Mottier, V., 2004, 'Feminism and Gender Theory: The Return of the State', in Gerald Gaus and Chandran Kukathas, eds., *Handbook of Political Theory,* New York: Sage, pp. 277-288.

Republic of Uganda, 1962, *The Uganda (Constitution)* Order in Council. London: HMSO.

Republic of Uganda, 1995, *Constitution of the Republic of Uganda,* Kampala: Uganda.

Republic of Uganda, 2009, Bill No. 19, *Marriage And Divorce Bill,* Republic of Uganda: Kampala

Rubongoya, J. B., 2006, 'The "No-Party" System and the Women's Movement in Uganda: Preliminary Observations',paper presented at the International Political Science Association (IPSA) Conference, Fukuoka, Japan.

Sawer, M. 2000. 'Representation of Women: Questions of Accountability', paper presented to the 18th World Congress, International Political Science Association, Quebec City.

Steady, C. F., 2006, *Women and Collective Action in Africa,* New York: Palgrave Macmillan.

Tamale, S., 1999, *When Hens Begin to Crow: Gender and Parliamentary Politics in Uganda,* Boulder, Colorado: Westview Press.

Tanzarn, N., 2003, 'Affirmative Action in Ugandan Parliamentary Politics', in Kwesiga J. C. et al, eds, *Women's Political Space: The Experience of Affirmative Action in Eritrea, Tanzania and Uganda,* Belfast: Centre for Advancement of Women in Politics (CAWP) Queens University; and Kampala: Department of Women and Gender Studies, Makerere University.

Tripp A. M., 2001, 'Women's Movements and Challenges to Neopatrimonial Rule: Preliminary Observations from Africa', *Development and Change,* Vol. 32.

Tripp A. M., 2000, *Women and Politics in Uganda.* Madison WI: University of Wisconsin Press; Oxford: James Currey; Kampala: Fountain Press.

Tripp, A. M., Casimiro I., Kwesiga J. and Mungwa A., 2008. *African Women's Movements: Changing Political Landscapes,* New York: Cambridge University Press.

Tripp, A. M., 1999. *New Trends in Women's Political Participation in Africa,* Madison: University of Wisconsin Press.

Vale, de Almeida, M., 1997, *'Gender, Masculinity and Power in Southern Portugal', Social Anthropology, vol. 5, No. 2, pp. 141-158.*

Virginia V., 1992, 'The Feminist Movement in Latin America: Between Hope and Disenchantment', *Development and Change,* Vol. 23, No. 3, pp. 195-214.

Waring, M., 2010, *Women's Political Participation,* Auckland: The Institute of Public Policy, Auckland University of Technology.

Zamfirache, I., 2010, 'Women and Politics – The Glass Ceiling', *Journal of Comparative Research in Anthropology and Sociology,* Vol. 1, No. 1, pp. 175-185.

10

HIV-Positive Women 'Virgins': The Complexities of Discourse on Issues of Sex and Sexuality in Zimbabwe

Molly Manyonganise

Introduction

This chapter focuses on the experiences of HIV-positive women virgins, as a way of challenging some of the contemporary discourses of the meaning of sexuality and the prevention of the HI virus. The reason for focusing on women virgins, despite my knowledge that there are, of course, men HIV-positive virgins, is that even though the women face the same medical condition as HIV-positive men without ever having had sexual intercourse, women remain often disadvantaged by the socio-cultural as well as religio-political structures of African societies which are largely patriarchal. Patriarchy itself entrenches hegemonic masculinities which justify men's dominant position over women. According to Tamale (2011:11)

> Researching human sexuality without looking at gender is like cooking pepper soup without pepper – it might look like pepper soup but one sip will make it clear that an essential ingredient is missing. In the same way, without a gendered analysis, the 'dish' of sexuality research simply can't rise to the occasion. It is flat, empty and morose.

As Bennett (2011:81) adds,

> When exploring issues of sexuality... it is still important to note the effect of European colonialisms – including the effect of Christianity – on the citizens of the territories conquered and administered between the late 19th and mid-20th centuries.

Thus, while the chapter looks at how socio-cultural and religious factors have influenced the sex and sexuality discourse in Zimbabwe, through the 'eyes' of young HIV-positive women virgins, it also explores how the church in Zimbabwe has responded to their plight in terms of their sexuality. While I am cognisant of both material and theological responses which the church have offered to the infected and affected children in Africa, I would also argue that religious institutions have been instrumental in the production of gender identities which, in turn, have a strong impact on questions of sex and sexuality.

The chapter draws from a study in which I used qualitative research methods to explore the experiences of young HIV-positive women who had never been engaged in sexual activities. Interviews with both mothers of these young women and the young women themselves were held, alongside some informal discussions with them outside of the interview space, and my observations within the school setting in which these young women were located became the core data for this project. A total of ten individuals were involved, five women whose children were born infected with HIV and five young women, born with HIV, whose ages range from 18-20 years. In interpreting the data, the study used content analysis.

HIV-Positive Women Virgins and the Discourse of 'Othering'

The traditional Shona conception of the virginity of a girl or young umarried woman is when their hymen is still intact. Such 'virginity', regardless of the girl's actual experiences with sexual activity, sexual desire, and interaction with ideas about sex and sexuality gleaned from friendship circles, the media, or reading, was and still is rewarded during marriage. While it needs to be noted that the meaning of the term has evolved, especially so in the context of HIV & AIDS, it remains the case that virginity is highly prized, while no amount of education on the humanity and value of HIV-positive people has managed to erase the stigmatisation of sero-positivity. Being an HIV-positive person and a virgin places young women in contested spaces where they have to negotiate their identities between the 'value' of their virginity and the negativity associated with being HIV-positive.

Within these spaces, the HIV-positive women virgins are, however, often confronted with yet another discourse of 'othering'. 'Othering' offers an important perspective on social relations in the context of HIV & AIDS (Rule and John 2008:80) since it is a central energy within AIDS-related stigma and as a practice, it effectively increases the distance between groups of people (Van Breda 2012:180). Ackermann (2005:388) argues that [HIV & AIDS] stigma effectively brands 'the other' as undesirable. In this case, the HIV-positive female virgins are 'othered' because they are perceived as presenting an impossible challenge in discourse on issues of sex and sexuality in Zimbabwe. They can neither be assimilated into discourses about 'good,' 'innocent' and 'desirable' young women as virgins, nor can they be placed within the discourses of taintedness and 'undesirability' which surround those young people who become HIV-positive as a result of sexual activity. This 'contradictory' discursive space means that these young women are excluded from what Birungi (2008) recommends as the need to give HIV-positive adolescents information and practical support to enable them deal with the potential identity of being HIV-positive but also to make informed choices and balance responsibility with sexual and reproductive desires. She further argues that the HIV & AIDS counselling being received by these children is not balanced since it only focuses on responsibilities and not their rights and lives.

Discourses on Sex and Sexuality in Zimbabwe: The Challenges

Discussion on sex and sexuality has largely remained imbued with secrecy and a sense of privacy in African societies (Arnfred 2004; Tamale 2011), although the need to address the HIV epidemic entailed efforts to place it within the public domain. In Zimbabwe, the subject of sex and sexuality continues to be surrounded by taboos, misconceptions and cultural myths. As Madongonda and Chirimuuta (2006) note, 'the subject of sex and sexuality is avoided amongst family members and the community at large in Zimbabwe.' In Shona culture, any public discussion about sex and sexuality is considered vulgar. When one dares say the Shona terms for 'penis', 'vagina' or even the sexual act itself, people shy away, unless those contexts are deliberately 'sexual' among peer-groups, particularly men's peer groups (see Manyake, this volume). Manyonganise (forthcoming) suggests that:

> Married couples though engaging in sexual acts would/do not openly discuss the subject. When expressing their satisfaction after having sex, the Shona resorted to what they called *madanha* and *zvirevereve* (classified under praise poetry) in which figurative language was used. These poems were done in the darkness of the night revealing the general African concept of sex as an act performed in obscurity. When referring to issues of sex the Shona have the general belief that *zveusiku hazvitaurwe* (what happens during the night should), not be spoken about.

Hence, when calling for the demystification of the sex and sexuality in Zimbabwe, one needs to be conscious of the challenges of language, and I am not in total agreement with some scholars (both Western and African) who have tended to romanticise the traditional attitudes towards sex and sexuality. Arguments that are usually put forward are that traditional African societies were open to this subject since they had organised institutions that dealt with these issues when preparing boys and girls for marriage. Such arguments deliberately turn a blind eye to the fact that these were private institutions whose activities and teachings were held in strict secrecy and those taught were bound to remain silent. It was their deeds that would show if they had understood what was taught, not their future conversation.

The problem of secrecy and silence over issues of sex and sexuality has been compounded by the advent of HIV & AIDS in most African societies, and Zimbabwe is no exception. If it was difficult to talk about sex and sexuality before the coming in of HIV & AIDS, how much more now with the 'deadly' disease? The Zimbabwean society at large is guilty of associating HIV with moral failure. The linking of sex with morality tends to lead to the stigmatisation of those affected by HIV & AIDS (Lindow cited in Kamau 2009:199). The fact that HIV & AIDS have been persistently linked with sexuality, promiscuity, poverty and death has led to a deafening silence around the world (Kamau 2009:118). However, McFadden (1992:158) argues that 'The AIDS pandemic has brought to the fore the essential and extremely problematic nature of sex and sexuality. Perhaps for the first time in living memory, we are faced with the imperative of having to examine what sex and sexuality really mean in their numerous socio-cultural contexts; how sexuality is constructed and played out in both the public and private areas of life.'

The sex and sexuality discourse within efforts to constrain AIDS becomes more loaded if it is women who are involved, especially so if young women are involved and, broadly speaking, this is due to the influence of patriarchal norms According to Machera, 'Generally, in Africa, male and female sexualities have been patterned by cultural definitions of masculinity and femininity. Female sexuality is seen as something to be contained and controlled; this can be traced to the well-known dichotomy of labeling 'good' women as virgins and 'loose' women as whores. Such labels depict female sexuality as evil and dangerous if not constrained and imply that 'good females' should repress their sexual feeling (Machera 2004:167).

This same scenario obtains in Zimbabwe where women are expected to be ignorant of sexual issues if they are to be considered respectable women. Cultural prescriptions for masculinity and femininity dictate how men and women explore their sexuality in the era of HIV & AIDS. For example, the dominant ideology of femininity in Zimbabwean society casts women in a subordinate position with virginity, chastity, motherhood, moral superiority and obedience as key virtues of the ideal women. Travers and Bennet (1996) cited in Tallis (2002:20) posit that 'patriarchal relationships involve, to varying degrees and within different sites inequalities of power, and without power women are likely to experience little control over sexual relations with men'. It, therefore, becomes a given that social and cultural definitions of gender shape women's and men's behaviour, particularly in the realm of sexuality.

In a bid to empower young people with much-needed information on issues of HIV prevention, the government of Zimbabwe introduced life skills and sex education in its school curricula in 2000. However, there has been resistance from parents who feel that it encourages their children to engage in the sexual act itself. The teachers themselves are not well-trained to deal with the subject due to the influence of their cultural as well as religious backgrounds. An additional challenge of the sex and sexuality discourse in Zimbabwe is the perception of heterosexuality as the normative sexuality. Such perceptions tend to blend sexuality and reproduction, co-identifying them into one idea. Undie (2011:521-22) muses over young people living with HIV and the ways in which their choices are constrained and their sexuality forcibly shaped by censoring much-needed sexual and reproductive health information, or by prescribing what sexuality should mean for them. She asks 'what are the realities of "choice" in African settings and how do these shape sexualities?'. Such questions are thorny especially when discussng the lives of young HIV-positive women who are virgins.

HIV-Positive Virgins, Sex and Sexuality: The Dilemma

In this era of HIV & AIDS, societies have been encouraged to be open when dealing with issues of sex and sexuality, and it is ironic that these calls have turned a blind eye on children who are born HIV-positive. These children have been made vulnerable at birth before they face the oppressive cultures in their respective African societies. Madongonda and Chitando (2009:161) note that when confronted with the problem of children living with HIV, care organisations become helpless. In spite of the fact that children are valued in Zimbabwe, its society appears oblivious of their plight in the context of the HIV pandemic (Madongonda and Chitando 2009:159) For example, very little research has been done on the experience of children who have been born with the HI virus and there has been little or no interest in these children's sexuality issues. The only possible explanation for this is that before the introduction of anti-retroviral drugs, the general belief was that children born with HIV had a short life span, hence there was no need to consider other issues that would affect them in their later life. However, McFadden (1992:166) noted twelve years ago, 'the problem of AIDS has not only confronted our societies with an unknown virus, it has begun to unravel some of the myths and mystifications surrounding sex and sexuality at a general level, as well as at the more specific levels of female sexuality/male sexuality; adult sexuality /adolescent sexuality, and it is forcing us to deal with the issues in conceptual, practical and ultimately very essential terms of human survival.'

In reference to children born with the HI virus Mavolwane (http://www.zbc. co.zw) argues that 'A lot has been said about abstinence, behavioural change and the decline in the HIV & AIDS prevalence rate, but there has been a deafening silence on the plight of children who years ago were born with the virus' and goes on to argue, 'with some of the children born with the virus now in their teens and others in their early 20s, complications have now arisen regarding knowledge of their status and issues relating to dating and marriage'.

This suggests that Zimbabwean society has been caught unprepared for the children who are born infected with HIV. To a large extent, these have remained a forgotten generation living in troubled present while at the same time facing an uncertain future especially on issues that have to do with their sexuality. While both boys and girls who are born with the virus may face similar challenges, the female ones are mostly affected. The fact that Zimbabwean society is patriarchal means that these children do not only face the effects of HIV but also those of being female in a male dominated society. In this case, there is a need for Zimbabwe to pay attention to how these virgins, especially the female ones, experience sex and explore their sexuality. There is a need also to look at how the sex and sexuality discourse can be made meaningful in their condition. For example, (a) If, as alluded to earlier, virginity is respectable for the girls as it proves chastity and decency, does the same apply to the infected-at-birth girls? (b) If sexuality in Africa is largely defined in terms of procreation, what choices are there for the infected girls to simply explore their sexuality and embrace the pleasurable aspects of sex without focusing on conception? We definitely need to pay attention to the way Zimbabweans define marriage, motherhood, womanhood and reproduction. As McFadden (1992:161) sai, there is a need to pause and ask what motherhood has become in the context of the HIV scourge, especially in light of HIV-positive female virgins.

All parents interviewed indicated they were afraid and ashamed of talking to their daughters about sex and sexuality issues. These feelings were based on the premise that they were responsible for the condition of their children. One of the interviewees said:

Ndingataure sei nemwana wandakapa chirwere ndichimuudza nezvebonde?
Ndinonyara uye ndinotya kuudza mwana wangu zvakadaro.
(How can I discuss with my child whom I infected telling her issues of sex?
I am ashamed and I fear telling my child such things) (Interview with an
HIV-positive female virgin's mother in Harare, 26 May 2013).

Another interviewee retorted, 'I do not expect my infected daughter to be sexually active because I was infected in the same way. She should just focus on at least living longer.'

These two responses show that the infected mothers themselves now have a negative attitude towards sex and sexuality. Apart from regretting having indulged in the sexual act that eventually resulted in the infection of the child through birth, the mothers do not expect their daughters to have any desire to have sex with anyone. If anything, they should actually put these issues aside and concentrate on living a longer life. What needs to be established is whether the positive condition kills the libido of the HIV-positive virgins or maybe we have a case of adults trying to impose their expectations on them? Jackson (2002:272) notes that:

> In many cultures in sub-Saharan Africa, children are greatly valued yet treated in ways that encourage silence, obedience and submission. They are not encouraged to express their own views and individuality but to respect their elders and do what they are told to without complaining. The assumption is that the adults know what is best for the children.

For example, in the above cases, the mothers would think that the decisions they are making for their children are in the best interests of their health, yet probably the needs of these children go beyond the realm of sickness and well-being. The only way to understand these children is to allow their voices to be heard at family, community as well as national level so that the sex and sexuality discourse could be structured to have a proper meaning in their lives.

Experiences, Dreams and Fears of the HIV-Positive Virgins

Existing scholarly works on African sexualities/sexualities in Africa provide insightful analysis on the genuine issues that surround the discourse in Africa. However, what is conspicuous in these works is the absence of spaces for interactive engagement with HIV-positive female virgins in Zimbabwe. Also noticeable is the absence of the voices of HIV-positive female virgins on sex and sexuality. Providing spaces for this kind of engagement is crucial as it opens up avenues through which the HIV-positive female virgins can effectively deal with critical issues that shape their existence. When the Zimbabwean society stops and listens to this people, it will encourage them to remove sex and sexuality discourse from the private domain and place it in the public arena. In other words, such an endeavour is key to breaking the silence and secrecy that has for long shrouded the discourse in Africa and, particularly, in Zimbabwe. In my opinion, the discourse on sex and sexuality is incomplete with the exclusion of HIV-positive female virgins. An inclusive discourse should pay attention to the experiences, dreams as well as fears of this group.

Data gathered from the HIV-positive female virgins shows that they have contemplated suicide at one time or the other. One of the interviewees said:

> Life for me as a young adult has not been easy. I cannot enjoy life in the same way as my colleagues. I cannot date a young man because the moment I disclose my status, they leave me. I have contemplated suicide several times. What is the purpose of living if I cannot live a normal life. (Interview with an HIV=positive female virgin in Harare, 28 May 2013).

The revelation by this interviewee shows that, like any other young adult, she desires to have close heterosexual relationships. Normal life for her implies being able to explore her own sexuality like any other child of her age. In this case, the restrictions on doing so is frustrating, condemning her to a place of helplessness.

It is also evident that being HIV-positive has led to these girls to living in seclusion. Despite HIV & AIDS awareness campaigns being held in the country, the stigma and discrimination against the victims still abounds. This is particularly worse if it involved unmarried women. While communities in Zimbabwe have been forthcoming in giving moral and material support to the victims, parents guard jealously against their children (especially the boys) crossing the boundary of mere concern to that of getting acquainted with the infected girls. The fear of getting infected also compels the young men to be guarded as they associate with the victims. In most cases, it is this inhuman treatment in the social arena that forces the young women to condemn themselves to self-imposed solitude. It becomes clear in this case that being HIV-positive gives the infected an indelible mark. Despite the awareness campaigns, stigma and discrimination against the victims is reinvented in the sexuality arena irrespective of how they got infected. This is not to criticise the efforts of the Zimbabwean government or the NGOs working tirelessly to ensure that HIV-positive people can access much needed treatment and reproductive health information in the country. What is coming out of this research suggests, rather, that these institutions should revisit their models of information dissemination so that HIV-positive, but sexually inexperienced people are not excluded from their messages of treatment and hope.

In a society where the virginity, especially of girls, is highly valued, the existence of HIV-positive young women places the country in a quandary. Can society celebrate the virginity of these girls? As one interviewee puts it:

> My being a virgin does not make me any better than the rest who are not virgins. Society continues to treat me like an outcast because of my HIV-positive status. Even if someone were to marry me, their family would not accept me because I am always looked at as a moving grave. I am not expected to give birth because there are high chances that I may infect the child. So what's the point of celebrating my virginity if it can't give birth to new life. It is pointless.

Does the society, at large, expect these young women to remain asexual? The lack of recognition that sexuality is an important part of everyone's being has resulted in silences around the implication of HIV-positive people's sexual lives. The young women in my study are invisible, and treated as though they should remain so. Discourses on healthy, pleasurable and safe sexuality exclude them and even when discussions on these issues are going on around them, they feel wounded from within and often shy away from contributing. One of interviewees shared an experience in which she was told to 'shut up' after she had ventured to make a contribution on 'girls' talk' about sex.

While some HIV-positive women virgins felt the need to actively take part in the discourse, others feared getting involved. The fear came from the dread of the virus itself and from the implications of revealing their positive status among their friends. One interviewee revealed that she cannot even envision herself indulging in sex because of her condition. The fact that her body is often weak means she cannot think about being sexually active. From her perspective, sleeping with a man requires enormous energy which she does not have. I would argue that such a perception reflects badly on Zimbabwean society where heterosexuality is elevated above all other forms of sexuality. Even then, in heterosexuality, the only perceived way for one to express their sexuality is through penetrative sex. Hence, in order to remove the fear of HIV-positive female virgins on sex issues, there is a need to emphasise other sexual activities such as kissing, caressing, fondling, etc. Jackson (2002:120) suggests, for example, that masturbation should also be encouraged in the era of HIV & AIDS, and it was clear from my preliminary research that the young woman and parents I engaged with had a very weak grasp of the full range of activities which could be considered 'sexual' and through which a young woman's sexual desire could be expressed with, and without, partners.

Conclusion

The purpose of this chapter has been to highlight how the experiences of HIV-positive young women, who are considered as virgins, complicate the dominant discourses on sex and sexuality in contemporary Zimbabwe. What came out clearly in the research is that Zimbabweans need to pay particular attention to this group of people and introduce policies and programmes that address the sexual needs of HIV-positive female virgins and transform dominant ideas about what 'sex' involves, and why sexual desire is a healthy and essential facet of our lives. The chapter also challenged Zimbabweans to rethink their perception on virginity and motherhood in the era of HIV & AIDS. Moreover, it called on the government and the NGOs to revisit their models of information dissemination on sex and reproductive health issues. The chapter tries to give a voice to the invisible young women, who are HIV-positive even though they have no sexual experience. This provides a platform from which they can share their experiences, fears and dreams. We need new discourses on questions of sexuality and health where people's experience cannot be simply ignored – as long as we have among us those who are born infected with the virus, we cannot categorise them as 'other' or 'beyond our understanding', but embrace them as they also explore their sexuality and live their lives fully as healthy and knowledgeable people.

References

Ackermann, D.M., 2005, 'Engaging Stigma: An embodied Theological Response to HIV and AIDS', *Scriptura: International Journal of Bible and Theology in Southern Africa*, 89, pp. 385-395.

Arnfred, S. 2004. 'African Sexuality/Sexuality in Africa: Tales and Silences', in Arnfred, S., ed., *Rethinking Sexualities in Africa*. Sweden: Almqvist & Wiksell Tryckeri AB.

Bennett, J., 2011, 'Subversion and Resistance: Activist Initiatives', in Tamale, S., ed., *African Sexualities: A Reader.* Cape Town: Pambazuka Press

Birungi, H., 2008, Strengthening Family Planning Services. Operations Research. USAID.

Chitando, A., 2012, *Fictions of Gender and the Dangers of Fiction in Zimbabwean Women's Writings on HIV and AIDS*, Harare: Africa Institute for Culture.

Kamau, N., 2009, *AIDS, Sexuality, and Gender: Experiences of Women in Kenyan Universities*. Eldoret: Zapf Chancery Research Consultants and Publishers.

Jackson, H., 2002, *AIDS: Africa, Continent in Crisis*. Harare: SafAIDS.

Machera, M., 2004, 'Opening a Can of Worms: A Debate of Female Sexuality in the Lecture Theatre', in Arnfred, S., ed., *Rethinking Sexualities in Africa*. Sweden: Almqvist & Wiksell Tryckeri AB.

Madongonda, A.M. and Chitando, E., 2009, 'Children Living with HIV in Zimbabwe: A Challenge to the Media, Schools and the Church', in Chitando, E. and Hadebe, N., eds, *Compassionate Circles: African Women Theologians Facing HIV*. Geneva: WCC Publications.

Manyonganise, M., forthcoming, '*Demystifying Sex and Sexuality Issues: Responses of a Bikita Community to HIV and AIDS*.

Mapuranga, T.P., 2010, 'Challenging Sexual Ethics: Gender, HIV and AIDS in Christianity-A Lesson from Canon Byamugisha', *Journal of Theology, Religion and Philosophy*, Volume 3, No. 2.

Mavolwane, D., 2010, 'The Plight of HIV Positive Virgins'. Available at http://www.zbc. co.zw. Accessed on 19 March 2013.

McFadden, P., 1992, 'Sex and Sexuality and the Problems of AIDS in Africa', in Meena, R., ed., *Gender in Southern Africa: Conceptual and Theoretical Issues*. Harare: Sapes Books.

Nyanzi, S., 2011, 'Unpacking the [Govern]mentality of African Sexualities', in Tamale, S., ed., *African Sexualities: A Reader*. Cape Town: Pambazuka Press.

Phiri, I. and Nadar, S., 2012, 'Charting the Paradigm Shifts in HIV Research: The Contribution of Gender and Religion Studies', *Journal of Feminist Studies in Religion*, September.

Rule, P. and John, V., 2008, 'Unbinding the Other in the Context of HIV/AIDS and Education', *Journal of Education*, No.43, pp. 79-100.

Tamale, S., 2011, 'Researching and Theorising Sexualities in Africa', in Tamale, S., ed., *African Sexualities: A Reader*, Cape Town: Pambazuka Press.

Undie, C., 2011, 'The Realities of "Choice" in Africa: Implications for Sexuality, Vulnerability and HIV/AIDS', in Tamale, S. ed., *African Sexualities: A Reader*. Cape Town: Pambazuka Press.

Van Breda, A.D., 2012, 'Stigma as "Othering" among Christian Theology Students in South Africa' *Journal des Aspects Sociaux* du VIH/SIDA. Vol 9, No. 4.

The Zimbabwean, 9-15 July 2009, p6.

11

Sexual Health Promotion in Tanzania: Narratives on Young People's Intimate Relationships

Claire Coultas

Introduction: The Sexual 'Behaviour' of Youths

Interest in studying the sexual behaviours of youths has gained momentum rapidly with the realisation that 41per cent of all new HIV infections worldwide are among young people aged 15 – 24 years (UNAIDS 2011). A Lancet review of qualitative studies on the sexual behaviour of youths worldwide showed similar forces at play despite the massively diverse settings highlighting seven common themes: (i) Young people assess potential partners as 'clean' or 'unclean'; (ii) Sexual partners have an important influence on behaviour in general; (iii) Condoms are stigmatising and associated with a lack of trust; (iv) Gender stereotypes are crucial in determining social expectations and, in turn, behaviour; (v) There are penalties and rewards for sex from society; (vi) Reputations and social displays of sexual activity or inactivity are important; and (vii) Social expectations hamper communication about sex (Marston *et al.* 2006). The authors, however, highlight the need for more information in addition to 'just understanding' the sexual behaviours of youths, looking at social contexts and influences as well as the need for 'more detailed questions' that help us to understand the reasoning and/or justification behind certain behaviours (Marston *et al.* 2006:1585).

There is a dearth of studies on youth sexuality in Tanzania. An explorative study into the association between HIV and intimate partner violence among youths in Dar es Salaam (the largest city in Tanzania) suggests a situation of high sexual activity that forms the basis of intimate relationships. These happen secretly and, therefore, the meetings are often rushed and arranged purposely to have intercourse. Moreover, these sexual liaisons commonly involve violence, demonstrate gendered power struggles with the expectations of women to make the liaisons enduring, which are usually notforthcoming, and they are usually non-monogamous (Lary, *et al.* 2004). A follow-on paper from this same research data also highlights the transactional elements of intimate relationships among young Tanzanians in Dar es Salaam (Maganja *et al.* 2007). My own experience working with Tanzanian youth through mixed method HIV prevention and peer education programmes and in field research work has also shown me a situation in which young people have the requisite knowledge to protect themselves during sex but refuse to apply it. It occurred to me, therefore, that peer education was falling short in its interventionist strategies; hence the need to look further into the reasons behind this.

To better understand the logic behind the sexual relationships that young people have, it is important to also discuss their sexual behaviours in an affirmative way: try to get an idea of what they aspire to in a relationship versus what they allow themselves to expect; how they view love; what they enjoy about their sexuality; and how they themselves define and frame their intimate relationships. A book of collected papers by Parker *et al.* articulates the need to move away from more rigid assessments of 'risk behaviours' that also carry colonial and neo-colonial connotations of 'correct' sexuality and behaviours and the presumption that there is cross-cultural consistency of sexual categories (2000). They go on to explain that this means that researchers must have an awareness and reposition themselves as political actors among others (including religious leaders, rights activists, politicians, journalists etc...), all '... with specific stakes in a contested field' (Parker *et al.* 2000:18).

It is for this reason that the word 'behaviour' in this introduction is in inverted commas. Tamale draws our attention to the racialised connotations based on colonial stereotypes that still remain today in the focus on African sexual 'behaviours' as if they are homogenous and different from Western practices, being 'insatiable, alien, and deviant' (Tamale 2011:14-17). Similarly, such prejudices can be seen in to the grouping of youth sexuality as 'risky' (Fine *et al.* 2006).

Sexual Behaviour Change and Health Promotion Approaches

Historically, the study of sexual behaviour began focusing on its development, dysfunctions, and finding the causes of 'deviant' behaviours (Money 2003:237). Large-scale sexual behaviour change 'fertility control' programmes then began in the 1950s in response to a fear of catastrophic population explosions (Ahlberg and Kulane 2011). It was the advent of HIV & AIDS in the mid-1980s, however, that sparked an interest in the study of sexual behaviour across essentially all disciplines and elicited a global 'public health' response (Parker 2001). The approach that the 'social cognition' tradition of psychology took towards tackling the epidemic (with theoretical models such as the Health Belief Model and Theory of Reasoned Action) – i.e., the premise that education and training could prompt individuals to change 'risky' behaviours – well suited biomedical positivist notions of objectivity and reductionism (Parker 2001; Campbell *et al.* 2003). It gave credence to a 'one-size-fits-all' approach that could be rolled out globally with measures of success and failure juxtaposed against the more contextual or social and cultural influences highlighted by anthropological and sociological disciplines.

The majority of sexual behavioural change (now interchangeably called 'health promotion') programmes fall under the umbrella of public health, and these social cognition foundations which focus on the individual are clearly visible. Curricula are often as pragmatic, comprehensive and factual as possible and so involve the provision of education focusing on disease and pregnancy under the premise that knowledge of these will cause behaviour change (Gresle-Favier 2010). However, sex, being such a politically- and morally-contested issue, makes maintaining objectivity highly difficult. In reality, what we often see is education on sex being laden with values, the kind of which depends on *who* the service provider and/ or donor of the project is, and the two main opposing approaches have been broadly labelled as 'sex-negative' and 'sex-positive' (although many programmes fall somewhere between these).

'*Sex-negative*' approaches are based on fear and morality-based messages, teaching 'that sexual activity outside of the context of marriage is likely to have harmful psychological and physical effects' and 'that bearing children out-of-wedlock is likely to have harmful consequences for the child, the child's parents, and society' (Bay-Cheng 2003:64). The supporters of sex-negative education approaches are among proponents of more conservative and religious philosophies and such programmes are popular and heavily subsidised by groups in USA (Gresle-Favier 2010; Weaver *et al.* 2005). Their influence can be seen globally, and an example of this is the changing of the Ugandan President's Initiative on HIV & AIDS Strategy on Communication to Youth (PIASCY) from one that included discussions on condoms and sexual negotiation to information that '... characterised sexual intercourse as an act that should be confined to marriage... [and] inserted messages intended to scare students away from having sex... [such as] 'condoms are not 100 per cent perfect protective gear against STDs and HIV infection. This is because condoms have small pores that could still allow the virus through" (Jones *et al.* 2010:159-160).

Advocates of the much more liberal '*sex-positive*' approaches criticise the sex-negative programmes, arguing that their focus on sexuality as violence, victimisation and morality '... hinders our ability to provide teens with needed knowledge, guidance and support... [and] argue for the presentation of sexuality as a positive and healthy aspect of life... and for the need to help adolescents determine not only when to say 'no', but when to say 'yes', as well' (Bay-Cheng 2003: 64-65). In this way, sex-positive approaches see sexual behaviour as having the potential to have a positive influence on a person's life, largely based around the pursuit of pleasure. And '... products [e.g. condoms] that are to be used in sex should not be separated from sexual excitement and pleasure... [but] should be promoted and used for positive reasons (sexual enjoyment) rather than negative ones (fear of infection)' (Poole *et al.* 2000:2058).

These discussions have, also been linked to continuing debates over rights-based perspectives to sexuality and sexual health. Petchesky details this issue that started gaining recognition at the International Conference on Population and Development (ICPD) in Cairo, 1994, where sexual health was, for the first time, explicitly included as a human right, defining its purpose as 'the enhancement of life and personal relations, and not merely counselling and care related to reproduction and sexually transmitted diseases' (Petchesky 2000:83-4). The Cairo Declaration (along with the Convention of the Rights of the Child) also make reference specifically to adolescents, acknowledging their competence to make decisions in a mature way regarding their sexual health, provided that they have been fully informed and had education in these matters (Holzner *et al.* 2004:41). These statements are left rather open-ended with no express qualification regarding age, marital status, sexual orientation, etc., and are strongly contested by religious and more conservative organisations and advocates (Petchesky 2000). Nevertheless they are significant in terms of identifying the need for more discussions on diverse relationships in peoples' own voices, and particularly pertaining to young people who, falling through the gaps between children and adults, have until very recently often not been included in human rights discourse, in many countries.

Unfortunately, research and practice in all sexual health promotion approaches are generally weak, lacking the inclusion of critical appraisal, reflection and evaluation. There is still much discordance between groups using and developing sexual health education programmes and also in relation to discussions on sexual and reproductive rights, debates continue about the age that is appropriate to start the education, how it should be delivered, and by whom, as well as *how much* of a mention is given to pleasure and desire in relation to sexual relationships and sexuality (Blake 2008; Ingham 2005).

Sexual Behaviour Change and Health Promotion in the 'Developing' World: The ABC Approach

The most common strategy used in 'developing' countries is the ABC approach: A(bstain); B(e faithful); and C(ondomise) – a comprehensive public health approach that covers the main ways for protecting oneself from HIV. The idea is that people can choose whichever of the methods suit them best and so the approach can be applied to the population as a whole (not just the youths). However, with regard to young people, this approach predominantly positions teenage sexuality as a risky behaviour and so programmes generally focus on abstinence, the extent of this (i.e. abstinence-only versus the more comprehensive) vary between countries and implementing organisations (Kane 2008:6).

The major promoter of this method – the US donor agency, the President's Emergency Plan for AIDS Relief (PEPFAR) – pushes for abstinence with 33 per cent of their budget having to be spent on promoting abstinence until marriage among youth (Coates *et al.* 2008:673). This was stopped in 2008 with the coming to power of President Obama; however still an abstinence focus remains. There has been much controversy over this continued promotion of abstinence-only programmes, especially regarding the lack of evidence and disagreement over their efficacy, and also the associated moral intimations in that the ABCs are not presented as three separate ideas but run in a set hierarchy with abstaining being the 'best' and using a condom the last resort for those who are unable to be 'virtuous' and abstain (Kirby 2008).

Uganda and Thailand have been heralded as success stories of the ABC approach with both countries seeing a fall in HIV rates in synchronisation with implementation of the approach. To this end, Uganda has seen a rise in the numbers of monogamous partnerships, and Thailand, an increased use of condoms among sex workers (Dworkin *et al.* 2007). However, there is much debate over this 'success' and the role that the ABC approach has played in the fall in HIV rates. Barnett *et al.* suggest that ABC is not in actuality a defined and/or unified 'approach' and is often one of many messages, but that it has been 'misused' by abstinence advocates to give credence to their more limited, simplified, and education-focused initiatives (Barnett *et al.* 2005). In fact, both these countries have – post their 'success' story – seen a rise in HIV rates once more (Dworkin *et al.* 2007).

There is, in fact, much discordance over the effectiveness of the strategy in general regarding whether people are able to change their behaviour on their own volition (Barnett *et al.* 2005). Other criticisms have included the inappropriateness of 'infantilising slogans' or moralising sexual behaviours that ignore wider complex social situations affected by gender, economics, and migration, and that also essentially impose Western Judeo-Christian heteronormative sexuality paradigms in a way that individualises 'blame' on those who are unable to effect a change in behaviour (Collins *et al.* 2008; Dworkin *et al.* 2007; Esacove 2010).

In Tanzania, national and international government and non-governmental organisations (NGOs) alike have enormously stepped up their programmes towards promoting healthy sexual behaviours including widespread education programmes and social marketing campaigns. Generally, sex education programmes along the ABC model (that also often touch on gender and life skills topics), are widespread across Tanzania, both within schools and also community groups. Therefore, a large proportion of young people in Tanzania are being taught about the biology of sex; on how to protect themselves from HIV; life skills and gender topics such as girls are equal to men and that girls have a right to say 'no'; and that in a good relationship partners listen and are honest with one another, and so on. Another source of sex and relationship education and advice in Tanzania, are the youth-focused magazines that include *Fema* and *Si Mchezo!* run by the NGO FeminaHip, that use the 'edutainment' approach to promote behaviour change (FeminaHip Annual Report 2008).

Nevertheless we still know very little regarding the reasons why the spread of sexual diseases such as HIV is so high in this demographic group and in what ways the current health promotion efforts are falling short. Increasingly, there are calls for a more combined approach to behaviour change that is more context-specific and localised, and developed in participation with communities (Merson *et al.* 2008). This research seeks to contribute to that appeal regarding the needs of youth in urban Tanzania.

Research Methods for Studying Sexual 'Behaviour'

In response to the AIDS pandemic in the mid-1980s, studies into sexual behaviour and intervention research boomed. Such studies were mainly driven by global public health agencies that followed the biomedical model using mainly quantitative methods that focused '... on surveys of risk-related behaviours and on the knowledge, attitudes, and practices that might be associated with the risk of HIV infection', that could then be used to inform disease control strategies (Parker *et al.* 2000:4). Inquiring into sexual behaviour is not a simple process, however, and people are often apprehensive and/or uncomfortable talking about something so private, they are prone to answer questions in a way that makes them look good rather than be honest when they feel judgement and/or stigma might be passed on them, and many people refuse outright to talk about it (Thomas *et al.* 1997).

Regarding the survey method, these factors can cause significant measurement error with only more sexually-experienced persons volunteering to participate. Participants who decline to respond to certain questions thus reduce the representativeness of the study just as participants recalling and reporting themselves in a way they would like to present themselves, as opposed to the way they actually behave (Fenton *et al.* 2001). Numerous studies show the survey method to facilitate the problem of participants under-, over- and/or mis-reporting themselves. For example, in one case, a significant number of women stated that they had never had intercourse yet later tested positive for HIV

(Gallo *et al.* 2007; Plummer *et al.* 2004). Ahlberg and Kulane also discuss how questionnaires reinforce detachments between service providers and communities because by being top-down and pre-conceived they '… mirror the worldview of the researchers or their perception of the research question', and so erasing the 'worldview' of the researched (Ahlberg and Kulane 2011:327).

In this way, the contribution of more qualitative methods quickly became recognised in terms of exploring the sexual context of STI transmission, for example, discovering the importance of 'bath houses' in the transmission of HIV among homosexual men in San Francisco, and the preference for 'dry sex' in a number of communities in Africa (Fenton *et al.* 2001). Such studies also highlighted the 'difficulties of translating or adapting research protocols for cross-cultural application… in the face of often radically different understandings of sexual expression… in different societies and even in different subcultures of a broader society', and the need for more explorative work into sexualities (Parker *et al.* 2000:5).

In a qualitative study of sexualities great care must be taken to ensure that the participant feels comfortable and safe, firstly, because there is a risk that they may have experienced a trauma or form of abuse in the past and/or present; and secondly, to make them feel free to talk honestly without fear of judgement. Poulin suggests that in poor and/or rural communities where people often cannot read and have rarely had formal interviews, '… flexible talk facilitates trust between a respondent and an interviewer, a trust that gives [the participant] comfort, and grants them freedom to divulge private information, like premarital sex' (Poulin 2010:18). This holds particular relevance to the study of young people, especially in a society such as Tanzania where open sexuality outside of marriage is frowned upon and carries great stigma.

The Narrative Study of Sexual 'Behaviour'

Commonly used qualitative approaches include focus groups that are useful in identifying shared and common knowledge (yet also can silence individual voices of dissent and compromise confidentiality), and in-depth interviews that can be analysed in a variety of ways. The two main approaches for studying sexual behaviour through in-depth interviews are sexual script and narrative studies: sexual script studies focus mainly on the interpersonal level, looking at '… mutually shared conventions that allow two or more actors to participate in a complete act involving mutual interaction'; while narrative studies are more expansive being able to look at intra-, inter-, and extra-personal levels, and for this reason was selected to be best suited for this study (Seal *et al.* 2008:626).

Interests in narratives within the social and medical sciences are based on the perspective that an enacted narrative is '… the most typical form of social life', and this 'typicality' is all the more important when trying to move away from generalised 'one-size-fits-all' initiatives and understand the localised contexts and cultures (Czarniawska 2009:1-3). In this way, narrative analysis is '... the study of general social phenomena through a focus on their embodiment in specific life stories' (Chase 2003:274). Bruner conceptualises narrative as a 'natural instrument' that we all use for differentiating between action, effect and thought, and reintegrating them, that therefore helps us to 'make sense' of what we experience in our lives and also, at the same time, is a representation of culture (Bruner 1991:8).

When working with young people, who commonly frame their worlds and use language differently, narrative is an especially useful method in that it allows insight into these shared meanings by giving the participant free reign in construction of the story (Green et al. 2007). In Malawi, a narrative study was performed to understand better the language and metaphors that young people use when talking about sex and relationships so that these could be incorporated into education efforts (Undie et al. 2007). Farrer, whose ethnographic narrative study looks at the 'opening up' of youth sex culture in Shanghai, states that in uncertain and changing times '... established cultural strategies and discourses become a 'cultural tool kit' for youth constructing and legitimating new tactics of social action... [and that] storytelling is a key rhetorical tactic in sexual culture... [configuring] a social world in terms of ethical value and moral action' (Farrer 1998:9).

The idea is that people are at ease and familiar with the narrative / storytelling form as it is used in all aspects of making sense of our lives. Storytelling is greatly enjoyed in Tanzania and a common feature in social interactions, and so approaching the participants in the language of stories was anticipated to help make them more comfortable.

Given this backdrop, my overall aim was to gain a greater understanding of the ways the urban-poor youths in Dar es Salaam conceptualise their sexuality and intimate relationships. I was interested in identifying the social forces and systems of meaning that affect youth sexual relationships through the collection of personal narratives on young peoples' 'love life' experiences. I also wanted to begin to consider how an awareness of this sexual culture can be used to improve current health promotion strategies directed at youths.

Methodological and Contextual Issues

Dar es Salaam, the largest city in Tanzania was chosen as the setting for this research because it offered cultural diversity with people from over 120 tribal backgrounds living together (along with a significant number of foreigners), and also because of the high levels of access and exposure that young people have to the various health promotion efforts. To further ensure the latter, participants were recruited from three different inner-city youth camps (youth-initiated groups that have been trained on HIV and conduct seminars within their community).

An introductory meeting gave interested participants information on the study, reassured them on issues such as confidentiality, and went through the consent forms in recognition that some might not be able to read. Purposive sampling was then used to select participants displaying a range of characteristics: six young people (three male; three female) were chosen; ages ranging from 19-27 years; with educational backgrounds ranging from a Primary School, Form 4 (GCSE), to a School Certificate; two were married, and the rest were in relationships (out of all the people who showed interest in the study, nobody presented themselves as single); a range of tribal origins; and occupations that included unemployed, traditional dancer, street vendor, seamstress, and carpenter.

In-depth narrative interviews, described as '... a qualitative research method used to stimulate interviewees or study participants to express their experiences and views of the topic being studied through stories or narratives' were held with participants (Bates 2004:16). The following topics were chosen after a process of refining through pilot interviews: relationships; love; and marriage. In addition to this 'free-form' of interviewing the participants were also asked for each of these topics to help construct a story based on a vignette which Hughes describes as '... stories about individuals, situations, and structures which can make reference to important points in the study of perceptions, beliefs, and attitudes... Participants are typically asked to respond to these stories with what they would do in a particular situation or how they think a third person would respond' (1998:381). These were still designed to be as open as possible so that terms like 'sex' and 'relationships' could be defined by the participants, but were included to help participants who might struggle with speaking openly on these sensitive issues, and also because the '...application of vignettes offers the opportunity to compare and contrast different groups' interpretations of a 'uniform' situation while at the same time providing the opportunity to identify and isolate certain structural factors such as gender, age, and ethnicity' (Barter *et al.* 2010:320-21).

All interviews were held in the native language Swahili with th researcher and a Tanzanian interpreter (one man for all interviews with men; and one woman for all interviews with women), both of whom I had already had experience working with in sexual health peer counsellor / educator roles, and who are fluent in English. I am fluent in Swahili, however, after the pilot interviews I decided it was best that these interpreters lead the interviews, and their previous work experience qualified them for this. Much literature has been written on the power relations between interviewer and interviewee associated with race, gender, class, and age, and it was clear that the participants built a rapport (which is so important in narrative interviewing) much more easily with the interpreter than myself (a White foreigner). After each interview the interpreter and I discussed our thoughts about what had been discussed along with any ideas on improvements for the next one.

All interviews were recorded, transcribed in Swahili, and labelled by a numerical figure rather than the participants name to ensure confidentiality. I analysed the data while still in Swahili and the chosen sections for inclusion into the write-up were then translated into English through discussions between the interpreters, myself, and a bilingual Tanzanian academic. Each narrative was studied as a whole along Muller's five overlapping stages of narrative analysis: 'entering the text (reading and preliminary coding); interpreting (finding connections in the data through successive readings and reflection); verification (searching the text and other sources for alternative explanations and confirmatory and disconfirming data); representing (writing up an account); and illustrating (selecting representative quotes' (Greenhalgh 2006:70). In this way, each narrative could be reflected on and interpreted individually, though simultaneously also be connected with others through 'narrative linkage' to produce a more broad (meta)-story for all identified themes (Gubrium *et al.* 1998).

Ethics Committee Approval was obtained from the Tanzania National Institute for Medical Research in February 2011.

Discussion

All participants except one responded extremely well to the narrative method, speaking freely and without need for much, if any, prompting. Participants also 'performed' their narratives, drawing in the researchers like an audience by acting out their stories with direct speech and 'putting on' voices. This demonstrates the importance of the audience and the dialogic aspects to storytelling (Reissman 2008). The interviews generated a wealth of data yet for the purposes and scope of this chapter the following themes have been identified: Swahili language; societal structures, religion and poverty; dependence; and *upendo wa kweli* ('real' love).

Swahili Language

Swahili is a Bantu language that dates back to the 13th Century, developing as the most common coastal and trading language in the region of East Africa and consequently displaying influences from Arabic as well as Hindi, Persian, Portuguese and English (Githiora 2010:163). Still today, remnants of a hierarchical society and culture can be seen in the language, and this has an influence on the ways that young people converse and relate to one another in their intimate relationships. For instance, unequal gender dynamics are demonstrated through the verb 'to marry', indicating men as active and so marrying (*kuoa*), and women as passive so 'being married' (kuolewa).

ROSE: He is the one that marries her, he is the one that brings food and because of that he is everything and head of the family and a woman must follow him and do what he says.

Much literature has been written on the gendered and oppressive power of language on women, yet linguistic analyses of Swahili or other Bantu languages from feminist perspectives are virtually non-existent and would be an interesting area of future study.

More than just endorsing gendered hierarchies, however, we see from the narratives that the Swahili language is also limiting in terms of 'names' for an intimate partner with the only commonly used alternative to husband and wife being *mpenzi* (singular) *wapenzi* (plural) that comes from the verb *kupenda* (to like / love), so therefore translates to 'lover'. This is not a word that would be used in front of elders and does seem to carry an element of stigma i.e., out-of-marriage sexual relations, and connotations of a lack of commitment and/or trust: often it was found that participants who had been in a relationship for a long period of time, referred to their partners as husband/wife even though they had not yet got married.

This 'serious' / marriage-focused language can also be seen from the very beginning of intimate relationships among young people, with girls responding badly or ignoring boys approaching them unless they say *nakupenda* (I love you):

INTERV: Benja told a girl nakupenda yesterday. Can you make up a story for us about what you think the situation was like for Benja to say this?

DAUDI: [silent]. Ok... [pause]... Um... What happened was that these words nakupenda, are very easy for the mouth to say... [pause]... Benja... [silent]... dah...!!... It's possible that Benja just saw this girl today... These days my friend, girls look really good and dress really nice... And because of this guys are made to say 'dah..! Nakupenda so much!', but this isn't true, they only desire the girl. Because these words nakupenda are very easy to say, and if you tell a girl you desire her or find her attractive you won't get her.

All the participants identified the paradox in this scenario of a boy approaching a girl by saying *nakupenda* in that none of them thought the words to be genuine or the sentiment true. From the male, perspective they acknowledged that this was the only way 'to get' a girl and for the girls it seemed to relate to the fact that they must not be seen as promiscuous and only receive attention from men with serious / potential marriage intentions. Accordingly, the female participants also described restrictions on the use of *nakupenda* i.e. that it can only be said by males, and the expectations of them to not be forthcoming:

ROSE: It is hard for a girl to tell a boy nakupenda in our culture because she will be called a prostitute just because she has said, 'Musa nakupenda, I'm attracted to you, maybe you should be my boyfriend, let's have sex, or we should get married'. In our life, saying things like this is really hard. There are people who are trying to be free with their feelings but these are very few. [pause]... Our community doesn't believe that everyone has the capability of thinking for themselves and thinking in their own way. [silent].

Societal Structures, Religion and Poverty

The powerful influence of 'our community' is displayed throughout the young people's narratives. Excepting Rose (whom I will discuss more about in the next sub-section), all the participants aspired to being married. This wish to marry was not once described in reference to love but by all participants seemed more to do with changing their positioning in the hierarchy of the Tanzanian society, and for men, making the transition from child to adult.

SUZANNA: Marriage for young people here in Tanzania, of all religions, is something to be very happy about. For us girls, we are very lucky because you go from being a person with no respect to being the wife of someone and given respect... [pause]... Therefore it's important to respect the husband because he brings you respect from neighbours and other men.

RAMA: Men may want to marry so as to gain respect in their home and from their family... [pause]... For us men, you may have [attained] many years of age but if you don't have a woman your family will look at you just as if you are a child... [pause]... In our culture, if you have a younger brother, because he has already married and has children, he will be listened to in family meetings, and you the elder one will be sent to fetch him for the meeting... [pause]... when he arrives he will be asked to share his ideas with the elders but you the eldest you are not asked to say anything because you don't have a woman... This is one thing that will make young people marry without love or even before they feel ready.

For girls, we also see a desire to marry stemming from the need for security and protection, and also the way in which men 'marry' and women wait 'to be' married:

INTERV: Are there many young people who want to marry?

REHEMA: Eeeh, there are many, you will find a girl is tired to stay by herself.

INTERV: So there are people who want to be married because they are bored of staying by themselves?

REHEMA: Yes, because she will be tired of being with many men... [pause]... now she will wait for the one to settle with.

INTERV: So girls are married because of the problems of having a difficult life?

REHEMA: Yes, they are tired of a difficult life, then they need to be married.

INTERV: And what about guys?

REHEMA: [Pause]... Guys marry when they are ready and if they have planned their life well.

We also can see how even with a decline in arranged marriages, that societal structures and familial hierarchies still have a strong influence on partner choice:

DAUDI: If the father of a girl or of a boy refuses Benja or the girl, then there is a real problem for their love because it won't be able to continue as here many people follow and make the decisions that their parents want.

Yet these same structures that still play a role in joining marital partnerships appear to have broken down in regards to supporting young couples in their relationships, possibly owing to urbanisation and young people moving out of villages and/or living further away from their elders:

RAMA: In the old days, the elders of a family were used to stop fights between a husband and wife. The grandfathers and grandmothers of the two families would sit the husband and wife down and remind them of how big their two families are together and would also tease them. The grandfather would say to the husband if you like to beat your wife and you are tired of her, I can take her because she is still pretty and you can have my old wife. Everybody would laugh and at the end the grandfather would give them a cock and maize for them to take away and people respected old people and would stop fighting like this... [pause]... but these days people have already forgotten their customs and traditions. They argue inside and curse each other until people outside know the secrets of their house and if they start to beat one another, friends become involved... [pause]... These days we have lost our customs meaning that there are now many problems in marriages.

This breaking down of societal support structures has already been recognised in relation to the 'coming of age' ceremonies (*unyago* for girls and *jando* for boys) that were common in coastal regions where elders taught adolescents about sex and relationships (Mbonile *et al.* 2007; Fuglesang 1998). Various NGOs and health promotion initiatives have worked to incorporate these structures into sex education efforts, however the lack of relationship support and advice-giving as opposed to the educational aspects has not yet been acknowledged. In terms of the current available sources of advice-giving in Tanzania, the most explicitly focused is the peer counselling that various NGOs offer as a part of their peer education programmes, however concerns have been raised over the ethics of requiring peer educators to act as counsellors: they will have had little if any training on counselling and also will themselves be constrained by gendered power relations and the social dynamics of poverty, meaning that such an interaction could potentially be very traumatic and damaging for both the peer counsellor and the youth seeking help (Price *et al.* 2008:8).

While planning this research study, I sought out centres which offer counselling services in Dar es Salaam that participants could be referred to if needed, and could only find four such places: two offered SRH counselling from a medical perspective; one offered legal and human rights advice; and the other offered peer counselling. None offered comprehensive relationship counselling. Advice can however be found in the 'Agony Aunt' page of the youth-focused magazines (as described on page 10), (NOT CLEAR. OF THE MAGAZINE? IS THIS A CONSTANT/REGULAR PAGE IN EACH EDITION?) however the quality and usefulness of such advice is questionable, as shown in the following example (from '*ema* July-September 2010 edition, p. 23):

Dear Aunty,

I am a boy of 22 years old. My girlfriend is called Suzan and we have loved each other for a long time now. My problem is that one of Suzan's friends wants me as her lover and she has told me that if I don't agree to her she will break up my relationship with Suzan. Aunty, this problem is killing me, what should I do?'

Norbert.

Dear Norbert,

I am sorry for your problem [sic]. Well done[sic] for being faithful and honest/ genuine. Remember that there is HIV and other STIs and that it is a dangerous habit to have more than one partner.

Aunty

In this reply we see the influences of sex-negative approach with the use of scare tactics, and poor Norbert's plea for help remains completely unanswered regarding how to negotiate his way out of this situation with his girlfriend's friend. Boynton discusses the issue of Agony Aunts and the lack of regulation and governance over the advice and education given through them, as well as the potential for authors of such columns to give incorrect or unhelpful views (2007).

From the narratives, we also see a situation where young people are unable to marry due to poverty and so if in an intimate relationship, must face the view that they are 'living in sin before their God', and are also disgraced in the eyes of their society and community.

DAUDI: God tells us that love should not be done illegally but should be done legally. By law when you reach 18 or 20 years you are able to marry.

INTERV: Yes…

DAUDI: Therefore in Tanzania the religious laws allow you to marry when you reach this age and it doesn't matter whether you have a job or not. But for today's situation, if you want to marry, to keep your woman at home, what are you going to feed her if you don't have a job?… If you don't have work you can't marry here, it will only bring you more problems.

Considering the centrality of marriage to the construction of masculinity and the security/protection of women that we have seen in these narratives, one can imagine the drastic effects that this inability to marry has on gender dynamics and youth relationships (discussed further in the next sub-sections). Therefore, this loss of a cultural support structure for relationship counselling (the elders' involvement), would perhaps not even be relevant to the current environment, yet we see no effective replacement having developed. A longitudinal randomised trial study assessing the impact of an HIV prevention programme in Mwanza, Tanzania also demonstrates the inadequacy of education efforts in this respect, showing that while those young people who received the training had better knowledge on healthy sexual behaviour, there was no significant difference in the rates of pregnancy, HIV and other STIs between the group of young people in the study and those who didn't receive the training (Mema kwa Vijana 2008-Technical Briefing Paper 3). The authors relate this to the '… contradictory norms about sexual activity' that young people face between what is 'approved' by the community and the *actual* environment that they are faced with and lack of support in dealing with this (ibid 4:1).

These contradictions mean that intimate relationships for young people must often be hidden, and therefore lack time for getting to know one another and develop an emotional bond, have no support mechanisms, and involve rushed and often unsafe sex:

JACOB: He chases after her at 6am in the morning when she goes to school and in the evening when she returns home so that he can see her and seduce her. The girl will tell Simon 'I don't have time or opportunity to leave my home and I don't have a phone therefore if you love me you will have to be tolerant,' [in a high-pitched voice] and Simon will reply to her 'no worries, nakupenda'...

INTERV: And what about sex?...

JACOB: Well they can't meet at their houses so it could be any place that they get an opportunity. If she is coming back from school, maybe a guest house or even just outside in the wild... if they do get to meet it will be rushed and maybe they can only do it once or they might not even finish properly and their desires will not be satisfied but because of the short time that they have there is no other way.

None of the participants responded to prompts asking for more details on what the sex was like, yet all of them indicated sex to be an expected part of intimate relationships that happens very early on:

SUZANNA: A big percentage of young people in relationships right now expect sex... [pause]... there are very few who stay for a while without talking about having sex.

Dependencies

Gender inequalities is a much discussed topic in development and sexual health paradigms, and we have already seen examples of this in the stories given so far:

the verb 'to marry' and also reasons for marrying; the use of the words *nakupenda*; and also the man as provider '*if you want to marry, to keep your woman at home*' (Daudi). The narratives from the participants elaborated much further on this last point, describing a situation in which dependencies, that result from gender inequalities, have an enormous impact on both young women and men, and consequently also their partner-partner communication, and relationship as a whole.

SUZANNA: A woman has the right to tell her boyfriend that he needs to buy things like sanitary pads... [pause]... this happens every month for us therefore we need money to buy such things as this and you can't tell your parent to give you money for this... [pause]... therefore you must look for a boyfriend so that you can ask him for money.

DAUDI: A girl knows 'if I get a boyfriend, then he must help me with all my little problems'... [pause]... For example if she is on her period there are things that she needs... [pause]... now if this happens and you have nothing in your pocket and she needs you to buy things for her but you fail to give her what she needs, and you have to tell her wrap yourself in a kanga, how do you think this girl is going to see you? [laughs].

Hunter describes this as the transformation of men '... from being 'providers within marriage' to less reliable and less esteemed 'providers outside of marriage'', as a form of 'emergency response' to the economic barriers to marriage (2010: 190). All the male participants discussed this expectation and enormous pressure on them to provide for their partner, and stories showed that often the common way of dealing with this was by lying. Another common feature in their stories was their accepting, often with an ironic sense of humour, of how if they failed to give their girl what she needs, that she would look for another, often claiming how if she really loved her 'poor' boyfriend, she wouldn't leave him but would hide him from this new, wealthier lover.

DAUDI: Sometimes my girl wants to meet with me but I have nothing in my pocket so I can't go meet her... [pause]... so I try to postpone seeing her by lying, saying 'tomorrow, tomorrow, tomorrow...' until the day comes when I get some money that she can enjoy a little... but definitely there is a big possibility that my girl has another man with money and that she hides me, you just don't know, and she could be bringing you diseases also but you can't spread these to anyone else because you can't get another girl, you don't have any money!

Daudi was laughing quietly whilst saying much of this, and note how he switches from saying 'I / my' to 'you / your' as if trying to separate from himself when discussing the potential consequences of this aspect to his relationship that he has accepted, and possibly is forced to accept because of his, and his partner's, poverty.

Swidler *et al.* discuss transactional sex in Malawi and suggest that it is not just a result of vulnerable women in economic desperation, but '... that patron-client ties and a moral obligation to support the needy, which are fundamental to African social life, are central elements of transactional sex' (2007:147). In this way, they suggest that men and women are constituted '... by the system in which they participate, a political economy in which ties of dependence are crucial and ubiquitous... providing opportunities for upward mobility... [and] also provide a cushion against a time when unpredictable events may threaten a downward mobility. In a patron-client society, being a patron to as many clients as possible and simultaneously being a client to many patrons are clearly advantageous strategies.' (ibid 2007:150).

Thomas *et al.* suggest that in many African cultures, there has always been a transactional element to 'courting' relationships with brideprice exchanges demonstrating a woman's productive and reproductive value, but that '... a more general shift from economies of production to those of consumption... [along with] the social consequences of money entering exchange relations and replacing cattle or other items', and the increasing desire and societal pressure to attain Western commodities has caused the circumstances that we see today in which many young people (especially girls) use their relationships to obtain resources (in Cole *et al.* 2009:22-23). Hunter also discusses the hold that this consumerist linkage between masculinities and affluence has on young men: 'As a consequence of the increasingly winner-takes-all sexual economy 'in which wealth can secure many girlfriends and poverty none' men marginalised from the productive economy also face marginalisation from the sexual economy... [with] class consciousness... [being] constructed today in the sexual and not simply the productive economy' (2010:167-8). A study among Zimbabwean students paints this picture, with both young men and women using transactional relationships to compete for social status within their peer groups as well as '... to fashion themselves as high-status, successful modern subjects... [and that often] involves more than a straightforward exchange of sex for money' (Masvawure 2010:857).

ROSE: Even if the husband tells his wife 'right now I don't have anything but wait, if I get money I will buy these things for you so you look fashionable like our neighbour's wife', but because of her desire she cannot wait, it will feel like a very long time, so she will get another man to buy things for her and this man will want services also, therefore she will be with three men: the man at the market to give her food to eat at home; and the man at the shop to give her clothes to wear so that she is fashionable.

However, Thomas *et al.* remind us to look at the term 'transactional sex' with caution as '... the long-standing Euro-American folk dichotomy between emotional and economic concerns [i.e., that these should not become entangled]...

not only stigmatises 'African' intimacy, but also fails to recognise how all human intimacy rests on a complex blend of the material and the ideal, compunction and choice' (in Cole *et al.* 2009:21;24). Also, Rose in this last narrative is not only demonstrating a woman's dependence on men for money, but is also showing the husband's dependence on his wife: if no work or money can be found, then the woman must find another means of getting food for the family to eat. As described by Rama in the previous sub-section, marriage gives young men respect in their community, and this respect is also partly related to what a woman gives and can do for a man (things that men cannot or are not taught to do for themselves).

JACOB: In marriage... [pause]... you will definitely develop because if you are by yourself you will work hard and all your money will be spent fast but in a marriage you will remember dah! my wife knows to save money in case we need to go to the hospital or buy things and she knows how to budget money well, so also you will eat well, and wear nice and clean clothes.

The complexities and strong foundations of these gendered dependencies and inequalities, and therefore the consequent difficulties in trying to combat them from a personal level, can be seen in the narratives of Rose. She is a young woman who has been with her partner since Primary School, has a child with him, but they have not married because he is Muslim and she Christian. She has had trainings on gender and life skills, and is a confident young woman who works small jobs to support her family as her partner has no education and cannot find work. Her stories directly reveal very little about her relationship with her partner, but they are heartfelt, and for the most part spoken with vigour and tears in her eyes. You are able to sense how she continually must fight for her independence against his religion, the constructs of marriage, and also against the wider cultural and societal constructs that hold a woman dependent.

ROSE: For some guys, if you tell them 'let's use a condom', he will tell you 'aahh, me I don't need to use a condom' and he will ask you 'why should we use a condom, it means that you don't trust me' and you find that he will be saying this even though they have never once met before and don't know anything about each others' relationship histories... But you think about how she must consider money, you will see how it is difficult to refuse because if you refuse you will fail to get what you need from the man... [pause]... I know if I go to a man and agree to do what he wants that I will get money for going to the Salon and 2,000TSH to buy flip-flops. To be a woman is to be dependant so you must agree in these situations... [pause]... and this has effects. Therefore in relationships in terms of sex the person who gets hurt a lot is a woman because she has no decisions... [pause]... decisions she doesn't have.

... ...

ROSE: In a marriage, the woman is the one to stay at home and listen to the man and nothing else. For example, in the religion of Islam, a woman can't go to see her mother if she is sick or even if she dies until the man allows you... he can also not let you and you can't do anything. These are the things that will make a person say 'haa... wow, to be married is slavery'... [pause]. So there is no need to being married, I don't want to be a slave, its better I am happy with this guy or I change him to another, have fun with him and then leave him, because to be kept like a slave I don't want that.

         ... ...

ROSE: The law is patriarchal and women must follow it... even if it happens that the husband has a relationship with another woman she will be forced to tolerate it because she is in his compound. If they don't understand each other he can beat you, ok, you can't do anything. You can want to return to your home but your parents, from the laws and customs, won't let you because you have already been sold. Therefore the woman gets hurt. They have no opportunity for planning like men and many, we wait, we are trained to wait, our lives are dependent on men. There are women who know their rights and they can leave a man... but then you remember what will the children eat and will fail to leave the man because you are scared to bring problems to your family. Therefore it's not good to leave.

Upendo wa kweli ('Real' Love)

Kweli is Swahili for real, genuine, true, honest etc.., and upendo means love. This was something that all of our participants claimed there was none of (or at least very little) among young people like them.

REHEMA: Way back, even before our parents there was *upendo wa kweli*... [pause]... but in this century... Mmmhh!! I don't know if you can say there is *upendo wa kweli*, many young people are lying to each other... [pause]... it's possible that in every 10 people, 1 person will have *upendo wa kweli*.

INTERV:1 in 10! Wow 1 in 10 will have love [laughs].

REHEMA: Yes... [pause]... The love right now is different... [pause]... I say 'I love you' but then, wow, I have three other men [doesn't laugh].

Love as a phenomenon has been greatly under-researched particularly in African contexts. A book of collected papers edited by Cole *et al.* identify the reasons for this stemming from early anthropologists' (perhaps unconscious yet) evident avoidance of the loving and intimate aspects of relationships in Africa despite being clearly demonstrated in songs, poems, love medicines, etc…, and ascribes this to rooted colonial ideas that situated '… blacks as morally and spiritually inadequate', and also their fascination with the 'other' and so a focusing on differential values of kinship and exchange in marriage (2009:6-8). As can be seen throughout the narratives, this current absence of love is rationalised by young people in view of their poverty and gendered struggles to accessing money, resulting in girls engaging in 'transactional sex' and boys lying.

RAMA: In terms of love, where I come from, girls don't have love… [pause]… if they have boyfriends then its business, not love, but about developing/ furthering themselves… [pause]… This is because they have a weak foundation. And for boys in the area where I stay, they also don't have love because they don't have money. You will find that the boys go with little children and this is just because it is easy to lie to and get a little child and even if the boy doesn't have money it is easy to have sex with a little girl… [pause]… And for girls, they agree to be married to old men because they have money.

DAUDI: Young people, both boys and girls, have lots of lovers, for girls we call it *vidumu* or *mafiga matatu*. There are some who can give a girl money, others who are attractive… but also now things are changing. There are old men who are not attractive but they have money and they can give a girl even 200,000TSH! A person like me can't give a girl 200,000TSH, it's alot of money, I could use it to start a business selling chips… [pause]… yeah, 200,000TSH is enough to start a chip shop! [laughs].

INTERV: [laughs].

DAUDI: [laughs more]. We're talking about love, but there is no love here.

Nevertheless, as I have begun to discuss in previous sections, there is more to this than just survival strategies in situations of poverty. Thomas *et al.* discuss how modernisation theories identified smaller nuclear families based on strong 'love' bonds between couples as an important indicator of a modernising society towards Western industrialised ideals: '… many scholars concluded that African societies were transitional- somewhere between older patterns of African kinship and marriage and those expected to emerge with modernisation' (in Cole *et al.* 2009: 10-12). And while modernisation theory has itself been heavily criticised for its teleological and evolutionary assumptions, this construction of 'love' as a modern thing, only found in companionate relationships has remained, maintained by the spread of Christianity, school education, and media which endorsed that '… certain intimate and emotional relations were depicted as 'civilised', 'modern', and 'Western' and contrasted with others deemed 'primitive', 'traditional', and 'African'" (Cole *et al.* 2009:13-16).

Yet Hirsch *et al.* suggest that this is not just a case of people being 'swept up' in cultural globalisation towards 'modernity', but is instead related to changing *material* structures of power which positions companionate marriage as a 'deliberate strategising' used by actors who consciously want to claim a 'modern identity' (2006:14). A number of studies do demonstrate how middle-class youths in a variety of cultures worldwide are distinguishing themselves from their parents' generation through companionate 'love' relationships (Clark *et al.* 2010; Spronk 2009; Nehring 2012). Also, the narratives have certainly shown us how commodities and consumption are a way of defining one's status in today's society.

Yet importantly, as Hunter points out, love is also presented through HIV & AIDS campaigns in terms of individualistic notions of choice using '… romantic love to celebrate individuals' ability to move in and out of relationships at will', which assumes a certain degree of agency that for the majority, other than the 'sassy middle-class' could prove problematic (Hunter 2010:199). It could be for this reason that we see in these narratives how the participants view *upendo wa kweli* as something that although they themselves cannot have, that it does exist and is attainable for others: (Western) foreigners.

SUZANNA: Jenny will choose to be with an mzungu [European person], because these wazungu [European people], they have upendo wa kweli, wo-

INTERV: [laughs]. So wazungu have upendo wa kweli, but us Tanzanians don't?

SUZANNA: There is no upendo wa kweli here, I completely refuse to believe that there is. There is no Tanzanian man who is in 'real' love... [pause]... So many of them are liars.

Conclusions and Ways Forward

This study has looked at the intimate relationships of urban poor youth in Dar es Salaam, and through the collected narratives described a situation in which young people are sexually active and having relationships that are based on deception, dependence, are considered immoral (being out of wedlock), and also that cannot be 'real' love because of endemic unfaithfulness and poverty. We see that young men cannot find work and, therefore, are unable to marry at the expected age as they cannot provide for a wife, and so pursue young girls with pretences of love and marriage intentions, forced to lie about their economic abilities. These girls, in turn, are also desperate to believe and/or accept these pursuits owing to their need for financial support that starts essentially as soon as they hit puberty, and the young man's consequent inability to completely provide for the girl then forces her to seek other men. All in all, a culture of concurrent and deceitful relationships is bred, and we see an acceptance by this group of young people at the way that their lives are and their helplessness to change it.

Even though this study was small and localised, it contributes to the growing amount of evidence highlighting the need to re-evaluate current health promotion strategies that presume every individual's ability to change their behaviour. 'Focus on individual behaviour change assumes that individuals execute their preferences or choices regardless of societal pressures around them, the complex contexts within which reproduction takes place and the colonial histories that disrupted the many cultural systems of regulating reproduction' (Ahlberg and Kulane 2011:327).

Campbell *et al.* from a social psychological perspective stress the importance of 'health-enabling contexts' and the need to look further towards identifying what constitutes them in different settings: 'This level of analysis is important because local communities are key mediators between the macro- and micro-social. They often form the contexts within which people negotiate their social and sexual identities, and often play a key role in enabling or constraining people to take control of their health' (2003:149-150). However, in order to incorporate concepts like this there needs to be a change in how sexual health promotion is approached, namely a de-medicalisation of the sexual body, and in 'development' contexts a move away from foreign (Western)-designed didactic curricula in which reductionist oversimplifications of complex issues such as gender are inevitable.

The narratives have given us a glimpse into the highly complex gendered relations among youth in urban Tanzania, and strikingly the powerless young men who accept and even expect their partner's infidelity do not fit with the dualist images central to gender and development paradigms of the exploited victimised woman versus the oppressive and abusive man. Ratele argues for the need to look more in-depth and inclusively at masculinities within the field of gender and African feminine studies, because there are many different forms of masculinity which at a personal level are constantly changing (often being only aspirational), are historically and culturally predicated, and highly contingent on gaining access to power not only in terms of man versus woman, but also man against other men (Ratele 2010; Shefer 2008). This also aligns with Crenshaw's concept of *intersectionality* that highlights social inequalities and oppression as being more than just man versus woman, black versus white, but rather involving complex interactions of biological, social, economic, and cultural categories, thus, creating multiple grounds of identity in terms of how the social world is constructed and experienced.

Furthermore, consideration needs to be put towards how these 'health-enabling contexts' can be integrated into existing structures and organisational cultures. Humphreys, discussing sex education in schools, identifies that while '... [educational institutions] constitute an identified location to teach about HIV/AIDS and to challenge particular configurations of (hetero)sexual and gender relations; on the other hand, they often perpetuate the very gender/sexual ideology that they are ostensibly aiming to disrupt' (Humphreys in Dunne 2008:22). This does not necessarily have to mean that alternate venues should be found, but could instead be tackled by a more problem-solving approach to education in which gender relations are discussed and historically framed rather than 'taught'. Freire's theory of conscientisation proposes that genuine and positive behaviour change can only occur among marginalised groups if they have an insight into the social conditions which foster their disadvantage, and that this understanding must come from an education programme which is 'dialogical' (so not what he calls the 'banking' concept of education in which students are 'receptacles to be filled', but rather where men and women are 'linked' through discussion which transforms their individual and collective ability to recognise and bring about action and change) (2011; 2005:72,89).

The narratives provided by these young Tanzanians highlight the complexities of sexual relationships and how they intrinsically link us to our collective cultures and histories. The responsibility of having influence on such relations cannot be reduced to the individual, especially those who are marginalised by society whether because of age, gender, socio-economic status, sexual preference, etc... In this way, while there are undeniably objective facts related to sexual health and relationships, there are also wide arrays of continuously changing subjective experiences that can in no way be addressed through a 'one-size-fits-all' education approach. The current tokenistic 'cultural awareness' often only included as a justification for the limitations of a factual public health education project is massively insufficient and verges on being subliminally racist.

Each of these narratives are clear declamations for the need of more critical, contextualised and *collective dialogue* around the subjective experiences that make it hard for these youth to protect their sexual health: what gender relations and power mean in their own lives and changing communities; the need for support and advice on how to negotiate their highly complex relationships deeply affected by poverty; the role of transactional sex in their community as a whole (not just the individual); to continuing debates about the *rights* of young people, their 'place' in society, and also their country's place in the world and relationship with 'development'. Enabling '...young people to negotiate effectively their emerging sexualities and sexual relationships within a rapidly-changing society... [is essential towards] establishing meaningful sexual citizenship in which young people have real choices over their sexuality and sexual relationships' (Hampshire *et al.* 2010: 228-29). And this cannot occur until health promotion efforts bind together the subjective and objective experiences of intimate relationships, and open up localised dialogue around young people's sexualities.

Acknowledgements

This research was undertaken towards an MSc and developed with the illuminating and expert guidance of Dr Sylvia Tamale, the Director of the 2012 Gender Institute at the Council for the Development of Social Science Research In Africa (CODESRIA) in Senegal. The support and resources from CODESRIA and Dr Tamale gave me access to transform this research. I would also like to acknowledge the hard work of Ramadhani Mohamedi and Jacqueline Nkwamah whose commitment and passion contributed greatly to the study. My university tutors Dr Petra Boynton and Ceri Butler must also be credited for their expert guidance and continued support at every stage of the research process. Also many thanks to Dr. Joe Lugalla for his unfailing support and to his organisation Health Development International Consultants, my local contact institution.

References

Ahlberg, B. M. and Kulane, A., 2011 'Sexual and Reproductive Health and Rights', in Tamale, S., ed., '*African Sexualities: A Reader*', CapeTown: Pambazuka Press.

Barnett, T., and Parkhurst, J., 2005, 'HIV/AIDS: Sex, Abstinence, and Behaviour Change' in *The Lancet Infectious Disease* 5, pp. 590-593.

Barter, C. and Renold, E., 2010, ' "I Wanna Tell You a Story": Exploring the Application of Vignettes in Qualitative Research with Children and Young People' in *International Journal of Social Research Methodology* Vol. 3, No. 4, pp. 307-323.

Bates, J. A., 2004, 'Use of Narrative Interviewing in Everyday Information Behaviour Research', in *Library and Information Science Research* 26, pp. 15-28.

Bay-Cheng, L. Y., 2003, 'The Trouble of Teen Sex: The Construction of Adolescent Sexuality Through School-Based Sexuality Education', *Sex Education* Vol. 3, No. 1, pp. 61-74.

Blake, S., 2008, 'There's a Hole in the Bucket: The Politics, Policy and Practice of Sex and Relationships Education', *Pastoral Care in Education* Vol. 26, No. 1, pp. 33-41.

Boynton, P. M., 2007, 'Advise for Sex Advisors: A Guide for 'Agony Aunts', Relationship Therapist and Sex Educators Who Want to Work with the Media', *Sex Education* Vol. 7, No. 3, pp. 309-326.

Bruner, J., 1991,) 'The Narrative Construction of Reality', *Critical Inquiry,* Vol. 18, No. 1, pp. 1-21.

Campbell, C. and Cornish, F., 2003, 'How Has the HIV/AIDS Pandemic Contributed to Our Understandings of Behaviour Change and Health Promotion?', in Ellison, G, Parker, M. and Campbell, C., eds,) *Learning from HIV and AIDS*, Cambridge: Cambridge University Press, UK.

Chase, S. E., 2003 'Taking Narrative Seriously: Consequences for Method and Theory in Interview Studies', in Lincoln, Y. S. and Denzin, N. K., eds, '*Turning Points in Qualitative Research: Tying Knots in a Handkerchief*', Lanham, Maryland: AltaMira Press, Rowman and Littlefield Publishers.

Civic, D., and Wilson, D., 1996, 'Dry Sex in Zimbabwe and Implications for Condom Use', *Social Science and Medicine* Vol. 42, No. 1, pp. 91-98.

Clark, S., Kabiru, C., and Mathur, R., 2010, 'Relationship Transitions among Youth in Urban Kenya', *Journal of Marriage and Family* 72, pp. 73-88.

Coates, T. J., Richter, L., and Caceres, C., 2008, 'Behavioural Strategies to Reduce HIV Transmission: How to Make Them Work Better', *The Lancet* 372, pp 669-684.

Cole, J. and Thomas, L. M., eds, 2009, '*Love in Africa*', Chicago: University Chicago Press.

Collins, C., Coates, T. J., and Curran, J., 2008, 'Moving Beyond the Alphabet Soup of HIV Prevention', *AIDS* (suppl. 2):S5-S8.

Crenshaw, K. W., 1991, 'Mapping the Margins: Intersectionality, Identity, Politics and Violence Against Women', *Stanford Law Review* Vol. 43, No. 6, pp. 1241-1299.

Czarniawska, B., 2009, 'Narratives in Social Science Research', London: Sage.

Dunne, M., 2008, Gender, Sexuality and Development: Education and Society in Sub-Saharan Africa, Rotterdam: Sense Publishers.

Dworkin, S. L., and Ehrhardt, A. A., 2007, 'Going Beyond 'ABC' to Include 'GEM': Critical Reflections on Progress in the HIV/AIDS Epidemic' *American Journal of Public Health* Vol. 97, 1,1 pp.3-18.

Esacove, A. W., 2010, 'Love Matches: Heteronormativity, Modernity, and AIDS Prevention in Malawi', *Gender and Society* 24, pp. 83-109.

Farrer, J., 1998, *Opening Up: Youth Sex Culture and Market Reform in Shanghai*, Chicago: The University of Chicago Press.

Femina Hip, 2008, *Annual Report*. Available at: (): http://www.feminahip.or.tz/fileadmin/pics/research/Femina_HIP_Annual_Report_2008_for_web.pdf. Accessed on 1 May 2011.

Fenton, K. A., Johnson, A. M., McManus, S., and Erens, B., 2001, 'Measuring Sexual Behaviour: Methodological Challenges in Survey Research', *Sexually Transmitted Infections* 77, pp.84-92.

Fine, M. and McClelland, S., 2006, 'Sexuality Education and Desire: Still Missing After All These Years', *Harvard Educational Review* Vol. 76, No. 3, pp.297-338.

Freire, P., 2005, *Pedagogy of the Oppressed*. New York: The Continuum International Publishing Group Inc.

Freire, P., 2011, *Education for Critical Consciousness*, New York: The Continuum International Publishing Group Inc.Fuglesang, M., 1998, 'Lessons for Life – Past and Present Modes of Sexuality Education in Tanzanian Society' *Social Science and Medicine* Vol. 44, No. 8, pp. 1245-1254.

Gallo, M.F., Behets, F.M., Steiner, M.J., Thomsen, S.C., Ombidi, W., Luchters, S., Toroitich-Ruto, C., Hobbs, M.M., 2007, 'Validity of Self-Reported 'Safe Sex' among Female Sex Workers in Mombasa, Kenya-PSA Analysis', *International Journal of STD & AIDS* Vol. 18, No. 1, pp. 33–38.

Githiora, C., 2010, 'Sheng: Peer Language, Swahili Dialect, or Emerging Creole?' *Journal of African Cultural Studies* Vol. 15, 2, pp. 159-181.

Green, J., and Thorogood, N., 2007, Qualitative Methods for Health Research, London: Sage Publications Ltd.

Greenhalgh, T., and Hurwitz, B., 1999, 'Why Study Narrative?' *British Medical Journal* Vol. 318, No. 48.

Greenhalgh, T., 2006, What Seems to be the Trouble? Stories in Illness and Healthcare, Oxford: Radcliffe Publishing.

Greenhalgh, T., Robb, N. and Scambler, G., 2006a, 'Communicative and Strategic Action in Interpreted Consultations in Primary Health Care: A Habermasian Perspective' *Social Science and Medicine* 63, pp.1170-1187.

Gresle-Favier, C., 2010, 'The Legacy of Abstinence-Only Discourses and the Place of Pleasure in US Discourses on Teen Sexuality' *Sex Education* Vol. 10, No. 4, p. 413-422.

Gubrium, J. F. and Holstein, J. A., 1998, 'Narrative Practice and the Coherence of Personal Stories' *The Sociological Quarterly* Vol. 39, No. 1, pp.163-187.

Hampshire, K., Porter, G., Mashiri, M., Maponya, G., and Dube, S., 2010, 'Proposing Love on the Way to School: Mobility, Sexuality, and Youth Transitions in South Africa' *Culture, Health and Sexuality* Vol. 13, 2, pp. 217-231.

Hattori, M. K., and Dodoo, F. N. A., 2007, 'Cohabitation, Marriage, and "Sexual Monogamy" in Nairobi's Slums' *Social Science and Medicine* 64, pp. 1067-1078.

Holzner, B. M., and Oetomo, D., 2004, 'Youth, Sexuality and Sex Education Messages in Indonesia: Issues of Desire and Control' *Reproductive Health Matters* Vol. 12, No. 23, pp. 40-49.

Hooks, B., 1994, *Teaching to Transgress: Education as the Practice of Freedom* ,New York: Routledge.

Hughes, R., 1998, 'Considering the Vignette Technique and Its Application to a Study of Drug Injecting and HIV Risk and Safer Behaviour' *Sociology of Health and Illness* 20, pp. 381–400.

Hunter, M., 2007, 'The Changing Political Economy of Sex in South Africa: The Significance of Unemployment and Inequalities to the Scale of the AIDS Pandemic' *Social Science and Medicine* 64, pp. 689-700.

Hunter, M., 2010, *Love in the Time of AIDS: Inequality, Gender and Rights in South Africa*, Indiana: Indiana University Press.

Ingham, R., 2005, ''We Didn't Cover That in School': Education against Pleasure or Education for Pleasure' *Sex Education* Vol. 5, No. 4, pp. 375-88.

IRIN News, 2009, 'A New and Improved PEPFAR under Obama?'. Available at: http://www.irinnews.org/report/82494/global-a-new-and-improved-pepfar-under-obama. Accessed on 22 August 2012.

Jones, S., and Norton, B., 2010, 'Uganda's ABC Program on HIV/AIDS Prevention: A Discursive Site of Struggle', in Higgins, C., and Norton, B., eds, *Language and HIV/AIDS*. Critical Language and Literacy Series, Bristol: Multilingual Matters.

Kane, R., 2008, 'Sex and Relationship Education: Bridging the Gap Between Research and Practice' *Health Education* Vol. 108, No. 1, pp. 5-9.

Kirby, D.B., 2008, 'The Impact of Abstinence and Comprehensive Sex and STD/HIV Education Programmes on Adolescent Sexual Behaviour', *Sexuality Research and Social Policy* Vol. 5, No. 3.

Lary, H., Maman, S., Katebalila, M., and Mbwambo, J., 2004, 'Exploring the Association Between HIV and Violence: Young People's Experiences with Infidelity, Violence and Forced Sex in Dar es Salaam, Tanzania', *International Family Planning Perspectives* Vol. 30, No. 4, pp. 200-206.

Maganja, R.K., Maman, S., Groves, A., and Mbwambo, J.K., 2007, 'Skinning the Goat and Pulling the Load: Transactional Sex Among Youth in Dar es Salaam' *AIDS Care* Vol. 19, No. 8, pp. 974-981.

Marston, C., and King, E., 2006, 'Factors that Shape Young People's Sexual Behaviour: A Systematic Review', *The Lancet* 368, pp. 1581-1586.

Masvawure, T., 2010, ''I Just Need to be Flashy on Campus': Female Students and Transactional Sex at a University in Zimbabwe', *Culture, Health and Sexuality* Vol. 12, No. 8, pp. 857-870.

Mbonile, L., and Kayombo E. J., 2008, 'Assessing Acceptability of Parents/Guardians of Adolescents towards Introduction of Sex and Reproductive Health Education in

Schools at Kinondoni Municipal in Dar es Salaam City' *East Africa Journal of Public Health* Vol. 5, No. 1, pp. 26-31.

Mema kwa Vijana, 2008, *Technical Briefing Papers*. Available at : http://www.memakwavijana.org/publications/2008.html. Accessed on 1 May 2011.

Merson, M. H., O'Malley, J., Serwadda, D., and Apisuk, C., 2008, 'The History and Challenge of HIV Prevention' *The Lancet* 372, pp. 475-488.

Money, J., 2003, 'History, Causality and Sexology' *The Journal of Sex Research* Vol. 40, No. 3, pp. 237-239.

Nehring, D., 2012, 'Love in Changing Times: Experiences of Intimate Relationships among Young Female Professionals from Mexico City' *Asian Journal of Latin American Studies* vol. 25, No. 1, pp. 75-96.

Parker, R., Barbosa R.M., and Aggleton, P., eds, 2000, *Framing the Sexual Subject: The Politics of Gender, Sexuality and Power*, California: University of California Press.

Parker, R., 2001, 'Sexuality, Culture and Power in HIV/AIDS Research' *Annual Review of Anthropology* 30, pp. 163-179.

Petchesky, R., 2000, 'Sexual Rights: Inventing a Concept, Mapping an International Practice', in Parker, R., Barbosa R.M., and Aggleton, P., eds, *Framing the Sexual Subject: The Politics of Gender, Sexuality and Power*, California: University of California Press.

Plummer, M.L., Ross, D.A., Wight, D., Changalucha. J., Mshana, G., Wamoyi, J., Todd, J., Anemona, A., Mosha, F.F., Obasi, A.I.N., Hayes, R.J., 2004, 'A Bit More Truthful: The Validity of Adolescent Sexual Behaviour Data Collected in Rural Northern Tanzania Using Five Methods' *Sexually Transmitted Infections* 80 (suppl 2), pp. ii49–ii56.

Poole, R., Whitworth, J., Green, G., 2000, 'Ambivalence, Sexual Pleasure and the Acceptability of Microbicidal Products in South-West Uganda' *AIDS* 14.

Poulin, P, 2010, 'Reporting on First Sexual Experience: The Importance of Interviewer-Respondent Interaction' in *Demographic Research* Vol. 22, No. 11, pp. 237-288.

Price, N., and Knibbs, S., 2008, 'How Effective is Peer Education in Addressing Young People's Sexual and Reproductive Health Needs in Developing Countries' *Children and Society* 2, pp. 1-12.

Ratele, K., Shefer, T., Strebel, A., and Fouten, E., 2010, "We Do Not Cook, We Only Assist Them': Constructions of Hegemonic Masculinity through Gendered Activity' *Journal of Psychology in Africa*, Vol. 20, No. 4, pp. 557-568.

Reissman, C. K., 2008, *Narrative Methods for the Human Sciences*, London: Sage Publications.

Rose, T., 2003, 'Longing to Tell: Black Women Talk about Sexuality and Intimacy', New York: Picador.

Seal, D. W., Smith, M., Coley, B., Perry, J., and Gamez, M., 2008, 'Urban Heterosexual Couples' Sexual Scripts for Three Shared Sexual Experiences' *Sex Roles* 58, pp. 626-638.

Shefer, T., Ratele, K., Strebel, N., and Shabalala, R., 2008, *From Boys to Men: Social Constructions of Masculinity in Contemporary Society*, Claremont: Juta and Company Ltd.

Spronk, R., 2009, 'Sex, Sexuality, and Negotiating Africanness in Nairobi' *Africa* 79, pp. 500-519.

Swidler, A., and Watkins, S. C., 2007, 'Ties of Dependence: AIDS and Transactional Sex in Rural Malawi' *Studies in Family Planning* Vol. 38, No. 3.

Tamale, S., ed., 2011, *African Sexualities: A Reader*, Cape Town: Pambazuka Press.

Thomas, C., Greenfield, S., and Carter, Y., 1997, (Chapter 6), in ' Carter, Y. and Thomas, C., eds, *Research Methods in Primary Care*,' Oxford: Radcliffe Medical Press.

Undie, C. C., Crichton, J., and Zulu, E., 2007, 'Metaphors We Love By: Conceptualizations of Sex among Young People in Malawi' *African Journal of Reproductive Health* Vol. 11, No. 3, pp. 221-235.

UNAIDS (Joint United Nations Programme on HIV/AIDS), 2011, *Securing the Future Today: Synthesis of Strategic Information on HIV and Young People*, Geneva: UNAIDS.

United Nations Fund for Population Activities (UNFPA), 2010, 'Youth in Tanzania: Data from the Tanzania Demographic and Health Survey (TDHS)'. Available at: http://countryoffice.unfpa.org/tanzania/drive/FinalYouthDHS.pdf. Accessed on 3 September 2012.

Weaver, H., Smith, G., and Kippax, S., 2005, 'School-based Sex Education Policies and Indicators of Sexual Health among Young People: A Comparison of the Netherlands, France, Australia and the United States' *Sex Education* Vol. 5, No. 2, pp. 171-88.

Index

Q

www.ingramcontent.com/pod-product-compliance
Lightning Source LLC
Chambersburg PA
CBHW050646280326
41932CB00015B/2796